European Review of Service
Economics and Management

2022 – 1, n° 13

European Review
of Service Economics
and Management

Revue européenne d'économie
et management des services

PARIS
CLASSIQUES GARNIER
2022

The *European Review of Service Economics and Management (ERSEM)* is an international pluridisciplinary Journal devoted to services studies in the field of economics and management. Papers can be submitted in English or in French. The journal is led by an editorial board bringing together economists and management scientists who were involved in the thematic series "Économie et Gestion des Services" (EGS) of the Journal "Économies et Sociétés". Keeping the editorial policy unchanged, it continues EGS which ceased publication in September 2015.

The *European Review of Service Economics and Management* is devoted to those activities that constitute the main sources of employment and wealth in contemporary economies. ERSEM publishes original high-quality contributions that aim at improving our knowledge of service activities, on the theoretical and empirical as well as on the managerial and public policy viewpoint. It also publishes, in a "Debate and Viewpoints" section, shorter articles which develop personal viewpoints addressing specific economic, policy or management issues regarding services. The Journal covers any type of service activity: market and non-market but also services within manufacturing firms. It has no thematic boundary.

ERSEM is simultaneously published in paper format and in an electronic version available through the website of Classiques Garnier.

Papers should not exceed 70,000 characters (including notes and spaces). Author's name, affiliation and full contact details (postal address, telephone, Email) should be provided. Submitted articles should include a title, an abstract (maximum 900 characters including spaces), and main keywords.

Papers should be submitted by Email (in Word format) to:
ersem@univ-Lille.fr

See the editorial guidelines on the journal's website:
https://ersem.univ-lille.fr

La *Revue européenne d'économie et management des services* est une revue internationale pluridisciplinaire, qui publie en français ou en anglais des articles d'économie et de gestion sur le thème des services. Elle est portée par un comité éditorial constitué d'économistes et de gestionnaires issus de l'ancienne série « Économie et Gestion des Services » (EGS) de la revue « Économies et Sociétés ». En maintenant une ligne éditoriale inchangée, elle prend la suite de EGS qui a cessé de paraître en septembre 2015.

La *Revue européenne d'économie et management des services* est une revue dédiée aux activités qui constituent les sources principales de richesse et d'emplois dans les économies contemporaines. *La REEMS* accueille toute contribution originale de qualité qui permet d'améliorer nos connaissances des services, sur le plan théorique et empirique, mais aussi managérial et en termes de politique publique. Elle publie également, dans une rubrique « Débats et points de vue », des articles courts, qui développent un point de vue personnel sur une question d'économie, de politique économique ou de management des services. La revue couvre l'ensemble des activités de services : qu'il s'agisse de services marchands ou non marchands ou de services internes aux firmes industrielles. Elle ne connaît aucune limite thématique.

REEMS est publiée sous forme papier et électronique. Elle est mise en ligne sur le site des Classiques Garnier.

Les propositions d'articles ne devront pas excéder 70 000 signes (notes et espaces compris). Outre une identification des auteurs (adresse postale, téléphone, Email), elles devront comprendre : un titre, un résumé inférieur à 900 signes (espaces compris) et quelques mots clés.

Les projets doivent être adressés par courrier électronique
(en format Word) à l'adresse Email suivante :
ersem@univ-Lille.fr

Voir les consignes éditoriales sur le site web de la revue :
https://ersem.univ-lille.fr

ISBN 978-2-406-13089-5
ISSN 2497-0107

CONTENTS

ARTICLES

DEBATES AND VIEWPOINTS

SOMMAIRE

ARTICLES

DÉBATS ET POINTS DE VUE

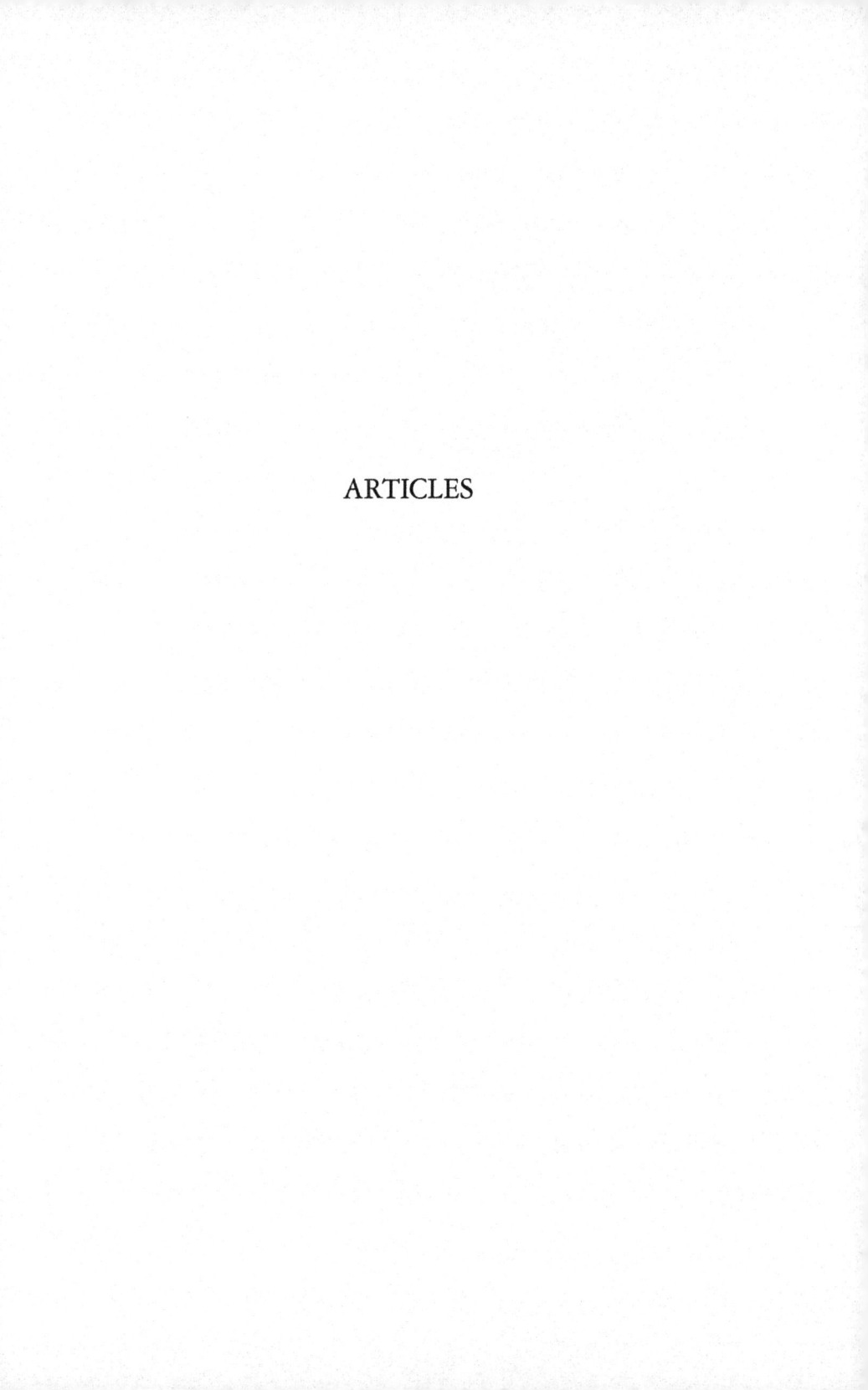

ARTICLES

INSIDE THE BLACK BOX OF PUBLIC SERVICE INNOVATION NETWORKS FOR SOCIAL INNOVATION (PSINSIs)

A Public Service Logic perspective

Benoît DESMARCHELIER[a],
Faridah DJELLAL[a],
Faïz GALLOUJ[a],
Luis RUBALCABA[b]
[a]University of Lille (France)
[b]University of Alcala (Spain)

INTRODUCTION

Social innovation is an umbrella-concept characterized as much by its great success as by the persistent fuzziness of its definition. It is generally agreed that this is an innovation that is social in its "means and ends": a collaborative innovation whose objective is to improve quality of life for individuals and communities, introducing social justice and respect for the environment, rather than to maximize profit (Pol and Ville, 2009; Mulgan et al., 2007; Moulaert and MacMallum, 2019; Gallouj et al., 2018; Djellal and Gallouj, 2012). Social innovation covers all socio-economic activities, whether market-based or not. However, this article is devoted to social innovation in the field of public services, targeting the so-called "wicked" complex human problems (aging, environmental issues, etc.) that demand collaborative systems.

Recent years have shown an increasing number of studies about social innovation in public sector/services, mostly addressing particular services (O'Byrne et al., 2014; Lévesques, 2012; Lyon, 2012; Van der Have and Rubalcaba, 2016). Muli-actor collaboration and co-creation have been identified as cornerstones for social innovation in the public sector (Voorberg et al., 2015; Torfing, 2019; Terstriep et al., 2020). Social innovations can drive societal change and empower actors to deal with societal challenges. However they are not by themselves catalysts for systemic change, as their impact is constrained by structural conditions and institutional factors beyond their control (Avelino et al., 2019; Sinclair et al., 2018). To generate a more substantial impact, social innovations would require public services and governments to be aligned with them (Haxeltine, 2016; Sinclair et al., 2018). The importance of this concept has generated research that seeks integrating findings in this field. This includes literature on social innovation frameworks, theoretical and practical implications of social innovations and studies about social innovation process (Aksoy et al., 2019; Marques et al., 2018; Oeij et al., 2019). Social innovation has also been discussed within the Quadruple Innovation Helix framework (involving public sector, private sector, academia, and civil society). Social entrepreneurs and activists contribute to a fifth helix, operating in the borders by connecting the four entities as pollinisers and cross-sectoral ambassadors and thus, making social innovation determinant for this Helix framework (Carayannis et al., 2018; Calzada, 2018; 2020).

In this context, this paper focuses on the network dimension of social innovation in public services, what Desmarchelier et al. (2020a, 2020b) call "Public Service Innovation Networks for Social Innovation" (PSINSIs). It seeks to unlock the black box of PSINSIs in order to understand their internal dynamics and identify what actions and interactions are driving factors for a successful PSINSI.

If only because social innovation is often, by definition, both an innovation produced in a network and a network innovation, these networks are nothing new as operational arrangements. Indeed, this collaborative or network dimension of social innovation is considered not only a characteristic of how social innovation is produced, but a fundamental element of its nature and definition (O'Byrne et al., 2014; Ziegler, 2017; Vickers et al., 2017). What is new about these networks is that they are now being taken seriously by academic research and public policy. From a theoretical point of view, it can be said that the PSINSI concept is the ultimate declination of the innovation network concept, following a double trajectory of servitization (or tertiarization) and de-marketization, reflecting the rise of market and non-market services and public-private relationship in collaborative innovation (Desmarchelier et al., 2020a). The servitization dynamics, which falls within the scope of the public service logic paradigm (Osborne, 2018, 2020; Strokosch and Osborne, 2020; Engen et al., 2020), is aligned with the social innovation focus as more services mean more interaction/coproduction, not just in bilateral relationships between public administration and individual citizens, but also among different multiactor service networks (involving public, private, third sector agents and users), leading to the strengthening of social means for innovation.

Using a rich set of empirical material collected within the Co-VAL European project and consisting of 24 in-depth PSINSIs case studies undertaken in five European countries, this article attempts to get in the black box of PSINSIs in a bid to better understand the nature of social innovation at work and the modes of formation and functioning of these networks.

The article is organized into four sections. In the first section, we discuss, from a theoretical point of view, i) how the notion of innovation network is enriched by a two-fold shift in analytical focus: from manufacturing to services (servitization) and from market to non-market and social spheres (de-marketization); ii) how this can be complemented by the use of the PSL approach. The notion of PSINSI is thus discussed in relation to other expressions of the notion of innovation network and other ways of understanding public governance for networks. Section 2 is devoted to the presentation of the research methodology. Section 3 and 4 are given over to a discussion of the 24 PSINSIs cases collected. We focus on the analytical variety of the types of social innovations implemented (section 3) and discuss the modes of formation and functioning of the corresponding networks (section 4).

1. SERVITIZATION AND DE-MARKETIZATION
OF NETWORKS: FROM TINs TO PSINSIs

Among the 20 advances in "innovation studies" of recent decades, Ben Martin (2015) mentions the shift "from individual actors to systems of innovation". This advance reflects the idea that innovation is increasingly the result collaborative networks – it is no longer solely the work of individual entrepreneurs or corporate innovators. For their part, Djellal and Gallouj (2018) consider that, in the field of *"service* innovation studies", service innovation in its relationship to innovation networks and systems is one of the 15 major challenges for the future. This means that, while networks are already at the heart of "innovation studies" focused on manufacturing industry, their concrete implementation – and, above all, their theoretical application – to services is still in its infancy and deserves greater attention (Mustak, 2014; Desmarchelier et al., 2020a). Another invitation to focus on service innovation networks comes from a completely different theoretical corpus, namely that of public administration. Indeed, the "new public governance" paradigm is based on the rise of production and innovation networks in public services (Kelly et al., 2002; Osborne, 2006, 2010, Desmarchelier et al., 2019, 2020b). The servitization of innovation networks highlighted and called for by "service innovation studies" is thus supplemented here by what could be called a de-marketization of innovation networks (i.e. a shift of focus from market to non-market).

1.1 A TYPOLOGY OF INNOVATION NETWORKS

An innovation network is *a structure that brings together a number of agents interacting in different ways within an innovation project.* Such a definition may, at first glance, seem simple – yet it both hides a number of difficulties and covers a wide variety of configurations. Thus, the number of agents involved may vary. These agents may be independent individuals, or various organizations represented by individuals. The links between agents are also very heterogeneous (collaboration, cooperation, coordination, partnership, co-creation...), and have been the subject of semantic discussions that are far from being exhausted (Keast et al.,

2007; Agger & Hedensted Lund, 2017; Voorberg et al., 2015; Pestoff et al., 2006; Alford, 2014; Bovaird, 2007; Sicilia et al., 2016; Loeffler, 2009). Innovation, which is the target of the network, can vary in terms of both form and degree. It may be designed and produced by the network itself, or, more simply, designed by other agents then adopted by the network.

Beyond this great diversity, several types of networks can be identified. These illustrate the two trends we mentioned earlier, namely servitization/tertiarization and "de-marketization" of the notion of innovation network (Desmarchelier et al., 2020a). The main criterion of this typology is the *sector* concerned by the innovation in question. This sector defines production activity, which is the network's main output: goods, market services, public services. *Sector* focus is identified using two axes: manufacturing *focus vs. service focus*, on the one hand, and *market focus vs. non-market focus*, on the other (Figure 1). This criterion makes it possible to highlight several types of innovation networks: Traditional Innovation Networks (TINs), characterized by a two-fold focus on the manufacturing and market sector, Market Service Innovation Networks (MSINs), focused on the market services sector, Public Service Innovation Networks (PSINs), devoted to non-market (public/social) services, and Public Service Innovation Networks for Social Innovation/PSINSIs, a sub-category of PSINs, located like them in the north-eastern quadrant of Figure 1 (i.e. service focus and public focus).

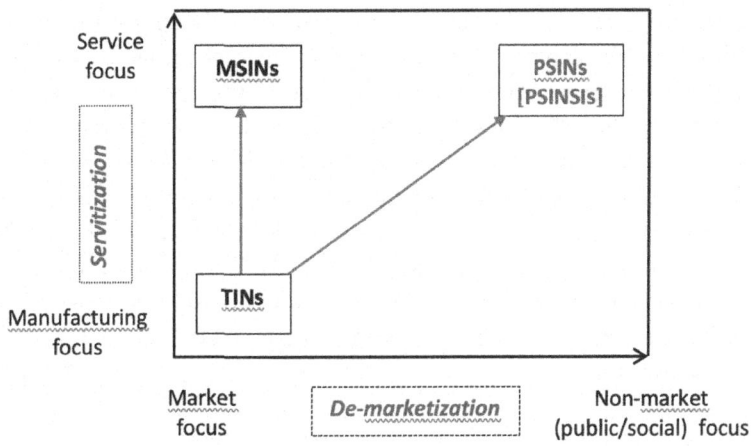

FIG. 1 – A typology of innovation networks: servitization and de-marketization.

Beyond sectoral focus, the different types of innovation networks we have identified can be more precisely described using the following criteria: types of agents involved in the network; role played by the public agent; nature of the innovation targeted by the network. These criteria are, of course, closely dependent on the sectoral focus considered.

- Regardless of the network type considered, the agents involved belong to the following categories: manufacturing firms; market service firms; public service organizations; third sector organizations; citizens/users/consumers. In theory, all of these actors can be involved in any of the abovementioned types of network. What distinguishes one type of network from another is the relative importance of some of these agents.
- In these networks, the public agent can, exclusively or jointly, play two different roles: as an operational co-producer of innovation and as supporter/facilitator of innovation or network formation (meta-governance).
- As already stated, these networks may be set up for the production or implementation of innovations having different forms, scales, and sources.

Based on these criteria, a simplified general definition of each of the innovation networks under consideration can be formulated. First, TINs are networks that focus on manufacturing and technological innovation and in which the public administration is engaged in facilitation and meta-governance activities rather than in co-producing innovation. The archetype for this type of innovation network is the triple helix model. MSINs are innovation networks focused on market services and service innovation, whatever form it takes (technological or non-technological). PSINs, for their part, focus on innovation in public services. The main actors in such networks are citizens, public sector and third sector organizations. Finally, PSINSIs, which we discuss further in the following paragraph, are a specific sub-category of PSINs, dedicated to social innovation.

1.2 A FOCUS ON PSINSIs

PSINSIs are the ultimate expression of the servitization and de-marketization processes of the innovation network concept (see Figure 1). They are set up to address major societal issues, such as aging, healthcare, education, transportation and mobility, unemployment, security, children at risk, etc. Their preferred field is the so-called "wicked" problems, i.e. those that are complex, multi-faceted, systemic, and often conflictual, which demand multi-agent collaborations because they cannot be solved by just one individual agent. This type of problem often lies at the intersection of the various major societal problems mentioned above. For example, caring for children at risk is at the intersection of education, employment, safety, health, etc.

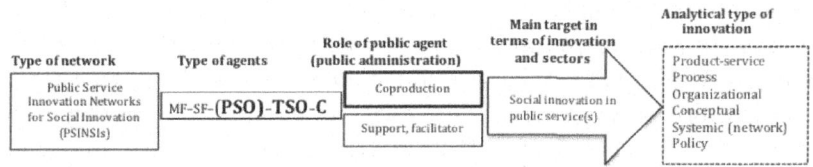

MF = Manufacturing Firm. SF = Service Firm. PSO = Public Service Organization. TSO = Third Sector Organization. C = Citizens, Users (Lead-Users), Consumers

FIG. 2 – Definition of a PSINSI.

Any type of agent can take part in a PSINSI, though the predominant actors are public service organizations, third sector organizations and citizens. In Figure 2, these are represented in bold and enlarged letters. PSO is bracketed in order to underline that the public agent may, in some cases, be absent from the innovation network – which nevertheless remains a public service innovation network insofar as it is dedicated to solving a social problem of general interest. When present in PSINSIs, this public agent is in charge of either co-producing (its dominant role) or supporting/facilitating innovation. The innovation in question is a social innovation.

Both innovation in public services and social innovation, and a fortiori social innovation in public services can encompass *product-service, process* and *organizational innovation* categories. However, they also cover other categories highlighted in the literature (Hartley, 2005; Halvorsen, 2005; Bekkers et al., 2006; Windrum, 2008), such as: *conceptual, systemic (network) and policy innovations. Conceptual innovation* encompasses the introduction of new concepts, new general frames of reference, new forms of rationale or even new paradigms. Examples include the concepts of "New Public Management" or "New Public Governance" (Bekkers et al., 2006) or "Big Society" (Lowndes & Pratchett, 2012). *Systemic (or network) innovation* refers to the establishment of new models of cooperation between organizations, or the improvement of existing models (Halvorsen, 2005). *Policy innovation* consists of the introduction of new laws and new modes of governance, i.e. new democratic institutions, and forms of participation (Bekkers et al., 2006; Hartley, 2005).

1.3 UNDERSTANDING PSINSIs FROM THE PSL PERSPECTIVE

Participation of different actors in the creation of value in public services has been emphasized in different public reforms since the 1960s. One of the most recent public management paradigm, the new public governance (NPG), emphasizes collaboration and seeks to transform relationships between established roles in public service delivery into trust and relational capital. Within NPG, citizens/service users and stakeholders are expected to co-produce public services with government and public managers through a horizontal relationship (Meijer, 2016). NPG provides room to consider public service not as a product but as a service. Service Dominant Logic – SDL (Vargo and Lusch, 2016) and its application to public services, PSDL (Osborne et al., 2013) are based on the hypothesis that any economic activity (both goods or services) is a "service offering". Today, PSDL is replaced by PSL (Osborne, 2018) as "this term maintains the link to service, rather than product-based theory, but distances it from being simply an offshoot of SDL."

Besides, PSL suggests that value co-creation process has both an intrinsic and an extrinsic side. On the one hand, value is created during the *use* and experience of public services, which extend across delivery and the service user's own lifeworld. Thus, users always participate in the intrinsic process, delivering *value-in-use* and *value-in-context*. On the other hand, PSL also reflects on the extrinsic processes of citizen participation where user participation depends upon the mechanisms established by the public service organization to facilitate genuine involvement, but also the willingness of each party to voluntarily engage in the process (Nabatchi et al., 2017), generating *value-in-production*. The extrinsic dimension is particularly useful to understand how value is created in PSINSIs, as innovation networks are driven by deliberate active cocreation engagements.

Figure 3 summarises our conceptual framework for understanding PSINSIs within a PSL perspective. Innovation networks are part of the extrinsic cocreation process aiming at generating public value (value-in-use and value-in-context) by adding value-in-production as output of the mere networked coproduction. There are other ways of extrinsic cocreation than networks, including bilateral relationships (between public administration an one individual or single organisation), and one-time short engagement (participation in one event). However, innovation networks are the structural arrangements in which the extrinsic role can be really multiactor and dedicated to cocreation over time. Determinants for this extrinsic activity of value co-creation include social needs and demands, regulatory changes, science and technology eco-systems or entrepreneurs and initiators particular stories.

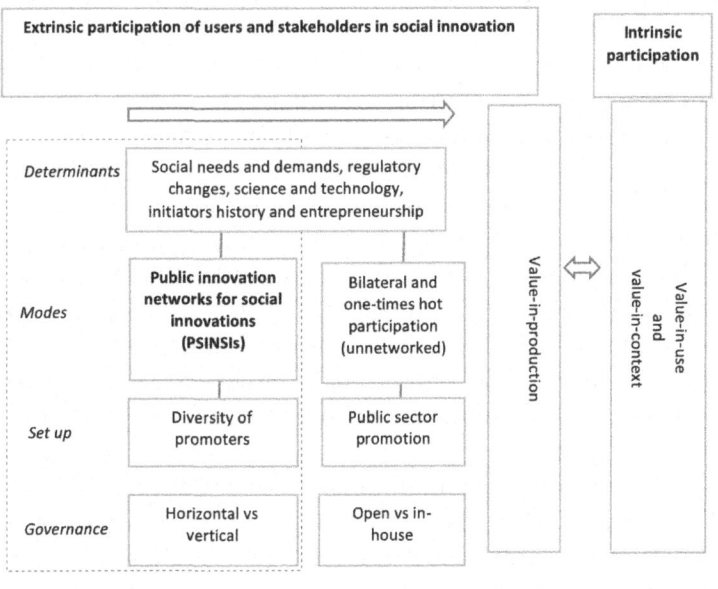

FIG. 3 – PSINSIs from a PSL perspective.

2. RESEARCH METHODOLOGY

Exploring empirical evidence on PSINSIs was achieved within the EU-funded Co-VAL project that made it possible to build a database of 24 case studies of social innovations developed within networked collaborations in the field of public services (Fuglsang et al., 2019; Merlin-Brogniart, 2019; Révész and Rosta, 2019; Magnussen and Rønning, 2019; Peralta and Rubalcaba, 2019). These case studies from five countries (Denmark, France, Norway, Hungary and Spain) cover the following five areas in which "wicked problems" are likely to give rise to social innovations: elderly issues, education, minorities, long-term unemployment, environmental protection.

In each country, case studies were selected according to three criteria: identification of a "wicked problem" within the five selected areas, identification of a social innovation to address this problem, and development of this social innovation by multi-agent collaboration.

Various sources were used for gathering information on the identified cases, including: existing gray literature, stakeholder websites when they exist, YouTube videos and TEDx conferences, focus group discussions, visits to facilities, and above all, interviews with stakeholders in each PSINSI. Across all the countries and cases concerned, the partners involved conducted more than 100 interviews (Fuglsang et al., 2019; Merlin-Brogniart, 2019; Révész and Rosta, 2019; Magnussen and Rønning, 2019; Peralta and Rubalcaba, 2019).

A joint methodology was defined across countries so that the case studies consisted of collecting data on dimensions such as types of social innovation, types of innovation network, drivers/barriers, institutional factors, and outcomes.

Annex 1 describes the social innovations and PSINSIs cases in the Co-VAL database. These cases are envisaged according to country, social problem(s) addressed, and a summary description of the social innovation at work in the network.

3. SOCIAL INNOVATION IN THE PSINSIs
OF THE CO-VAL DATABASE

It is not always easy to appraise the nature of a given social innovation, i.e. to translate its general description (Annex 1) into analytical categories (Annex 2). Indeed, the innovation carried out by the network may be multi-faceted, encompassing several innovations of different natures, and having different links between them. The line drawn between some traditional types of innovation (process innovation/organizational innovation) can be unclear, especially in service activities. Nevertheless, we carried out this typification exercise using the categories set out above: *product-service innovation, process innovation, organizational innovation, conceptual innovation, systemic (network) innovation, policy innovation.* (see Annex 2).

The vast majority of the social innovations selected are (or are also) *product-service innovations* (16 cases). They consist of the provision of new services to users, in response to a "wicked problem". At the time it is investigated, the network may be focused on a single product-service innovation (for example, in DK1, a rickshaw ride) or on several that make up a package (architectural innovation). For example, HU3 combines different training modules for older people with "a senior knowledge bank" containing the expertise and contact details of retired professionals willing to help the community.

As is often the case in services, *product-service innovations are often accompanied by innovative process and organizational changes.* For example, DK1 is based on the original use of rickshaws to walk the elderly and bring them out of their isolation, ES2 is an integration program through musical education, aimed at minority children, and is inconceivable without the digital technologies that allow musical collages, NO4 is based on closed-circuit vehicle driving.

Social innovation can however take the form of *a process, organizational or systemic innovation for a given service that is unchanged (or little changed) in its formal specifications.* In such a case, the innovation lies not in the service itself, but in how it is designed, produced, or delivered. Thus, in DK5, the two central elements are JOBiNTRA, the technological process innovation and the new network organization established between the municipal job center, employment agencies and citizens (systemic innovation). These elements make it possible to provide a flexi-job search service to citizens. Such a service is not new in itself, even though the innovations in question increase people's chances of finding flexi-jobs. In HU1, social innovation primarily takes the form of process innovation (an IT platform) to provide a service that already existed in other forms (letter to the mayor to report road problems).

Some of the technical systems used are technological process innovations in the truest sense. This applies, for example, to DK5 in which JOBiNTRA is an innovative IT platform designed by the IT company E-Bro, to HU1, which is also a new IT platform or to FRIDA in the case of NO1. In other cases, where the technology is not new, what leads us to qualify it as a process innovation is its use in a new and original context. Examples include the use of rickshaws to take senior citizens outside (DK1), and the use of vehicles in closed circuits as a way of caring for vulnerable young people (NO4), etc.

The notion of *systemic or network innovation* merits special attention. Indeed, all the social innovations in our database have an obvious and tautological relationship with networks, since they are, by definition, designed, produced, and implemented within networks. From this point of view, all are therefore systemic or network innovations. Nevertheless, we will limit the use of the notion of systemic or network innovation here to just two configurations: *Type 1 systemic or network innovation*: when the innovation lies, mainly or significantly, in the mode of collaboration, that is, in the constitution of the network, in other words when the innovation is the network itself (e.g. DK3, FR1, NO2, HU1); *Type 2 systemic or network innovation*: when the innovation produced by the network consists itself of new networks, in other words when the network produces new networks (e.g. DK4, NO5, HU3).

Social innovations, whether primarily product-service, organizational or network innovations, are also in some cases, *conceptual innovations* that reflect new world views that challenge the assumptions underlying existing services, products, processes and organizational forms (Windrum & Koch, 2008). Conceptual innovations are mentioned in six cases (see Annex 2). These include DK1 which is a simple idea (offering rickshaw rides to senior citizens to bring them out of their isolation) that has turned into a concept, becoming a worldwide movement in just a few years, FR2, that expresses a new business model that entails reallocating the costs of unemployment to employment.

Finally, two of the cases considered entail an explicit *policy innovation* dimension. One is FR1 (MAIA method), which is now a public policy, institutionalized in the Family and Social Action Code. The other is ES4, which is a public policy innovation aimed at improving the employability skills of young people, and long-term unemployed people, in the Spanish region of La Rioja.

4. FORMATION AND FUNCTIONING MODES OF PSINSIs

Although they differ from Traditional Innovation Networks and Market Service Innovation Networks, PSINSIs are not a homogeneous category, either in terms of their modes of formation or functioning.

4.1 PSINSIs FORMATION

PSINSI formation can be considered at two levels: general determinants and modalities. In both cases, the use of typologies makes it possible to order the variety of existing configurations.

4.1.1 PSINSI (and social Innovation) Determinants

– The Need

In public services, social innovation and corresponding networks emerge because of a social need or demand. This normally falls within the scope of the broadly defined public sphere (that of general interest, wherever it arises), but – for various reasons – is not addressed by the government. There may be a lack of competence and/or resources, or a political will to disengage from this social need.

The need reflects an aspiration to solve social problems. Insofar as PSINSIs are concerned, these problems are most often "wicked", i.e. systemic in their manifestation, and therefore demanding a systemic

resolution arrangement (network). Meeting the needs of an aging population thus raises issues in terms of health, housing, mobility, provision
of various services (examples: DK1, HU3), while meeting the needs
of minorities raises issues in the fields of education, unemployment,
security... (examples: FR4, HU4, HU5, NO2).

In the field of consulting, Milan Kubr (1988) distinguishes between
"corrective" problems for which innovation is a therapy undertaken to
rectify a difficult situation, "progressive" problems whose aim is to improve
a given situation that, while not yet bad, is expected to deteriorate in the
long term, and "creative" problems whose aim is to provide a totally new
and better solution, without there being any real problem to be solved
a priori. Such a typology seems applicable, at least partially, to societal
needs, social innovation and PSINSIs. In our database, most problems
are "corrective", insofar as networks are established to address tangible
problems that have a concrete manifestation (e.g. minority problems for
DK3, FR4, HU5, disabled problems for DK2 and NO5). But there are also
"progressive" (preventive) problems (e.g. DK1, DK4 and NO3). Conversely,
there do not seem to be any "creative" problems in the field of PSINSIs.
This is because their purpose is not to create a "demand" or a need (as may
be the case for economic and market innovations), but rather to making
the identified need disappear. Thus, the absolute indicator of the success
of a social innovation is the disappearance of the need that gave rise to it.
From this perspective, no innovation in our database is a success.

– Regulatory changes

In several of the cases in our database, legal reforms play an important
role. However, the relationship between PSINSIs (and corresponding
social innovation) and regulatory change can take various forms.

In some cases, regulatory change *determines* social innovation and the
creation of the PSINSI. For example, the formation of DK5 was determined by the Danish flexi-jobs law introduced in 2012; the formation
of FR2 (Zero Long-Term Unemployed Territory) was determined by
the 2016 law authorizing territorial experimentation to reduce long-
term unemployment; in NO1, the pilot experience was determined by
the 2017 amendment of the Health and Care Services Act, which gave
municipalities greater responsibility in supporting dependents.

Conversely, the regulatory change may itself result from the PSINSI and the corresponding social innovation. For example, in FR1, the MAIA method has become public policy and has been institutionalized in the Family and Social Action Code.

In other cases, PSINSIs are aimed at social innovation that is also a political innovation, i.e. an innovation that consists of the introduction of new laws and new modes of governance, i.e. new democratic institutions and forms of participation (Bekkers et al., 2006; Hartley, 2005). This modality is illustrated by the ES5 case in which the innovation is the implementation, through collaboration between public organizations and trade unions, of a regional plan to promote professional education and combat unemployment.

– Science and technology

In contrast to economic innovation, which is most often associated with tangible technological artifacts (products or processes), social innovation is often regarded as an intangible, non-technological object. In reality social innovation in PSINSIs can have a scientific and technical dimension, and it can also be brought about by scientific and technical determinants. Thus, with regard to relationships between PSINSIs and science and technology, the Co-VAL database makes it possible to highlight the following different, though not necessarily independent, configurations.

1. PSINSIs in which *the technological platform is a key element*. In HU1, for example, from the outset, the IT platform Járókelő. hu forms the backbone of the network. Another example is DK5, in which JOBiNTRA, the platform for communication between the various actors involved in the process of allocating flexi-jobs to the long-term unemployed, plays a fundamental role in the functioning of the PSINSI.

2. PSINSIs in which IT systems are *one element of innovation, among others*. Examples include FR1 (MAIA Method), in which the shared information system is one element of a multiform innovation, and NO1 (Flexible Relief for Dependents), where the FRIDA computer system allows career coordination (though this could otherwise be achieved by telephone).

3. PSINSIs based on a *philosophical, sociological or psychological theory.* Several cases fall into this category, including DK1 (Cycling Without Age), which is driven by a particular conception of leadership called "purpose makers" and by the philosophy of the "random act of kindness", centered on the value of free acts of benevolence and kindness; and DK4 (Bybi/Citybee), driven by Donna Haraway's thought (2016) and her analysis of an era (Chthulucene) in which humans and non-humans are inextricably linked, and sympoiesis (making-with) replaces auto-poiesis (self-making).

4. PSINSIs driven by a *research activity.* This configuration differs from the previous one in that here it is researchers implementing the results of their own research via a PSINSI, as opposed to citizen initiators of networks, who mobilize existing theories. Examples include FR1, the MAIA method, developed by two researchers at the Georges Pompidou European Hospital (Paris), and HU3, the formulation of the CédrusNet/CedarNet concept by the Hungarian sociologist Erika Sárközy at the Erasmus Research Institute (Budapest).

– Personal history of the PSINSI initiator and founding myths

A number of PSINSIs seem to owe their existence to a personal history, which can turn into a founding myth (as frequently happens in traditional entrepreneurship). The idea of offering rickshaw rides to seniors (DK1) came spontaneously to the founder in the fall of 2012, because he regularly came across an old person sitting on a bench in front of his care center, while cycling to work. DK3 was initiated by Agnete Grenness who wanted to improve the living conditions of her own learning disabled sister. The founder of Drive for Life (NO4) was European rallycross champion in 2009. Like the young people to whom he is a role model, he has personal experience of problems related to school *refusers.*

4.1.2 PSINSIs Modes of Formation

Network theory distinguishes two modes of network formation: *spontaneous* and *planned*. In the spontaneous mode, networks emerge in a self-organized way as a result of the convergence of the activities of agents faced with a given problem, in a given context (a neighborhood, city, region...). In the planned mode, their establishment is driven by an initiating agent who convinces other agents to join the network (Table 1).

TAB. 1 – Modes of formation and governance of PSINSIs[i].

Governance		Public initiator	Individual initiation	Organization initiation
HORIZONTAL	Stays horizontal	FR5 (2017); HU4 (2012); HU5 (2011); NO1 (2016); NO3 (2015); NO5 (2013); ES1 (2015)	DK4 (2009); HU1 (2012); HU3 (2015);	FR2 (1995/2011); FR3 (2012); FR4 (2018); HU2 (2016); NO2 (2018); ES2 (2017)
	Move towards vertical		DK1 (2012); DK2 (1977);	DK3 (2010)
VERTICAL	Move towards horizontal	DK5 (2012); FR1 (2008)		
	Stays vertical	ES4 (2016)	NO4 (2011)	ES3 (2008)

i.   Date of creation into brackets.

Despite some spontaneous manifestations[1], all the PSINSIs in the database were planned. The narratives of the various cases make it possible to identify the initiating agent as well as the precise context of the PSINSI initiation and the modalities of the constitution of the collaborative system. This "bias" (in favor of planned PSINSIs) in our database can be explained by the fact that the very existence of a specific initiating agent (often producer of a discourse – or even a

---

1   In FR5 and HU2, for example, the PSINSI idea emerged in the course of public events (discussion following a film screening in the municipal hall for FR5, and a forum at which the main stakeholders met, in HU2).

mythology – about him/herself) makes it possible to identify a planned PSINSI more easily than a spontaneous one.

The initiator of a planned network can be a public or a private agent. As we have already pointed out, in any innovation network it is ultimately a matter of individuals interacting with others. However, it is important to distinguish between the individuals as they work on behalf of the organization that employs them (in this case, it is their organization, rather than the persons themselves, that is considered the initiator) and the individual who takes part in the network in a personal capacity. If the distinction between private and public initiator is considered without taking into account the institutional dimension (individual vs. organization), then it can be observed in the Co-VAL database (see Table 1) that the initiator is a private agent in 14 cases and a public agent in 10 cases. Yet across both private and public spheres, the initiator is an individual in 6 cases and an organization in 18 cases (8 private organizations and 10 public organizations).

It should be noted that, in our database, where the initiating agent of a PSINSI is private, the individual or organizational nature of the initiator does not pose any problem. Indeed, this agent is either an individual or a third sector organization. It should be noted that (although theoretically possible), the database does not contain any case where the private initiator is a manufacturing or service company. On the other hand, when the initiating agent is public, it is always an organization. In some cases, it should however be noted that although initiated within a public organization, social innovation is developed by an individual who seems to express him/herself as an individual citizen, on the fringes of their professional activity. This situation is illustrated by DK5, where a civil servant takes innovative initiatives that quickly lead him to leave the administration to set up a company, FR1 (MAIA method) where the initiators of both network and method are two researchers from the Georges Pompidou Hospital, and HU4, where the starting point is the personal initiative of a school principal. In these cases it is particularly difficult to draw the line between a civil servant's activity as a citizen (private agent) and as a representative of a public organization (public agent). Thus, we attribute all initiatives to the organization that employs him or her, rather than to the individual.

4.2 PSINSIs MODES OF FUNCTIONING

The PSINSI can function in either horizontal or vertical mode (Table 1). However, it is not always easy to determine its mode of functioning. Indeed, the functioning mode is not always homogeneous within the network.

For example, the network may function in different ways with regard to relationships between the main stakeholders and the relationships between those stakeholders and users/recipients. When considering recipients, network functionality will vary according to its nature. For example, the most vulnerable users are most often in a vertical relationship with the main stakeholders. In HU2, for instance, relationships between the main PSINSI partners are horizontal, whereas those with users (weakened by their disability) are vertical. In NO1, if the recipients (the dependents) are not taken into account, the mode of operation between stakeholders is horizontal (it is a research project). Initially, then, the project operated in a top-down mode vis-à-vis the users. As the project evolved, the mode of operation became vertical, integrating the "dependents" to a greater extent, in order to correct certain mistakes made in defining their needs and implementing solutions.

Similarly, especially when the PSINSI is large, its main stakeholders are not necessarily homogeneous and may include more or less involved subgroups working together in different ways. For example, the mode of functioning may be horizontal at the core of the network, but vertical in terms of relationships between the core and the periphery. Thus, in DK2, there is a horizontal mode of functioning between the Grennessminde Foundation and the private partners (manufacturing and services firms) that offer internships or jobs to young people within the context of legislative change. It is probably more vertical in the subcontracting relationship established between the government (principal) and Grennessminde.

For the sake of simplicity, in our analysis and assessment of PSINSIs modes of functioning (see Table 1), we will only take into account users/citizens if they are actively involved in the network. Neither will we take into account possible differences in functioning modes within subgroups of the network. In other words if, for example, the mode of functioning within a component of the network is horizontal, yet this component is linked via vertical relationships with other components, we will consider that the network as a whole is vertical.

In our analysis of the mode of functioning of PSINSIs, where sufficient hindsight is available, we tried to identify the mode of functioning in the infancy of the network and its mode of functioning at the time of the empirical investigation (see Table 1).

In the Co-VAL database, 19 cases are initiated in a horizontal mode and 5 in a vertical mode, wherein the initiator is most often the conductor. Of the PSINSIs that were horizontal at the outset, 3 have evolved toward a vertical mode of functioning. One of these is DK1. This PSINSI, which initially functioned in a bricolage way, coped with its own success by setting up two coordination structures (associations) – one for the Danish national network (CUA), the other for the international network (CWA). The others are DK2 and DK3, where the founding associations play a central role and have clear leadership. Of the PSINSIs that were vertical at the outset, 2 have become horizontal. These are DK5 and FR1. In total, at the time of our investigation, 18 PSINSIs functioned in a horizontal mode, and 6 in a vertical mode.

Regarding the mode of functioning of the PSINSIs, the following remarks can be made:

1. Verticality or horizontality does not depend on network size. Thus, both large and small networks can be observed to function in vertical or horizontal mode.
2. In some cases, the initiators of the PSINSI have made use of specialized coordinators. For example, in ES1 (Library of San Fermin), the project initiators commissioned design specialists social architects firms to organize the interactions, sessions and events. These actors of the network are Knowledge Intensive Business Services (KIBS) in the traditional sense of the term.
3. Some PSINSI actors, whether initiators of the network or not, appear as KISS (Knowledge Intensive Social Service) in Desmarchelier et al.'s sense of the term (Desmarchelier et al., 2020c). Like KIBS, they provide their partners with knowledge and assist them in innovation (here, social innovation) and build a bridge between multiple actors. Their disappearance can be particularly detrimental to the network. For example, in the case of DK2, the Grennessminde Foundation has all the characteristics of a KISS. Similarly, in HU2, the Civil

Center Public Benefit Foundation is described as a thinktank and coordinator for the PSINSI. The decision made by this KISS to leave the network in 2019 raised the usual question of network fragility in the event of the hub actor's defection.

4. The existence of a system integrator does not necessarily mean that the network functions vertically. On the contrary, this particular actor may in fact perform a coordinating function that ensures horizontal functioning.

CONCLUSION

The innovation network concept denotes a multi-agent structural arrangement established to produce innovation in collaboration. Over recent decades, it has been very successful in theoretical, empirical and policy terms (Gallouj et al., 2013). This success can be illustrated by the evolution/renewal of the concept along a dual trajectory of servitization and de-marketization. This has led academic research – as well as the operational management of organizations – to attach increasing importance to innovation networks in market services and public services. This article is devoted to the most recent result of this evolution, namely networks dedicated to social innovation in public services. Innovations supported by PSINSIs are social by their demarketized goals and by their means: bilateral coproduction systems (between public administration and individual citizens) give way to service multi-actor coproduction arrangements (involving public, private, third sector organizations and individual users).

This paper has proposed an analytical framework that makes it possible to distinguish PSINSIs from other expressions of the innovation network, that can be complementary, namely Traditional Innovation Networks, Market Service Innovation Networks and Public Service Innovation Networks. In the context of the PSL paradigm, addressing public services as particular services and not anymore as quasi-goods (Goods-Dominant Logic) or as undifferentiated services (Public Service-Dominant Logic), these PSINSIs reflect extrinsic value cocreation processes targeted towards value-in-production.

Besides, drawing on rich empirical material collected within the Co-VAL project, we have attempted to get inside the black box of this type of innovation network, seeking to better understand the nature of the social innovation developed and the modes of formation and functioning of these networks.

A number of managerial, policy and theoretical issues were not addressed in this work, although they would merit inclusion in a research agenda.

At the managerial level, though we have considered certain aspects of the determinants of social innovation and PSINSIs, we have not addressed the question of the obstacles they face. Our database provides factual elements relating to the various obstacles encountered in the constitution of PSINSIs. One such obstacle is the problem of aligning the institutional logics of the various actors. In the societal fields we have considered, the forces of alignment are powerful, since most PSINSIs have laudable social objectives (caring for the vulnerable, caring for the planet...), which can only lead to buy-in. Moreover, most of the time, PSINSIs are not in competition with other public and/or private actors, since they develop precisely in spaces left unoccupied. However, the forces of misalignment of institutional logics do exist, and the obstacles encountered are numerous (financial, cognitive, technical, human, institutional...); they deserve in-depth analysis.

Another important managerial and policy issue worthy of special attention is the evaluation of the performance of PSINSIs. The traditional indicators used in the technical world (volumes, productivity) are needed, however the tools of the market world (costs, search for financial resources) should not be excluded – even in the field of "wicked" problems. Above all, however, alternative evaluation tools relating to the civic and social, reputation and creativity worlds, must be considered (Desmarchelier et al., 2020b).

At the theoretical and policy levels, this question of social innovation and the corresponding networks needs to be taken out of its political and theoretical isolation. It is important to reflect on how we might envisage recognition of the existence of local and national systems of social innovation, and more broadly the articulation of these systems with traditional local and national innovation systems.

ACKNOWLEDGEMENT:

This work was undertaken within the EU-funded COVAL project [770356]: "Understanding value co-creation in public services for transforming European public administrations", H2020 project 2017-2020.

BIBLIOGRAPHY

AGGER A., HEDENSTED LUND D. (2017), "Collaborative Innovation in the Public Sector – New Perspectives on the Role of Citizens", *Scandinavian Journal of Public Administration*, vol. 21, n° 3, p. 17-37.

AKSOY L., ALKIRE L., CHOI S., KIM P. B., ZHANG L. (2019), "Social innovation in service: a conceptual framework and research agenda", *Journal of Service Management*, vol. 30, n° 3, p. 429-448.

ALFORD J. (2014), "The multiple facets of co-production: Building on the work of Elinor Ostrom", *Public Management Review*, vol. 16, n° 3, p. 299-316.

AVELINO F., WITTMAYER J., PEL B., WEAVER P., DUMITRU A., HAXELTINE A., KEMP R., JØRGENSEN M., BAULER T., RUIJSINK S., O'RIORDAN T. (2019), "Transformative social innovation and (dis)empowerment", *Technological Forecasting and Social Change*, 145, p. 195-206.

BEKKERS V., VAN DUIVENBODEN H., THAENS M. (2006), "Public Innovation and Communication technology: relevant backgrounds and concepts", in BEKKERS V., VAN DUIVENBODEN H., THAENS M. (Eds.), *Information and Communication Technology and Public Innovation*, IOS Press, p. 3-21.

BOVAIRD T. (2007), "Beyond engagement and participation: User and community coproduction of public services", *Public Administration Review*, vol. 67, n° 5, p. 846-860.

CALZADA I. (2018), "From Smart Cities to Experimental Cities?" in GIORGINO V. M. B., and WALSH Z. D. (Eds.), *Co-Designing Economies in Transition: Radical Approaches in Dialogue with Contemplative Social Sciences*, Springer, p. 191-217.

CALZADA I. (2020), "Democratising Smart Cities? Penta-Helix Multistakeholder Social Innovation Framework", *Smart Cities*, vol. 3, n° 4, p. 1145-1172.

CARAYANNIS E. G., GRIGOROUDIS E., CAMPBELL D. F. J, MEISSNER D., STAMATI D. (2018), "The ecosystem as helix: an exploratory theory-building study of regional co-opetitive entrepreneurial ecosystems as Quadruple/Quintuple Helix Innovation Models", *R&D Management*, vol. 48, n° 1, p. 148-162.

DESMARCHELIER B., DJELLAL F., GALLOUJ F. (2019), "Innovation in public services in the light of public administration paradigms and service innovation perspectives", *European Review of Services Economics and Management*, 2019-2(8), p. 91-120.

DESMARCHELIER B., DJELLAL F., GALLOUJ F. (2020a), "Towards a servitization of innovation networks: a mapping", *Public Management Review*, vol. 22, n° 9, p. 1368-1397.

DESMARCHELIER B., DJELLAL F., GALLOUJ F. (2020b), "Public service innovation networks (PSINs): an instrument for collaborative innovation and value co-creation in public service(s)", *European Review of Service Economics and Management*, 2020-2(10), p. 133-169.

DESMARCHELIER B., DJELLAL F., GALLOUJ F. (2020c), "Mapping Social Innovation Networks: Knowledge Intensive Social Services as Systems Builders", *Technological Forecasting and Social Change*, 157 (August) https://doi.org/10.1016/j.techfore.2020.120068. Accessed 3 January 2022.

DJELLAL F., GALLOUJ F. (2012), "Social innovation and service innovation", in FRANZ H.-W., HOCHGERNER J. and HOWALDT J. (Eds.), *Challenge Social Innovation Potentials for Business, Social Entrepreneurship, Welfare and Civil Society*, Springer, p. 119-137.

DJELLAL F., GALLOUJ F. (2018), "Fifteen challenges for service innovation studies", in GALLOUJ F., and DJELLAL F. (Eds.), *A Research Agenda for Service Innovation*, Edward Elgar, p. 1-26.

ENGEN M., FRANSSON M., QUIST J., SKÅLÉN P. (2020), "Continuing the development of the public service logic: a study of value co-destruction in public services", *Public Management Review*, vol. 23, n° 6, p. 886-905.

ETZKOVITZ H., LEYDESDORFF L. (2000), "The dynamics of innovation from national systems and 'Mode 2' to a triple helix of university-industry-government relations", *Research Policy*, vol. 29, n° 2, p. 109-123.

FUGLSANG L., HANSEN A. V., SCUPOLA A. (2019), *PSINSI Danish case studies*, COVAL project, WP6 Deliverable, June, European Commission.

GALLOUJ F., RUBALCABA L., TOIVONEN M., WINDRUM P. (2018), "Understanding social innovation in services industries", *Industry and Innovation*, vol. 25, n° 6, p. 551-569.

GALLOUJ F., WEBER M., STARE M., RUBALCABA L. (2015), "The future of the service economy in Europe: a foresight analysis", *Technological Forecasting and social Change*, 94 (May), p. 80-96.

HALVORSEN T., HAUKNES J., MILES I., RANNVEIG R. (2005), *On the differences between public and private sector innovation*, PUBLIN project, Deliverable 9, FP5, European Commission.

HARAWAY D. (2016), *Staying with the trouble. Making kin in the Chthulucene*, Duke University Press.

HARTLEY J. (2005), "Innovation in governance and public services: Past and present", *Public Money and Management*, vol. 25, n° 1, p. 27-34.

HAXELTINE A. AVELINO F., PEL B., DUMITRU A., KEMP R., LONGHURST N., CHILVERS J., WITTMAYER J. M. (2016), *A framework for Transformative Social Innovation* (TRANSIT project Working Paper # 5), European Commission.

KEAST R., BROWN K., MANDELL M. (2007), "Getting the right mix; unpacking integration meanings and strategies", *International Public Management Journal*, vol. 10, n° 1, p. 9-33.

KELLY G., MULGAN G., MUERS, S. (2002), *Creating public value: an analytical framework for public service reform*, Cabinet Office Strategy Unit, United Kingdom Cabinet Office, London.

KUBR M. (1988*), Management Consulting: a Guide to the Profession*, Geneva, BIT.

LÉVESQUES B. (2012), "Social Innovation and Governance in Public Management Systems: Limits of NPM and search for alternatives?" *Les Cahiers du Crises, Collection Études théoriques*, n° ET1116, March.

LOEFFLER E. (2009), *Opportunities and challenges for innovative service delivery*, OECD-CRC.

LOWNDES V., PRATCHETT L. (2012), "Local governance under the coalition government: austerity, localism and the 'Big Society'", *Local Government Studies*, vol. 38, n° 1, p. 21-40.

LYON F. (2012), "Social Innovation, Co-operation, and Competition: Interorganizational Relations for Social Enterprises in the Delivery of Public Services", in NICHOLLS A., MURDOCK A. (Eds.), *Social Innovation*, Palgrave Macmillan, p. 139-161.

MAGNUSSEN S., RØNNING R. (2019), *Norwegian case studies report*, COVAL project, WP6 Deliverable, June, European Commission.

MARQUES P., MORGAN K., RICHARDSON R. (2018), "Social innovation in question: The theoretical and practical implications of a contested concept", *Environment and Planning C: Politics and Space*, vol. 36, n° 3, p. 496-512.

MARTIN B. (2015), *Twenty challenges for innovation studies*, SWPS 2015-30, November, SPRU Working Paper Series.

MEIJER A. (2016), "Coproduction as a structural transformation of the public sector", *International Journal of Public Sector Management*, vol. 29, n° 6, p. 596-611.

MERLIN-BROGNIART C. (2019), *French case studies report*, COVAL project, WP6 Deliverable, June, European Commission.

MOULAERT F., MACCALLUM D. (2019), *Advanced Introduction to Social Innovation*, Edward Elgar.

MULGAN G., TUCKER S., RUSHANARA A., SANDERS B. (2007), *Social innovation: what it is, why it matters and how it can be accelerated*, Skoll centre for social entrepreneurship, Oxford Said Business school, working paper, The Young Foundation.

MUSTAK M. (2014), "Service innovation in networks: A systematic review and implications for business-to-business service innovation research", *Journal of Business and Industrial Marketing*, vol. 29, n° 2, p. 151-163.

NABATCHI T., SANCINO A., SICILIA M. (2017), "Varieties of Participation in Public Services: The Who, When, and What of Coproduction", *Public Administration Review*, vol. 77, n° 5, p. 766-776.

O'BYRNE L., MILLER M., DOUSE C., VENKATESH R., KAPUCU N. (2014), "Social Innovation in the Public Sector: The Case of Seoul Metropolitan Government", *Journal of Economic & Social Studies*, vol. 4, n° 1, p. 53-71.

OEIJ P., VAN DER TORRE W., VAAS F., DHONDT S. (2019), "Understanding social innovation as an innovation process: Applying the innovation journey model", *Journal of Business Research*, 101, p. 243-254.

OSBORNE S. P. (2006), "The New Public Governance?", *Public Management Review*, vol. 8, n° 3, p. 377-388.

OSBORNE S. P. (2018), "From public service-dominant logic to public service logic: are public service organizations capable of co-production and value co-creation?" *Public Administration Review*, vol. 20, n° 2, p. 225-231.

OSBORNE S. P. (2020), *Public Service Logic: Creating Value for Public Service Users, Citizens, and Society Through Public Service Delivery*, Routledge.

OSBORNE S. P., RADNOR Z., STROKOSCH, K. (2016), "Co-production and the co-creation of value in public services: a suitable case for treatment?", *Public management review*, vol. 18, n° 5, p. 639-653.

OSBORNE S. (Ed.). (2010), *The New Public Governance?* Routledge.

OSBORNE S. P., RADNOR Z., NASI G. (2013), "A new theory of public service management? Toward a (public) service dominant approach", *The American Review of Public Administration*, vol. 43, n° 2, p. 135-158.

PERALTA A. , RUBALCABA L., (2019), *Spanish case studies report*, COVAL project, WP6 Deliverable, June, European Commission.

PESTOFF V., OSBORNE S. P., BRANDSEN T. (2006), "Patterns of co-production in public services: Some concluding thoughts", *Public Management Review*, vol. 8, n° 4, p. 591-595.

POL E., VILLE S. (2009), "Social innovation: buzz word or enduring term?", *The Journal of Socio-Economics*, vol. 38, n° 6, p. 878-885.

RÉVÉSZ É., ROSTA M. (Eds.). (2019). *Hungarian case studies report*, COVAL project, WP6 Deliverable, June, European Commission.

SICILIA M., GUARINI E., SANCINO A., ANDREANI M., RUFFINI R. (2016), "Public services management and co-production in multi-level governance settings", *International Review of Administrative Sciences*, vol. 82, n° 1, p. 8-27.

SINCLAIR S., MAZZEI M., BAGLIONI D., ROY S. (2018), "Social innovation, social enterprise, and local public services: Undertaking transformation?", *Social Policy Administration*, 52, p. 1317-1331.

STROKOSCH K., OSBORNE S. P. (2020), "Co-production from a Public Service Logic Perspective", in Loeffler E. and Bovaird T. (Eds), *The Palgrave Handbook of Co-Production of Public Services and Outcomes*, Palgrave Macmillan, p. 117-131.

TERSTRIEP J., REHFELD D., KLEVERBECK M. (2020), "Favourable social innovation ecosystem(s)? – An explorative approach", *European Planning Studies*, vol. 28, n° 5, p. 881-905.

TORFING J. (2019), "Collaborative innovation in the public sector: the argument", *Public Management Review*, vol. 21, n° 1, p. 1-11.

VAN DER HAVE R., RUBALCABA L. (2016), "Social innovation research: An emerging area of innovation studies?" *Research Policy*, vol. 45, n° 9, p. 1923-1935.

VICKERS I., LYON F., SEPULVEDA L., MCMULLIN C. (2017), "Public service innovation and multiple institutional logics: The case of hybrid social enterprise providers of health and wellbeing", *Research Policy*, vol. 46, n° 10, p. 1755-1768.

VOORBERG W., BEKKERS V., TUMMERS L. (2015), "A systematic review of co-production and co-creation: embarking on the social innovation journey", *Public Management Review*, vol. 17, n° 9, p. 1333-1357.

WINDRUM P., KOCH P. (Eds.) (2008), *Innovation in public sector services. Entrepreneurship, Creativity and Management*, Edward Elgar.

ZIEGLER R. (2017), "Social innovation as a collaborative concept" *Innovation: The European Journal of Social Science Research*, vol. 30, n° 4, p. 388-405.

ANNEX 1
Social innovations and PSINSIs in the Co-VAL database

PSINSI case	Social issue	Description of social innovation
Denmark		
DK1: Cycling Without Age	Elderly issues	Rickshaw rides for elderly people living in nursing homes or receiving home care, aimed at bringing them out of isolation.
DK2: Grennessminde	Education, accommodation and disability	New educational, vocational training and residential services for mentally disabled young people + platform for social enterprises providing new services.
DK3: Mind Your Own Business	Education, unemployment, minorities	Support for entrepreneurship projects for young people in deprived neighborhoods. Development of professional and social skills.
DK4: Bybi	Social inclusion, environmental issues	Rental of beehives to create social connections and preserve the environment, training in beekeeping.
DK5: E-Bro and JOBiNTRA	Long-term unemployment	Reorganization by a job center of how to find flexi-jobs for the long-term unemployed, using an IT platform and changing the organization of work.
France		
FR1: MAIA method	Elderly issues	Method designed to improve care for seniors, based on the *integration* of support and care services, strategic and tactical coordination, management of complex cases.
FR2: Zero Long-Term Unemployed Territory	Long-term unemployment	Project aimed at reducing long-term unemployment by involving the unemployed in the creation of their own jobs.

FR3: The Booster Program	Education	The program aims to bring minors in difficulty back to school by alternating *community* civic service with high school refresher courses.
FR4: The Melting Potes Program	Minorities	Integration of discriminated groups (Roma, refugees) by means of community civic service (mixing Roma and French people).
FR5: La Fabrique Saillysienne	Environmental issues (mainly)	New form of cooperation between citizens and a municipality, to develop community projects.
Hungary		
HU1: Járókelő (passer-by)	Urban issues	Computer platform allowing citizens to report road problems and track their resolution.
HU2: Esélykör (Circle of Opportunity)	Disability care Long-term unemployment	Integrated care (regarding employment in particular) of the disabled, in a city.
HU3: CédrusNet (CedarNet)	Elderly care Adult education	Programs and projects for and with the elderly in Kecskemét city.
HU4: No Bad Kid – Pressley Ridge Hungary Foundation	Roma minorities Education	A new educational service designed to meet the integration needs of Roma children
HU5: BAGázs Public Benefit Association	Roma minorities Education Long-term unemployment	A set of services (mentoring, education, legal advice, retailing…) for the integration of the Roma community.
Norway		
NO1: Flexible relief for dependents	Elderly demented people and their families	Respite system for family caregivers of elderly demented people, relying on volunteers and supported by a computer platform.
NO2: Strength of connecting vulnerable groups	Long-term unemployment Minorities, drug addicts	Connecting two existing networks: long-term unemployed drug-addicted men, long-term unemployed immigrant women.

NO3: Refugees as resources in rural areas	Minorities	Method of integrating refugees in rural municipalities, as a way of combating rural desertification.
NO4: Drive For Life	Vulnerable youth	Social integration of vulnerable young people by offering closed-circuit driving lessons and basic training in car repair.
NO5: Re-establishing personal networks for demented people	Mental disability	Care for demented people, and respite for care givers, via the (re-)creation of networks around demented people.
Spain		
ES1: Library of San Fermin project	Excluded citizens (minorities)	Design of a new type of library, with multi-agent collaboration in setting up the library model (types of services), the building, and the surrounding public spaces.
ES2: Antropoloops project	Education of minority children	Arts education program for "minority children" that remixes fragments of traditional music to create musical collages. It uses new technologies to promote intercultural dialog, knowledge of traditional music and collective creation.
ES3: Alas Foundation project	Disabled elderly	Facilities for assisting mentally disabled persons in old age.
ES4: The Plan for Professional Education and Employment of La Rioja	Youth professional education and unemployment	Plan to facilitate access to employment for citizens of the La Rioja region.

ANNEX 2
An attempt to typify social innovations in the Co-VAL database

PSINSI case	Innovation type
DK1	- Product/service innovation (rickshaw ride) - Conceptual innovation (a simple idea that has become a worldwide movement) - Process innovation (the rickshaw as a means of mobility for elderly people) - Systemic innovation [Type 1] (new forms of collaboration)
DK2	- Product/service innovation (training services + new services offered by the social enterprises involved) - Process/organizational innovation (teaching methods) - Systemic innovation [Type 1] (new ways of collaborating with partners)
DK3	- Organizational innovation (horizontal organization and collective decision-making) - Systemic innovation [Type 1] (strategic collaborations with private partners) - Conceptual innovation (learning a business-oriented logic)
DK4	- Conceptual innovation (paradigm shift: beyond consumerism, new principles of production, consumption and life) - Product/service innovation (beekeeping and honey production courses) - Organizational innovation (new and inclusive modes of co-production) - Systemic innovation [Type 2] (social networks around the hive and its exploitation)
DK5	- Technological product innovation (JOBiNTRA from the point of view of the IT company) - Technological process innovation (JOBiNTRA from the point of view of other actors) - Product/Service innovation (improvement of the flexi-job search service offered to citizens) - Systemic innovation [Type 1] (simultaneous increase in competition and collaboration between the different actors involved in the search for a flexi-job for a given citizen)

FR1	- Organizational innovation (new work organization method, new functions/jobs: pilot, case manager) - Process innovation (new communication tools: multidimensional analysis form and multidimensional evaluation tool, individualized service plan, shareable information system) - Systemic innovation [Type 1] (networking and integration of actors based on other organizational and process innovations) - Policy innovation (MAIA is now a public policy)
FR2	- A conceptual innovation (a new business model: reallocating to employment the costs of unemployment) - Organizational innovations (a new recruitment method known as reverse recruitment [jobs created according to the skills of individuals and not traditional selection], creation of an Employment-based Enterprise (EBE), horizontal management within EBE). - Systemic innovations [Type 2]. EBE is often the node of a new network.
FR3	- Product/service innovation (new flexible training services and new services carried out as part of the civic service) - Organizational/process innovation (mixed teams associating minors and adults)
FR4	- Product/service innovation (new flexible training services and new services carried out as part of the civic service) - Organizational/process innovation (mixed teams of volunteers half Roma and/or refugees and half indigenous people)
FR5	- Systemic innovation [type 1 and 2]. The network is itself an innovation, which will give rise to network innovations - Product/service innovations (participatory garden, car sharing, magazine exchanges, beehives...)
HU1	- Technological process innovation (IT platform) - Systemic innovation [Type 1] (network between citizens, authorities, repairers...)
HU2	- Systemic innovation [Type 1] (it is the building of the network itself that improves services to disabled people)
HU3	- Product/service innovations (training modules for the elderly, a "senior knowledge bank" containing the expertise and contact details of retired professionals) - Systemic innovation [Type 2] (creation of "cedar circles", small self-organized informal networks that provide solutions to community problems)
HU4	- Product /service innovation (educational services)

HU5	- Product/service innovations (mentoring, education, legal advice, business activities...) - Conceptual innovation (giving a chance, not giving money; not accepting public funding) - Organizational innovation (permanent presence in the camps, mobile charity shop)
NO1	- Product/service innovations (respite services for people living with demented elderly, counseling services, training services) - Technological process innovation (improvement of an existing IT platform by adding a module for dependents)
NO2	- Product/service innovation (job search assistance for long-term unemployed drug addicts and immigrant women) - Organizational innovation (café where members of both networks meet) - Systemic innovation [Type 1] (connecting both networks)
NO3	- Organizational innovation (method for increasing the number of refugees in training or employment after finishing the introductory program)
NO4	- Product/service innovation (driving training, car mechanics training, personal development) - Process innovation (a car driven in closed circuit)
NO5	- Product/service innovation (dementia care service, respite service) - Systemic innovation [Type 2] ((re-)creating networks around old demented people)
ES1	- Conceptual innovation (a new library concept) - Product/service innovation (new services that go beyond those of a traditional library) - Systemic innovation [type 1]: (co-creation system with stakeholders)
ES2	- Product/service innovation (artistic training/education service) - Process innovation (use of digital technologies in music learning)
ES3	- Product/service innovation (facilities and services to address aging issue of mentally disabled people) - Systemic innovation [Type 1] (innovation in the way of dealing with other stakeholders) - Systemic innovation [Type 2] (The Alas foundation is the central node of several networks proposing different social innovations. ES3 is one of them)
ES4	- Policy innovation (aimed at improving the employability skills of young people and the long-term unemployed - Systemic innovation [Type 1] (innovation also lies in the way the different stakeholders work together)

RECENT DEVELOPMENTS IN EUROPEAN INTEGRATION FOR SERVICES

Peter M. Smith
KU Leuven

INTRODUCTION

In this paper the focus is on the common market for non-financial commercial services[1]. Financial services apply different accounting principles which preclude the type of estimates provided here. The paper extends and updates the earlier estimates for 18 Member States in 2008 for European integration in services published in the Service Industries Journal (Smith, 2015). The estimates now cover the EU-28 for 2017 and the individual countries for 2016. These are the most recent years available. For the original 18 countries, the paper examines how the different sources of supply have developed over the nine-year period by type of service. It also examines whether integration for services between Member States has converged or diverged within the EU over this period. It provides a simulation of the EU market for services with and without the United Kingdom and how this affects trade in services between the EU-27 and the UK.

Overall, there has been little change in the degree of integration for non-financial services within the EU. Permanent presence through

---

1   Sales of foreign affiliates, permanent presence and right of establishment are all used here to denote inward foreign direct investment (mode 3 under the GATS). Freedom to provide service covers cross-border trade irrespective of whether the supplier and user are situated in different countries or when either the supplier or the user moves physically to another country on a temporary basis to provide the service (modes 1,2 & 4 under the GATS).

foreign direct investment is still the dominant form of internationalization for services. Differentiation by level and type of integration
takes place at the level of the individual service where for some services
cross-border trade rather than permanent presence is the dominant
form of internationalization (transport and some knowledge intensive
business services). Developments over time for the 18 countries in the
original sample are somewhat mixed but with some positive elements
for cross-border trade. Overall levels of integration (imports plus sales
of foreign affiliates as % of apparent consumption) between countries
have converged between 2008 and 2016. This overall result disguises
movement in opposite directions with cross-border trade diverging and
permanent presence converging over time.

Now that the UK has left the EU, the Single Market for non-financial services shrinks by around 16% and becomes less integrated. Sales
of foreign affiliates are relatively lower in the EU-27 than in the UK
although import penetration is higher. Contrary to expectation, the
EU-27 runs a small surplus on cross-border trade in the non-financial
services covered by this paper because the large surpluses on transport
and travel exceed UK surpluses on knowledge intensive business services.
Future restrictions on the provision of high-level services from the UK
could potentially harm EU competitiveness because these services are a
key input for all businesses. Foreign direct investment of the EU-27 in
the UK for non-financial services exceeds that of the UK in the EU-27
by a substantial margin. This "static" picture will of course evolve over
time as the two economies adjust to much greater friction between the
two, especially for services since the UK rejected an EEA type agreement
in favour of a "Canada style" free trade agreement.

The next section presents some theoretical considerations relating
to integration. Section 3 examines how to measure integration applying the methodology of the previous paper. Section 4 discusses the
data requirements for the measure developed in section 3. Section 5
presents the results of the measurement exercise. Section 6 discusses
BREXIT in the context of integration for services. Section 7 presents
some concluding remarks on how to further the integration of the EU
market for cross-border provision of services.

1. MARKET INTEGRATION

The study of economic integration in general and as applied to the European case underwent considerable theoretical development in the post-war period pioneered by Tinbergen and Balassa. Tinbergen (1954) made an important distinction between negative and positive integration. Negative integration refers to the removal of existing barriers such as tariffs. Positive integration implies the creation of common rules to apply throughout the area in question. While both are required to successfully integrate national economies, positive integration is particularly important for the Single Market in services because barriers to trade in services take place behind the border and often arise from differing regulatory regimes. Balassa (1961) introduced the idea of different levels or stages of integration. Free trade areas denote a lower level of integration than a customs union which is lower than a common market and economic union (Sapir, 2011). While the predominant movement in Europe has been towards higher forms of integration, BREXIT takes the UK back to the beginning with a free trade area.

Following Balassa, economic integration refers to both a (dynamic) process and a (static) state of affairs. Most of the subsequent literature has been concerned with the dynamics, for instance the reduction of barriers to trade or the impact of successive enlargements of (what is now) the European Union (EU). Even though European integration is clearly an on-going process, adopting a static approach which looks at where the process has arrived at a specific point of time is a valuable and neglected one which this paper aims to fulfil. It provides in a sense a benchmark for the distance yet to travel and against which subsequent development can be measured.

Pelkmans (2006) defines economic integration as the elimination of economic frontiers between two or more economies. He makes the important point that:

> There is no a priori reason for assuming that economic frontiers coincide with territorial frontiers: countries are demarcated by territorial frontiers, and economies by economic frontiers. Thus, local economies need not always add up to one regional economy if economic frontiers between different local communities persist. Likewise, economic frontiers between regions

may inhibit national economic integration. European economic integration is driven by efforts to reduce or eliminate the public role of territorial frontiers with European neighbours as economic frontiers. But, as the definition implies, this is a necessary, not a sufficient, condition for economic integration. Demarcations within and between national economies may remain, perhaps as a result of natural barriers… the costs of which have not been sufficiently reduced by infrastructural and transport provisions, or perhaps as a result of great disparities in the levels of development, or perhaps as result of business collusion in a region or country. (Pelkmans, 2006, p. 3)

The objective of the Single Market Programme (SMP) is to remove barriers to market integration that stem from the existence of national borders. This does not imply that a single homogeneous market would necessarily emerge. Instead, local cross-border markets in frontier regions, markets that constitute more than one Member State but less than the whole can emerge on the basis of shared language, culture, climate or other factors. Market integration merely means that internal borders are no longer the most important feature of how to define a market and that market participants are behaving as if these borders no longer exist.

How is market integration expected to be achieved once barriers have been removed? Increased cross-border trade in goods, services, capital and labour are expected to drive integration through the desire to seek out new markets by those who wish to export and by those who wish to broaden their sources of supply by those who wish to import. Particularly for services, the concept of trade has to be broadened to include the sales of foreign affiliates through foreign direct investment.

Market integration should result in more competition on the different markets. This may come directly in the form of foreign trade and investment or indirectly through the threat that foreign suppliers may pose to previously protected national or local suppliers. Potential competition from foreign suppliers is analogous to the threat of entry for incumbents and can be linked to the literature on the contestability of markets (Baumol, 1982). In practice some actual trade will be required in order for the threat of entry by foreign suppliers to become credible. How much is required will of course be determined by the nature of the market in question.

For services where permanent presence is a very important form of internationalization, a measure based exclusively on cross-border trade is seriously incomplete. However, the impact of foreign direct investment on competition is unlikely to be similar to that of cross-border trade. One important motivator for FDI in goods has been tariff jumping, or the desire to avoid a protectionist measure by going behind it. For services the equivalent would be regulation jumping whereby a firm will try and circumvent regulatory impediments to trade by setting up under the host country's rules and regulations. Foreign investment may take place through greenfield investment, the acquisition of an existing firm, through joint ventures or arms-length modes such as licensing or franchising. In all cases the foreign firm will benefit from the protection accorded to domestic firms against the threat of imports from other countries.

Competition is not valued for itself but as a means to provide benefits in terms of cheaper prices, more variety and higher quality. Greater competition is also expected to drive gains in terms of productive efficiency and through higher productivity the ability to increase also incomes. Lastly the desire to escape competition on existing markets is expected to spur innovation. The Single Market Programme therefore is a means and not an end, expected to work through increased trade to stimulate more competition.

2. MEASURING MARKET INTEGRATION

Market integration is expected to lead to price convergence through the law of one price. In an integrated market this implies that international relative price differentials should be arbitraged away so that identical products in different countries should sell for the same price when expressed in a common currency (Pippenger, 2015). A key advantage of the law of one price for studying integration lies in the way that border effects can be controlled for directly by comparing prices. At European level, the availability of data from the purchasing power parities programme has made it a particularly attractive way of tracking progress under the Single Market Programme (European Commission, 1996, 2001, 2007). Monetary union and particularly the introduction of euro notes and coins with the attendant boost to transparency of prices across border also led to interest in the degree to which prices converge across the euro zone (ECB, 2002, 2005, 2006, 2007, 2009, 2014).

Using final demand prices and more generally consumer prices to measure integration is subject to (at least) four major drawbacks. First, numerous violations to the law of one price have been found for consumer products (Haskel and Wolf, 2001). Second, two thirds of goods and 45% of services were sold to other firms in the form of intermediate consumption in 2010 for the EU-28. Third for services, comparing prices is not at all obvious. Unlike commodities that can be traded on an exchange (soybeans), services are often highly differentiated. At the limit each service is unique (management consultancy) and there is a unique price for each act. Liberalisation of markets for telecommunications and air transport has led to an explosion of different prices in the form of a multitude of different types of package for telecommunications and prices that can change by the second for the same class of air ticket on the same route at the same time on the same day.

Fourth, price convergence does not need to be driven by market integration but may be the result of the Balassa-Samuelson effect, which suggests that productivity growth in the traded sector of an economy usually exceeds that in the non-traded sector. Generally speaking, the further the price level in a country is from the average, the higher the differential between prices of goods and services. The wave of EU enlargement since 2004 has considerably widened disparities in levels of development within the EU. Overall, therefore, differences in the prices of services within the EU can be expected to be heavily influenced by the Balassa-Samuelson effect rather than by the level of market integration achieved.

The degree to which services are traded domestically constitutes another avenue by which the degree and possibilities for market integration for services might be explored. If services are constrained to limited local markets close to points of consumption within otherwise integrated national markets, then removing barriers to trade across borders will not necessarily lead to more cross-border trade. This would be an example of the type of natural barrier mentioned in the previous section.

Jensen and Kletzer (2005) were the first to address the issue of the degree to which services are traded domestically through a pioneering study of co-location of production and consumption of services within US metropolitan areas. Subsequently their methodology has been applied to France, Denmark, Sweden and Finland and found to have wider applicability (Barlet *et al.*, 2010; Borchsenius et al., 2010; Eliasson *et al.*,

2012; Huovari, 2012). Services for which production is more concentrated geographically than demand can be deemed to be traded domestically – and therefore potentially traded also internationally cross-border[2]. Some confusion has arisen between the concepts of tradable and traded. While on the extended definition commercial services are all tradable, they are not always traded because it may not be worthwhile economically to do so. Summarising the results of the French and other studies for Europe, we can develop a list of different categories of services that are traded domestically from highest to lowest (Table 1).

Implicitly, all the work using co-location of demand and supply are using trade as a measure of integration while conceptually it should be treated as means to achieve market integration and not as a measure of integration per se. Using trade both cross-border and through permanent presence as a surrogate for integration is justified to the extent that increased trade is expected to result from efforts to implement a Single European Market for goods, services, capital and labour. As a first pass, therefore, it measures the extent to which the SMP has succeeded in its initial objective. As a second pass and to the extent that actual trade is necessary to credibly affect competition within Member States, it can be used as an indicator of whether the SMP is likely to have led to such an increase in competition.

TAB. 1 – Domestic trade of different types of services.

Most traded	Highly traded	Medium trade	Low trade	Least traded
Air transport	Rail transport	Road transport	Postal services	Retail trade
Water transport	Advertising & market research	Telecommunications	Rental & leasing activities	Public administration
R&D	Auxiliary transport services	Architecture and engineering services	Waste management	Health care
Computer services	Travel Agencies	Real estate	Security & services to buildings	Social services
Audio-visual services	Employment agencies	Hotels & restaurants	Wholesale trade	Personal services to households
	Professional services	Cultural, recreational and sporting activities		Education

Source: Own elaboration on basis of Barlet et al. (2010), Borchsenius et al. (2010), Eliasson (2012).

---

2   All commercial services can be traded by foreign direct investment unless forbidden to do so by, for example, ownership restrictions.

Trade as a measure of integration has a number of advantages over the other possible measures. It can be applied to different geographic and product levels of disaggregation. It can be used to measure developments over time as well as levels at a given point of time. It is flexible to the definition of trade and can be extended to include permanent presence as well as cross-border trade.

Using trade as a measure of market integration turns out to be anything but straightforward. Services are traded in a number of different ways and understanding trade in services is relatively more complex than trade in goods (Lejour and Smith, 2008)[3]. The General Agreement in Services (GATS) classifies trade in services according to four different modes and these have been widely adopted. The first way and the nearest equivalent to trade in goods is direct cross-border transactions in which the purchaser of the service is located in one country and the provider in another (mode 1). Transport services are usually provided in this way. Services also cross borders when the consumer moves to the country of the provider to obtain a service (mode 2). This is the typical way in which tourism operates. Instead of the consumer moving, the supplier can temporarily move to the country of a client to provide a service (mode 4). Professional services such as management consulting as well as construction are often traded this way.

Collectively modes 1, 2 and 4 under the GATS constitute cross-border trade in services. The EU applies the term freedom to provide services to cross-border exchanges of services irrespective of whether they take place under mode 1, 2 or 4. It should be noted that when the definition of cross-border trade is broadened to include these three modes all commercial services and many social services including health and education can be traded cross-border. The tradability of services cross-border therefore needs to be taken as a given. It may not be in the commercial interest of a firm to trade cross-border but this does not affect tradability of services. Restrictive regulations may also make it difficult or even impossible to trade cross-border but these restrictions again do not affect the inherent tradability of services.

---

3   It should be noted that intra-firm trade is important for both goods and services. While the USA has long collected data on intra-firm trade, other countries have been slow to follow its lead and the lack of up-to-date comparable data across countries unfortunately precludes adequate treatment of this important topic.

Services are commonly traded through a permanent commercial presence in the host country (mode 3 of the GATS terminology). The EU applies the term right of establishment to services that are provided through foreign affiliates (Canoy and Smith, 2008). The figures for FDI tend to underestimate the significance of permanent presence for the provision of services because non-equity forms of participation constitute an important means for foreign companies to penetrate the markets of third countries. They include such techniques as franchising, management contracts, concessions and public–private partnerships and are prevalent in industries as diverse as hotels, restaurants and fast-food, car rentals, retailing and construction (UNCTAD, 2011). For many professional services, partnerships composed of locally established professionals are often the dominant or even required form of operation. Ownership restrictions of airlines and grandfathered landing slots have led to the growth of alliances of major carriers.

Firms may decide to supply services abroad through a permanent presence because it is more convenient to do so when sustained interaction with clients is required, when they are better able to exploit firm specific competitive advantages through foreign investment than by exports or as a means to circumvent restrictive regulation or to take advantage of opportunities opened up by the privatisation of public services. New Member States of the EU for example were the recipient of major inward investments in the distribution and financial sectors following the fall of the Berlin wall and their conversion to market economies.

Member States have been far more willing to countenance market opening through right of establishment, by which they retain a degree of control over the operations of companies on the domestic market, than through freedom to provide services. This leads to a rather unbalanced process of market liberalisation in favour of foreign direct investment over cross-border trade, with a potential impact on the actual degree of competition (Mustilli and Pelkmans, 2013). The attention given to both forms of market opening justifies including both in any measure of integration. For this purpose, we use the methodology developed and published in the article 'Does integration of services differ from integration of goods?' (Smith, 2015).

We start from the market using apparent consumption to measure the size of EU markets for the different services and overall:

Apparent Consumption = Production on the domestic territory − exports + imports
      = Turnover − X + I

In order to measure market integration, freedom to provide services (cross-border trade) and right of establishment (permanent presence) are combined and related to the size of the EU market:

$$Market\ Integration = \frac{Domestic\ Sales\ of\ Foreign\ Affiliates + Imports}{Apparent\ Consumption}$$

3. DATA

In order to calculate market integration as previously defined, a number of different data sources from Eurostat need to be combined (Smith, 2015). Structural business statistics (SBS) provide data on turnover for the different types of services and separately for Foreign Affiliate Trade in Servies (FATS) for which 2017 is the latest year available. Data on trade in goods comes from Comtrade and that on services from the Extended Balance of Payments in Services classification (EBOPS). Country estimates require compensation for so-called "carry along trade" which are imports that are also exported. 2016 input-output tables are used to make this adjustment which also limits country level estimates to that year. At EU level, trade is little affected by carry along trade which is mainly intra-EU so that it is possible to provide EU estimates for 2017.

To combine the different elements in order to calculate market integration, it is necessary to match the different sources, specifically the trade data on the one hand and the turnover data on the other. Trade data relates to products while that for enterprises relates to activities. In order to match the two, correspondence tables from Eurostat are employed. Unfortunately, the trade category "travel" has no immediate correspondence with the activity data. It covers "Accommodation and food service activities" but also other activities as well such as recreational services. As a result, travel is covered in the overall calculation of services integration but not at the level of the individual service.

4. EU MARKET INTEGRATION FOR GOODS AND SERVICES

Comparing manufacturing to services, the key difference concerns the level of cross-border trade. Import penetration for manufacturing is nearly five times that of services while the share of sales of foreign affiliates (inward FDI) is the same (Figure 1). As a result, just under two fifths of the market for manufactures is supplied by domestic firms against over two thirds for services. Domestic suppliers predominate for all major service categories. Construction remains overwhelmingly a domestic activity. Integration for distribution essentially takes place through FDI (for cross-border e-commerce see Sleuwaegen and Smith, 2020). At the other extreme, import penetration for professional, scientific and technical services is nearly as high as for manufacturing while sales of foreign affiliates are lower. Even though digitalization facilitates cross-border trade for information and communication services, internationalization for these services occurs mainly through FDI. Transport occupies an intermediate situation with import penetration above sales of foreign affiliates and overall levels of integration between those of distribution and information and communication.

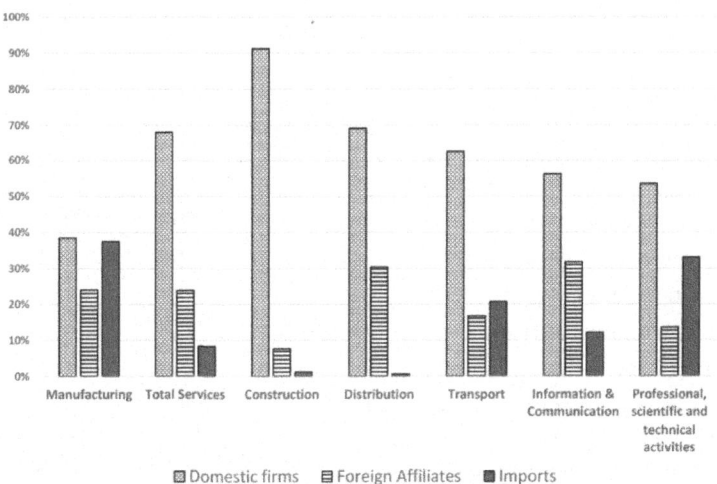

FIG. 1 – Levels of Integration for Manufacturing and Services, 2017.
Source: Own calculations based on Eurostat data.

With more disaggregated services, the contrast between integration through imports and permanent presence comes clearer into perspective (Table 2). Research and development, water and air transport are the services with highest levels of import penetration[4]. Public utilities and legal and accountancy services as well as construction and distribution have very little cross border trade and when they internationalize they do so via FDI. Air transport, management consultancy and advertising and market research internationalize both through cross-border trade and through right of establishment. For other professional services and information and communication services, permanent presence predominates.

TAB. 2 – Import penetration and sales of foreign affiliates by type of service, 2017.

	Domestic firms	Foreign Affiliates	Imports
Total Services	68%	24%	8%
Electricity transmission	76%	24%	0%
Waste treatment and de-pollution	85%	14%	0%
Construction	91%	8%	1%
Distribution	69%	30%	1%
Land Transport	76%	9%	15%
Water Transport	27%	8%	65%
Air Transport	34%	17%	49%
Auxilliary Transport services	59%	24%	17%
Postal and courier services	76%	18%	5%
Audiovisual and related services	64%	27%	9%
Telecommunications services	62%	29%	9%
Computer services	51%	30%	19%
Information services	48%	38%	15%
Legal & Accounting services	89%	4%	7%
Architects, engineers & technical services	69%	18%	13%
Advertising, market research, and public opinion polling services	43%	25%	32%
Management consulting and public relations services	43%	23%	34%

4   Because of the low level of imports, import penetration is presented on a log scale

	Domestic firms	Foreign Affiliates	Imports
Research and development services	7%	5%	88%
Other business services	65%	21%	14%
Operating leasing services	62%	28%	10%

Source: Own calculations based on Eurostat data

From the point of the view of the Single Market, the breakdown between intra and extra-EU imports and sales of foreign affiliates can also be important (Figure 2). Intra-EU imports constitute a majority of cross-border trade for both manufactures and for all major types of services. For manufacturing, information & communication and professional, scientific and technical services, sales of foreign affiliates originating outside the EU are the majority. For services in particular regulatory barriers can lead to third countries either preferring or being obliged to serve the EU market through a local presence.

At a more detailed level of services, three groups appear clearly (Annexe Table 1). The first group is composed of those services for which extra-EU trade is more important for both imports and sales of foreign affiliates (research and development and water transport). The second group is composed of those services for which intra-EU trade is dominant (construction, utilities and land transport). In between these two extremes are most services for which intra-EU imports are situated in the 50%-70% range and which are distinguished by the degree to which FDI originates from the EU or third countries. Third country control is more important than EU origin control for several professional and information and communication services (architectural and engineering, advertising, management consultancy, audiovisual, information and computer services). Sales of affiliates of EU multinationals are more important than those from third country ones mainly in certain forms of transport (air transport, postal and courier services and auxiliary transport services), distribution and other business services as well as telecommunications and legal and accountancy services. These services benefit from right of establishment dispositions under the Single Market and for which there may be specific ownership restrictions.

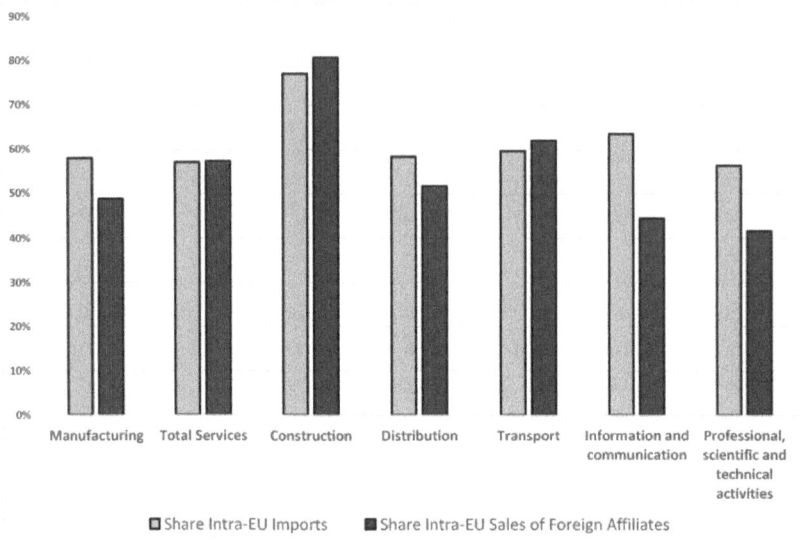

FIG. 2 – Breakdown of Intra and Extra-EU imports and sales of foreign affiliates, 2017. Source: Own calculations based on Eurostat data.

As developed in the previous sections, the relevant yardstick by which to judge whether trade in services is below the level that would be expected in an integrated single market is the degree to which services are traded domestically outside their region of production. Services that are traded domestically outside their area of production would be expected to be supplied from abroad by imports while services that are little traded domestically outside their area of production would be expected to be supplied by a local presence. Import penetration is measured against the domestic co-location Gini coefficient in Figure 3A and sales of foreign affiliates as a percentage of apparent consumption in Figure 3B.

The relationship between import penetration and the Gini coefficient of domestic trade is positive as expected. However, the goodness of fit as measured by a R^2 of 0.5385 is quite low. This would suggest that there are services that are not trading cross border to the expected extent. With regard to sales of foreign affiliates on the domestic market and the degree of domestic trade, the relationship is negative as expected but the goodness of fit with a R^2 of 0.0787 is very low so that there is little if any relation between the sales of foreign affiliates and the degree to which services are traded domestically.

By combining the information in Table 1 with that in Table 2, we can identify which services are traded as expected and which would be expected to be traded rather by imports but which in practice internationalize through sales of foreign affiliates. Research and development, water and air transport, advertising and market research and management consultancy are services that as expected display high import penetration. Distribution, waste management, and postal services are examples of services that would be expected to internationalize via FDI and which do in fact do so. Computer services, information services, audiovisual services, auxilliary transport services and legal and accountancy services are all services that would be expected to be highly traded cross-border but for which permanent presence is the preferred form of internationalization. Telecommunications, architectural and engineering services are also services that might be expected to trade more cross-border. We see therefore a heavy concentration of services in the digital economy and among some knowledge intensive business services (KIBS) that have yet to realise their potential for integration in the Single Market through cross-border trade.

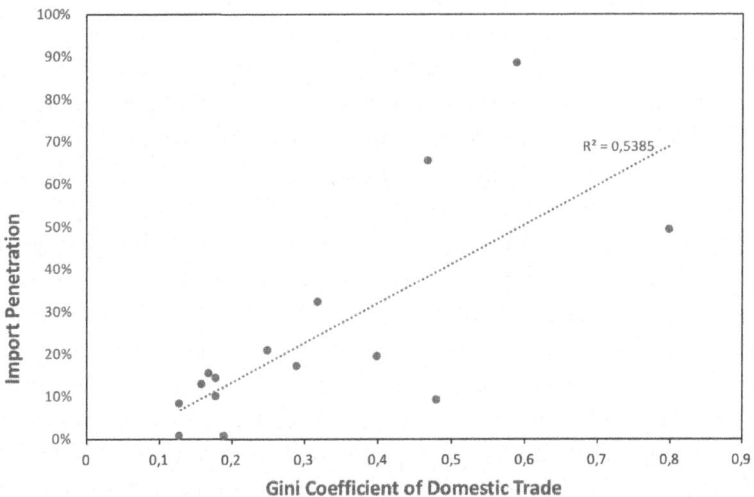

FIG. 3A – Import Penetration against Domestic Trade.

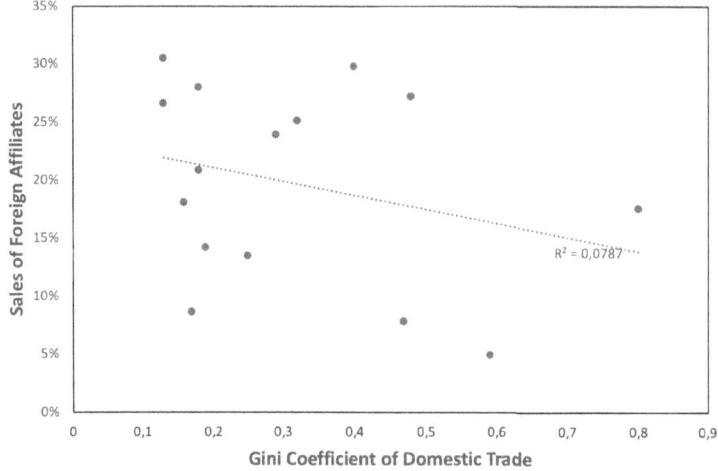

FIG. 3B – Sales of Foreign Affiliates against Domestic Trade.

To go beyond these general considerations requires a different approach. Two papers examine the role of service characteristics in respectively imports (Smith, 2017) and the choice between imports and FDI (Sleuwaegen and Smith, 2021). The first paper based on imports to 22 European countries for 8 years (2005-2012), indicates that the common effect of service characteristics on cross border trade does not play the prominent role usually ascribed to them in the literature. Rather it would seem that the degree to which a service involved fulfills a trade enhancing function for clients determines the extent of cross-border trade. The need for proximity between supplier and client continues to play an important albeit declining role in depressing the value of imports. Service characteristics appear to play a more significant role in the choice between exports and FDI than in cross-border trade. The importance of the requirement for proximity in the interaction between supplier and user of a service is again seen to be of particular importance. Other factors such as the ease with which it is possible to envisage a product rather than physical tangibility play an equally significant role. While the difficulty of evaluating the quality of a service before purchase does have the effect of dampening the choice of exports over FDI, the complexity of a service does not seem per se to limit the possibility of exporting.

Since digitalisation is rapidly developing the provision of on-line services and diminishing the need for physical proximity to exchange services, it is important to measure recent changes in the level of integration for services. For this we use the 18 countries in the original data set for 2008 updated to 2016. Since data for individual countries is less complete than that for the EU particularly at the detailed service level, reliability is lower than for the EU aggregates (Table 3).

TAB. 3 – Changes in Market Integration 2008-2016.

	Imports as % Apparent Consumption			Sales of Foreign Affiliates as % Apparent Consumption			Overall Integration		
	2016	2008	Change	2016	2008	Change	2016	2008	Change
Manufacturing	43.7%	36.2%	7.5%	19.5%	21.3%	-1.7%	63.2%	57.4%	5.8%
Total Non-Financial Services	7.0%	5.8%	1.3%	22.8%	23.8%	-1.0%	29.8%	29.6%	0.3%
Construction	1.0%	1.1%	-0.1%	7.3%	5.9%	1.4%	8.3%	7.0%	1.3%
Distribution	0.3%	0.3%	0.0%	28.7%	30.8%	-2.0%	29.1%	31.1%	-2.0%
Transportation and storage	*18.0%*	*18.1%*	*-0.2%*	*16.4%*	*13.5%*	*2.9%*	*34.4%*	*31.6%*	*2.8%*
Land Transport	13.8%	11.8%	2.0%	8.3%	6.5%	1.8%	22.1%	18.3%	3.9%
Water Transport	61.6%	69.0%	-7.4%	9.4%	5.0%	4.4%	71.1%	74.1%	-3.0%
Air Transport	46.0%	52.8%	-6.8%	18.9%	10.2%	8.7%	64.9%	63.1%	1.8%
Auxilliary Transport services	11.7%	14.2%	-2.5%	23.6%	20.1%	3.5%	35.3%	34.3%	1.0%
Postal and courier services	4.5%	5.1%	-0.6%	15.0%	8.5%	6.5%	19.5%	13.6%	6.0%
Information and communication	*10.9%*	*8.3%*	*2.5%*	*30.5%*	*29.0%*	*1.4%*	*41.3%*	*37.4%*	*3.9%*
Audiovisual & related services	6.0%	12.2%	-6.2%	30.1%	23.0%	7.1%	36.2%	35.2%	0.9%

	Imports as % Apparent Consumption			Sales of Foreign Affiliates as % Apparent Consumption			Overall Integration		
Telecommuni cations services	8.1%	5.9%	2.2%	34.3%	30.1%	4.2%	42.4%	36.0%	6.4%
Computer services	16.1%	8.9%	7.2%	28.2%	33.6%	-5.4%	44.3%	42.5%	1.7%
Information services	9.9%	1.4%	8.5%	36.4%	25.8%	10.5%	46.3%	27.2%	19.1%
Professional, scientific & technical activities	*18.0%*	*17.8%*	*0.2%*	*16.3%*	*14.6%*	*1.7%*	*34.2%*	*32.3%*	*1.9%*
Legal & Accounting	5.8%	4.9%	0.9%	3.0%	2.1%	0.9%	8.8%	7.0%	1.7%
Management consulting	20.3%	9.5%	10.8%	19.0%	22.4%	-3.4%	39.3%	31.9%	7.4%
Architectural, engineering & other technical services	15.5%	7.3%	8.1%	16.4%	15.4%	1.0%	31.9%	22.7%	9.2%
Research & development	61.2%	61.7%	-0.5%	14.5%	13.1%	1.4%	75.7%	74.8%	0.9%
Advertising & market research	25.0%	12.8%	12.2%	28.0%	22.7%	5.3%	53.0%	35.5%	17.4%

Source: Own calculations based on Eurostat data.

In terms of overall integration (imports plus sales of foreign affili-ates), integration for services hardly increased at all between 2008 and 2016 while that for manufacturing increased by 5.8% over the same period. Different forms of transportation saw large falls in import penetration except for land transport compensated for in the case of air transport by an increase in sales of foreign affiliates. Information and communication services apart from computer services witnessed large increases in sales of foreign affiliates. Both computer and information services saw substantial increases in import penetration. Among the professional, scientific and technical services there were major increases in import penetration by management consultancy, advertising and market research and architectural, engineering and other technical services. Management consultancy and advertising are among the least regulated of services. Heavily regulated legal and accountancy services remained much more nationally oriented with only small increases for import penetration and sales of foreign affiliates. Research and development had a small drop in import penetration and a larger increase in sales of foreign affiliates. This development would reflect a tendency of multinational companies to undertake R&D in affiliates to benefit from skilled researchers in these locations.

The final element in this presentation of the state of market integration concerns the country level in 2016. Previous data for 18 countries for 2008 identified a clear north-south divide for services among the EU-15 Member States with new Member States often exhibiting higher level of integration for both manufacturing and services. The situation in 2016 covering all 28 Member States presents a somewhat different picture. Southern European Member States from the EU-15 remain among the least integrated countries for both manufacturing and services but they are joined by Finland and Germany and for services only by Poland and Estonia. Among the other Member States no clear geographic pattern emerges.

Country size would be expected to influence both the overall level of integration and the form it takes (Table 4). Larger countries provide more choice and more competition between providers so it would be expected that this would discourage imports over domestic supply. This is a result that also applies to e-commerce (Sleuwaegen and Smith, 2020). Because of possible economies of scale and scope, larger countries would be expected to encourage foreign multinationals to set up subsidiaries in these countries. For the smaller countries, the opposite would be expected. Table 4 illustrates that while country size does seem to play the expected role for the largest and smallest Member States at least with regard to import penetration, there is no established pattern from the very small to the medium sized countries.

Tab. 4 – Country level integration, 2016.

Country	Import Penetration	Share Sales of Foreign Affiliates	Overall Integration	Population
Malta	73%	1%	74%	450,415
Luxembourg	25%	38%	62%	576,249
Cyprus	24%	14%	38%	848,319
Estonia	11%	17%	28%	1,315,944
Latvia	6%	42%	49%	1,968,957
Slovenia	9%	26%	35%	2,064,188
Lithuania	8%	24%	32%	2,888,558
Croatia	16%	21%	37%	4,190,669
Ireland	37%	26%	63%	4,726,286
Slovakia	7%	32%	39%	5,426,252
Finland	9%	19%	29%	5,487,308
Denmark	14%	19%	33%	5,707,251
Bulgaria	7%	26%	33%	7,153,784
Austria	9%	31%	40%	8,700,471
Hungary	10%	36%	46%	9,830,485
Sweden	9%	25%	34%	9,851,017
Portugal	9%	23%	32%	10,341,330
Czechia	7%	33%	39%	10,553,843
Greece	13%	14%	27%	10,783,748
Belgium	11%	24%	34%	11,311,117
Netherlands	13%	31%	45%	16,979,120
Romania	6%	39%	44%	19,760,585
Poland	5%	23%	29%	37,967,209
Spain	7%	22%	29%	46,440,099
Italy	5%	18%	23%	60,665,551
United Kingdom	6%	29%	35%	65,379,044
France	8%	17%	25%	66,638,391
Germany	6%	20%	26%	82,175,684
European Union	8%	23%	31%	510,181,874

Source: Own calculations based on Eurostat data.

Convergence describes the process by which different Member States come together over time. It can be interesting to also analyse convergence for market integration for services using the coefficient of variation (CV) as the measure. For the 18 Member States for which data exists for the earlier period, overall levels of integration (imports + sales of foreign affiliates as % of apparent consumption) did converge between 2008 and 2016 with a CV of 0.27 in 2008 and 0.20 in 2016. However, over this period convergence was driven entirely by sales of foreign affiliates (CV from 0.34 to 0.25) because import penetration diverged (CV from 0.41 to 0.49).

5. BREXIT

The UK left the EU on 1st February 2020 with the transitional period ending on 31st December of the same year. The most immediate impact of BREXIT is that the EU market becomes smaller and trade and investment between the UK and the EU that was previously internal to the EU becomes external. The EU's home market becomes 15.7% smaller for non-financial services against a drop of 10.7% for manufacturing. The largest fall is for audiovisual services (-30.5%) with above average reductions for construction, distribution, air transport, postal and courier services, travel and all categories of information and communication and professional, scientific and technical activities reflecting traditional areas of strength for the UK economy. Overall market integration (imports + sales of foreign affiliates) for EU-27 declines slightly because the UK has a higher level of sales of foreign affiliates than the EU-28 average (import penetration is lower).

We use national UK data rather than Eurostat data over the period 2016-2019 in order to look at the bilateral cross-border trade between the UK and the remaining EU-27, because the UK data appears more complete. As is well known, the UK runs substantial deficits on cross-border trade in manufactures both intra and extra-EU. The UK runs a substantial surplus on both intra and extra EU trade in services. This surplus depends mainly on financial services, for which continued access to the EU market will depend on the EU unilaterally granting equivalence post-BREXIT. However, the UK runs a small deficit on the non-financial trade in those services with the EU which are the subject of this paper while maintaining a surplus on extra-EU trade in services[5].

The UK deficit with the EU on non-financial services is accounted for by transport (except postal and courier services) and above all travel with smaller deficits on construction, waste treatment and operational leasing services (Table 5). The deficit on transport is composed of a small deficit on sea transport and much larger deficits on air transport and particularly land transport (mainly freight transport by road).

Telecommunications, computer and information services, professional services and technical, trade related and other business services from the UK are all in surplus with the EU reflecting the UK's comparative advantage in knowledge intensive business services. The largest UK surpluses with the EU are for legal, accounting and management consulting, computer services, advertising and market research, architectural, engineering, scientific and other technical services and other business services.

In terms of partner countries within the EU, the UK runs large surpluses on non-financial services with the Netherlands, Germany, Italy, Belgium, Denmark and Sweden and large deficits with Spain, Portugal, Greece and Poland (Annexe Table 2). Ireland (low cost air fares linked to tourism) is the main source of deficit for air travel with Hungary and the Netherlands also contributing. Poland, Romania and France are the major source of the UK's deficit with the EU on land transport. Spain followed by France, Greece and Portugal are the main contributors to the travel deficit. The largest UK surpluses for telecommunications, computer and information services are with Germany, France and the Netherlands followed by Sweden, Ireland, Spain, Denmark, and Italy. For professional and technical services, the largest UK surpluses are with Ireland, the Netherlands, Denmark, Luxembourg and Belgium.

---

5   When other non-financial services than those covered by this paper are included, the UK also runs a surplus on cross-border trade in services with the EU

TAB. 5 – UK cross-border trade with the EU, average 2016-2019 £ million.

	Credits	Debits	Balance
Total Services	116658	94306	22352
Financial Services	27103	6514	20589
Non-Financial Services	79313	81343	-2030
Transportation	13164	17218	-4055
Sea transportation	2324	2448	-124
Air transportation	9227	10377	-1150
Other modes of transportation	862	3644	-2782
Postal and courier services	750	750	1
Travel	17414	32116	-14702
Construction	1356	1450	-94
Telecommunications, computer and information services	10010	5818	4192
Telecommunications services	3011	2934	77
Computer services	5884	2348	3537
Information services	1115	536	578
Research and development services	2785	2588	197
Professional and management consulting services	17562	8367	9196
Legal, accounting, management consulting and public relations	12191	5623	6568
Advertising, market research and public opinion polling	5372	2744	2628
Technical, trade-related and other business services	16413	13407	3006
Architectural, engineering, scientific and other technical services	2335	1458	877
Waste treatment and de-pollution, agricultural and mining services	152	261	-109
Operating leasing services	59	147	-89
Trade-related services	1146	352	795
Other business services	12721	11189	1532
Personal, Cultural and Recreational	1426	526	900
Audiovisual and related services	611	381	230

Source: Own calculations based on UK data.

Using Eurostat data again for sales of foreign affiliates, for both manufacturing and non-financial services sales of affiliates of EU countries in the UK exceed those of UK companies in the EU (Table 6). While for manufacturing sales of UK affiliates in the EU reach 91% of those of EU affiliates in the UK, the situation is very different for non-financial services. Sales of UK affiliates in the EU only represent 37% of sales of EU affiliates in the UK. Half of inward FDI to the UK goes to the distribution sector with the electricity and transport sectors representing respectively a further 11% and 10%. UK sales of foreign affiliates in the EU are concentrated in information and communication (30%) and distribution (21%).

TAB. 6 – UK cross-border sales of foreign affiliates with the EU, 2017 Million euros.

	UK Sales of Foreign Affiliates to EU-27	EU-27 Sales of Foreign Affiliates to UK	UK Balance of Sales of Foreign Affiliates
Manufacturing	110,617	121,228.5	-10,611.5
Non-Financial Services	135,456.0	365,821.9	-230,365.9
Construction	11,840	16,784.8	-4,944.8
Distribution	28,696	181,587.0	-152,891.0
Accommodation & Food	4,534	7,164.9	-2,630.9
Transportation	11,704	37,526.0	-25,822.0
Information and Communication	40,698	29,027.9	11,670.1
Professional, scientific and technical activities	23,596	20,587.1	3,008.9
Administrative & support service activities	13,359	29,749.9	-16,390.9
Source : Own calculations based on Eurostat data			

When analysing the effects of BREXIT, we can rely on three types of sources at the time of writing. The first are anticipatory effects that occurred after the vote on the referendum but before BREXIT became effective after the end of the transition period on 1 January 2021 (Portes, 2020; Ahmad et al., 2020; Amuedo-Dorantes and Romiti, 2021). The second are the legal agreements between the UK and the EU that accompany BREXIT (Jacobsson, 2020; Barnard and Leinarte, 2021). For more recent developments, many of which are overclouded by the limitations placed on travel by the Covid-19 pandemic, we are obliged to rely on press reports (Hill, 2021; Foster and Barnes, 2021).

Ability to supply services cross-border cannot be separated from mobility of persons (Canoy and Smith, 2008). The mobility of natural persons is required whether to travel to a client to provide services on a temporary basis or for the user to travel to the point of supply or to send employees to a subsidiary abroad on a temporary or permanent basis or to set up as a self-employed service provider in another country. Indeed, one of the most far-reaching effects of BREXIT on trade in services between the UK and the EU concerns the impact of the loss of free movement of persons.

Three studies examine anticipatory effects of BREXIT. The first looks at trade in services in terms of regulatory restrictions outside the EU compared to those for EU members interacted with BREXIT probabilities between 2016Q1 and 2018Q4 (Ahmed et al., 2020). Increases in the probability of BREXIT lowered export values by between 20-49 log points and participation in trade by between 6 and 165 log points.

The second examines international student applications in the United Kingdom after BREXIT (Amuedo-Dorantes and Romiti, 2021). The UK higher education system is one of its most successful exporters of high value services ranking second only to the US in the numbers of foreign students. With the increase in student fees and the drive towards a more market-oriented university system since 2010, foreign students have become an important element in the financing of university courses. Among the highest rated, Russell group universities, 32% of students are of non-UK nationality. Changes in the volume of international student applications from the EU did not precede the BREXIT referendum but occured immediately after, persisting through the three year period that followed. The BREXIT referendum resulted in a 14% reduction in the growth of applications from the EU when compared to those from other international non-EU students (Amuedo-Dorantes and Romiti, 2021). The decline in applications was particularly important for STEM subjects, which the UK government is attempting to stimulate, compared to non-STEM subjects (17% reduction versus 13% reduction). Similarly, there was a greater reduction of EU applications to the most selective universities. Those students that have most choice where to study disproportionately decided to apply elsewhere. BREXIT therefore appears to be affecting negatively the quality of student applications as well as their number.

The third study of anticipatory effects examines immigration to the UK between the referendum and BREXIT (Portes, 2020). In the four years following the June 2016 referendum, net migration from the EU to the UK fell by three quarters or 150,000 persons. At the same time there was a significant rise in non-EU migration. While the largest numbers of migrants affected by BREXIT are EU citizens in the UK there has also been a movement of UK citizens to the EU in order to obtain settled status while it was still possible. OECD and Eurostat data show that migration from the UK to EU Member States increased by 16,810 in 2016-18 over the period 2008-15 or about 30%. Many of those along with already established British citizens in the EU also applied for citizenship in an EU Member State. According to Eurostat, 16,000 nationals of the United Kingdom obtained EU citizenship in 2018, six times higher than in 2015.

The EU-UK Trade and Cooperation Agreement (TCA) contains specific dispositions on services and investment, digital trade, intellectual property, public procurement and small and medium-sized enterprises as well as on aviation and road transport, social security coordination and visas for short visits, all of which are relevant for trade in services (European Commission, 2020). In spite of the wide-ranging list of areas covered by the TCA, the dispositions for services leave UK service providers with significantly less access to the EU market (and reciprocally) than previously. Service suppliers in the UK lost their automatic right to offer services across the EU. Instead, they need to comply with host country rules of each Member State because they lose the benefit of the country-of-origin approach or passporting in the case of financial services. For modes 1-3 under the GATS, all services are covered unless explicitly excluded. For mode 4 under the GATS (temporary presence of the supplier), a list of permitted activities is provided (Barnard and Leinarte, 2021). Among those services excluded are some air and water transport services and audio-visual services, the latter for which the UK runs a trade surplus. In addition, numerous reservations to liberalisation of services are listed in annexes to the agreement. Overall, UK suppliers to the EU will face considerable regulatory heterogeneity when exporting services. The fact that regulations often differ by market, means that the fixed costs of complying with regulations in an export market are in fact sunk market entry costs. Policy heterogeneity between countries has been shown to have a negative impact on bilateral service trade (Kox and Lejour, 2005).

For reasons inherent to services, much regulation applies to the provider rather than the service itself (Jacobsson, 2020). A very common form of regulation is to require that the service provider be in the possession of a specific qualification related to the service in question. The absence of a suitable qualification then constitutes an insuperable barrier to trade. The EU's Directive on mutual recognition of professional qualifications has been one of the most effective means to liberalise trade in services along with free movement of persons (Canoy and Smith, 2008). After BREXIT, UK nationals no longer benefit from mutual recognition and, irrespective of where they acquired their qualifications, need to have their qualifications recognised in each Member State in which they wish to do business. For professional services in particular, lack of mutual recognition is likely to constitute as great an inhibitor to trade as the limitations placed on provision of services supplied under temporary presence (mode 4 under the GATS).

The other major area where the ability to continue to provide services cross-border is likely to be impacted is through the limitations placed on mobility, often a requirement to provide services. With regard to the effect on mobility, the TCA must be read in conjunction with the Withdrawal Agreement. Under the withdrawal agreement, EU citizens who were already working in the UK and UK citizens in the EU will continue to enjoy settled status (Portes, 2020). For those wishing to migrate afterwards, free movement ended with the transition period. Instead, mobility under the TCA is temporary in nature and limited to those who are engaged in trade in services (Barnard and Leinarte, 2021). Visa free travel is an important corollary to the ability to provide services on a temporary basis. Both the EU and the UK allow visa-free visits of up to 90 days within any 180-day period as of 1 January 2021. However, this is not bound in the TCA and the EU decision is conditional on the UK continuing to provide for visa-free travel for EU citizens and on a non-discriminatory basis among Member States. Even so, Member States may require work permits for short stay visits if they are not covered by one of the service categories in the TCA such as musicians (Hill, 2021; Foster and Barnes, 2021).

The end of free movement will have a significant impact on the domestic provision of services in the UK. The UK has introduced a points based system for migrants emphasising skilled immigration. As a result, entry will be barred for migrants coming to work in low paid occupations which can be expected to affect health, social care, transport and construction particularly heavily (Portes, 2020; Plimmer, 2021; Neville, 2021). Hospitality is another area which relies heavily on migrants from the EU. The situation with regard to hospitality is less clear since many EU citizens with settled status left the UK during the pandemic and it is not certain that they will return afterwards.

An analysis of the respective trade and investment positions of the UK with respect to the rest of the EU demonstrates once again the weakness of the UK position. In particular for cross-border trade, the UK is exporting high value added services for which the Single Market is an important enabling factor while the UK is importing lower value added transport and travel services. Since exports are likely to face increased restrictions, it is possible that in spite of losing the advantages provided by the services directive for right of establishment, investing in the EU will become the preferred method of internationalization in the Single Market for UK service providers.

Direct consequences for the EU are less serious both because the UK represents a much lower share of trade and investment for the EU than for the UK and because the areas in which the EU runs a trade surplus on non-financial services are less likely to be affected by BREXIT (travel and some forms of transport). However, the longer term impact of BREXIT on the EU is less favourable. Knowledge intensive business service (KIBS) imports contribute to the competitiveness of domestic producers so that diminishing the quality and supply of service imports from the UK also affects negatively EU firms (Nordås and Kim, 2013; ECSIP, 2014; Ariu et al., 2019). In order to replace imports of KIBS from the UK the

EU can try to develop competitive domestic suppliers. This will require eliminating remaining barriers to cross-border supply in Member States and stimulating effective competition within the Single Market. The adverse effects on both the UK and the EU demonstrates that, at least in economic terms, BREXIT constitutes a lose-lose proposition.

CONCLUSION

Market integration for services remains dominated by permanent presence (right of establishment) rather than cross-border trade in services (freedom to provide services). As a means of integration, cross-border trade presents a number of advantages over permanent presence. It unambiguously increases competition since inward foreign direct investment may take over domestic suppliers without increasing competition on the domestic market. Cross-border provision is less costly for the supplier so that small and medium sized enterprises can more easily internationalize through this means and thereby assist them to grow. Services are more easily scalable when they can be supplied cross-border over the internet. The emergence of internet giants such as Google (Alphabet), Amazon and Facebook depended on scalablity. The fragmented nature of the EU's Single Market for services represents an obstacle to scalability.

There are many more firms supplying services cross-border than were previously believed including even firms with zero employees (Sleuwaegen and Smith, 2021). However, the large number of firms exporting services continue to remain small and export to few destinations. This would point to barriers to growth rather than barriers to entry for exporting. Compared to the US, the size distribution of firms in Europe displays a pronounced lack of a middle of medium sized firms for services such as distribution, transport, information and communication and professional scientific and technical services. In Europe, we observe large shares in employment for the smallest and largest size categories for these services while in the US shares in employment rise with each size category. A well-functioning single market for services should provide opportunities for small firms to grow into medium sized and ultimately large firms as occurs in the US.

Digitilisation offers the possibility to provide services that can be downloaded from the internet effortlessly and at marginal cost approaching zero. When the definition of cross-border trade is widened to increase temporary presence abroad of the service provider or client, all services can be provided cross-border unless prevented from doing so for instance by regulation. Even services that have traditionally been supplied via a local presence such as distribution can now be supplied cross-border through e-commerce. The willingness to purchase cross-border via e-commerce in the EU is quite low although this may now have changed as a result of the coronavirus epidemic (Sleuwaegen and Smith, 2020).

Certain services are already supplied predominantly cross-border within the Single Market. Cross-border trade is inherent in the provision of transport services. The case of professional services demonstrates that a wide range of high level business services can be supplied using temporary presence or via information technology. For those services, the key distinction is between the largely unregulated services such as management consulting, research and development and advertising and market research, which supply the market largely cross-border, and the more heavily regulated services, legal and accounting services and architectural, engineering and technical services with either very little cross-border activity or which tend to supply via sales of foreign affiliates.

Unlike goods, regulation of services generally applies to service providers rather than the service itself. This is why the recognition of qualifications is of such importance for services. The Services Directive remains the principal instrument for promoting market integration for most commercial services with the exception of certain areas with service specific regulation such as transport services, financial services, telecommunications and postal services (Flower, 2006-2007)[6]. It has some important provisions for right of establishment including for example the abolition of economic needs tests. In view of the very heterogeneous and fragmented nature of services, the decision to adopt a horizontal rather than service specific approach was inevitable. It had already been applied with regard to the Directive on the recognition of professional qualifications. The most controversial part of the original proposal for the Services Directive concerned cross-border trade in

---

6   As well as a number of areas that are excluded both from the Services Directive and other service specific regulation.

the form of the country of origin principle which was replaced in the adopted Directive by that of 'Freedom to provide services'. At the heart of the issue was the implication in the original proposal that providers were to rely on the rules of their home Member State in the access to and exercise of a service activity. Member States have been much more willing to countenance the setting up of foreign subsidiaries over which they maintain a high degree of control rather than delegating regulation over cross-border trade to foreign countries.

The country of origin provision can be viewed as a specific application of the general principle of mutual recognition in place of the alternative, harmonisation. Underlying mutual recognition is the belief that countries with similar levels of development and similar values will regulate to a similar standard. However, an EU of 27 Member States with very different levels of development and very different capacity of national administrations to apply laws and regulations compared to the EU of 15 Member States makes the acceptance of similar standards of regulation more difficult. The challenge of opening up markets for cross-border service provision for regulated services is therefore one of either making mutual recognition acceptable to Member States or replacing national regimes with EU level regulation.

The nature of that challenge is demonstrated by the fate of the Commission's services package of 2017 which proposed quite modest practical improvements for the functioning of the Single Market for services. Of the three elements in the package, a proportionality test before adoption of new regulation of professions, a services e-card and a services notification procedure similar to the one that has long existed for goods only the first has been adopted[7]. The two others have been withdrawn in the face of opposition from the Council and in the case of the e-card also from the European Parliament.

In view of the current situation, two main avenues to unblocking restrictions on cross-border restrictions on services present themselves: a non-regulatory approach which does not raise the same objections from Member States or further harmonisation and regulation established at EU level. As an example of the non-regulatory approach, the issuance of guidance documents by the Commission in the field of competition

---

7   Directive (EU) 2018/958 on a proportionality test before adoption of new regulation of professions

policy has proved successful. The Commission appears to be following that approach in its reform recommendations for regulation in professional services (European Commission, 2017). In that document the Commission restricted itself to architects, civil engineers, accountants, lawyers plus patent agents, real estate agents and tourist guides. The first four professions are are part of a set of professions which are heavily regulated in all Member States (health professions are also heavily regulated) and which will remain so in future. They have already received much attention through for example the OECD's product market regulation indicators (Nicoletti; Scarpetta; Boylaud, 2000).

However, it is the large number of services which are either not regulated or regulated to varying degrees in different Member States and for which the public interest nature of regulation is not always clear that should be the subject of most attention. Member States regulate up to 368 distinct professional service obligations with a quarter only regulated in one Member State (Dahlberg et al., 2020). The situation is similar in the US where access to professions is largely regulated at the state level. Following Dahlberg et al., it would be reasonable to assess the justification for regulations that exist in only one or a few Member States and why other Member States do not find it necessary to impose such regulations. The Commission's comprehensive regulated professions data base provides the necessary basis for such an evaluation exercise. In cases where access to a profession cannot be justified on public interest grounds, certification can be an attractive alternative to licensing. Licensing restricts access to a profession and constitutes a barrier to entry while certification offers practitioners the option to join a scheme that verifies that their skills meet certain standards (Koumenta and Pagliero, 2019).

Another line of non-regulatory approach would be an alternative dispute resolution (ADR) mechanism for services such as that being promoted for consumers. An ADR means settling a complaint out of court with the assistance of an impartial dispute resolution body without the need for infringement proceedings. In this case the ADR would attempt to settle disputes between the supplier wishing to provide a service cross-border and the host country which attempted to limit or prevent the service being provided rather than between a consumer and a supplier.

Even where regulation can be justified on public interest grounds, widespread "regulatory heterogeneity" between Member States adds to the costs of doing business across the entire Single Market (Kox and Lejour, 2005, 2006; Kox and Nordås, 2007). The mere fact of having to deal with different regulations is a cost in itself which can only be dealt with by harmonisation or direct regulation at EU level. At what level a service needs to be regulated and by whom is a major issue for the Single Market for services.

A fully integrated EU market for services requires a qualitative leap from the current situation. Recently the Commission has shown more ambition when presenting proposals for a Digital Services Act and a Digital Market Act[8]. However welcome the willingness to address problems that have emerged in the market for digital services, longstanding problems elsewhere still need to be dealt with. Within the sphere of digitally supplied services, the EU will be divided into 27 national markets for mobile communications as long as spectrum is allocated on a country-by-country basis. Longstanding problems for e-commerce stemming from geoblocking and the cost of deliveries across borders have been acknowledged but not adequately addressed. In particular issues relating to copyright and management of rights in an integrated market will need to be looked at afresh.

The initial push for the Single Market Programme enjoyed strong support from business and a major effort by the European Commission to present the benefits of the programme. These have been lacking in recent years. Overcoming regulatory fragmentation and opening up the markets for services to competition inevitably means that incumbents who have benefited from often well protected situations will react negatively to proposals coming from the Commission. These negative reactions need to be balanced by potential beneficiaries in the form of high growth firms and those that finance them such as venture capital funds and business angels whom must be mobilised before presenting proposals rather than afterwards. The Commission must also be sure to present concrete benefits from market opening to the public at large, which means giving more attention to B2C services.

---

8   Proposal for a Regulation of the European Parliament and of the Council on a Single Market For Digital Services (Digital Services Act) and amending Directive 2000/31/EC {SEC(2020) 432 final ; Proposal for a Regulation of the European Parliament and of the Council on contestable and fair markets in the digital sector (Digital Markets Act) {SEC(2020) 437 final}

REFERENCES

AHMED S., LIMÃO N., OLIVER S. and SHIKHER, S. (2020), *BREXIT Uncertainty and Its (Dis)Service Effects*, NBER Working Paper 28053, November 2020.

AMUEDO-DORANTES C., and ROMITI A. (2021), *International Student Applications in the United Kingdom after Brexit*, IZA Institute of Labor Economics, Discussion Paper Series, N° 14247.

ARIU A, JENSEN J. B., NILSSON HAKKALA K., and TAMMINEN S. (2019), *Service Imports, Workforce Composition, and Firm Performance*, NBER working paper 26355.

BALASSA B. (1961), *The Theory of Economic Integration*, Homewood, ILL. Richard D. Irwin Inc.

BARLET M., CRUSSON L., DUPUCH S., and PUECH F. (2010), "Des services échangés aux services échangeables: une application sur données françaises", *Economie et Statistique, 435-436*, p. 105-124.

BARNARD C., and LEINARTE E. (2021), *Mobility of Persons in the New UK-EU Relationship*, DCU Brexit Institute Working Paper N.6-2021.

BAUMOL W. J. (1982), "Contestable Markets: An Uprising in the Theory of Industry Structure", *American Economic Review*, vol. 72, n° 1, p. 1-15.

BORCHSENIUS, V., MALCHOW-MØLLER, N., MUNCH, J. R., SKAKSEN, J. R. (2010), "International Trade in Services - Evidence from Danish Micro Data", *Nationaløkonomisk Tidsskrift*, vol. 148, n° 1, p. 86-107.

CANOY M., and SMITH P. M. (2008), "Services and the Single Market", *Journal of Industry, Competition and Trade*, vol. 8, n° 3-4, p. 319-347.

DAHLBERG E., NAESS-SCHMIDT S., VIRTANEN L., MARCUS S., DI SALVO M., PELKMANS J., DALLA POZZA V., KUBOVICOVA K. (2020), *Legal obstacles in Member States to Single Market rules*, Policy Department for Economic, Scientific and Quality of Life Policies, Directorate-General for Internal Policies, European Parliament, PE 658.189 - November 2020.

ECSIP CONSORTIUM (2014), *Study on the relation between industry and services in terms of productivity and value creation*, Final Report. Study for the Directorate-General for Enterprise and Industry, European Commission, October 2014.

ELIASSON K., HANSSON P., LINDVERT M. (2012), "Jobs and Exposure to International Trade within the Service Sector in Sweden", *The World Economy*, vol. 35, n° 5, p. 578-608.

EUROPEAN CENTRAL BANK (ECB) (2002), *Price level convergence and competition in the euro area*, Monthly Bulletin, August 2002.

EUROPEAN CENTRAL BANK (ECB) (2005), *Sticky Prices in the Euro Area: A summary of new evidence*, Working Paper No. 563, December 2005.

EUROPEAN CENTRAL BANK (ECB) (2006), *Competition, productivity and prices in the euro area services sector,* Occasional Paper N° 44, April 2006.

EUROPEAN CENTRAL BANK (ECB) (2007), *How is real convergence driving nominal convergence in the new EU Member States?,* Working Paper N° 827, November 2007.

EUROPEAN CENTRAL BANK (ECB) (2009), *Determinants of inflation and Price level differentials across the euro area countries,* Working Paper Series n° 1129 December 2009.

EUROPEAN CENTRAL BANK (ECB) (2014), *One currency, one price? Euro Changeover-Related Inflation in Estonia,* Working Paper N° 1732, September 2014.

EUROPEAN COMMISSION (1996), *Price competition and price convergence,* DRI Europe, The Single Market Review Subseries V, Vol. 1, Office for the Official Publications of the European Communities, Kogan Page, Earthscan 1996.

EUROPEAN COMMISSION (2001), *Price levels and price dispersion in the EU,* European Economy, Supplement A - Economic trends, N° 7 – July 2001.

EUROPEAN COMMISSION (2007), *Price convergence in the enlarged internal Market,* European Economy, Economic Papers, N° 292 – November 2007.

EUROPEAN COMMISSION (2016), *Single market integration and competitiveness report.*

EUROPEAN COMMISSION (2017), *Commission Communication on reform recommendations for regulation in professional services* {SWD(2016) 436 final}.

EUROPEAN COMMISSION (2020), *Questions & Answers : EU-UK Trade and Cooperation Agreement,* 24 December 2020.

FLOWER, J. (2006-2007), "Negotiating European Legislation: The Services Directive", *Cambridge Yearbook of European Legal Studies, 9,* 217-238.

FOSTER P., and BARNES O. (2021), *Music industry decries first 100 days of Brexit deal as 'disaster',* Financial Times, 17 May 2021.

HASKEL J., and WOLF H. (2001), "The Law of One Price- A Case Study", *Scandinavian Journal of Economics,* vol. 103, n° 4, p. 545-558.

HILL, A. (2021), *Counting the real cost of Brexit,* Financial Times, 11/05/2021.

HUOVARI, J. (2012), *Globalization and the Location of Production,* Pellervon taloustutkimus PTT Reports 235.

JACOBSSON J. (2020), *Brexit and the Professional Services Sector – What Future for UK Professionals in Europe?,* DCU Brexit Institute Working Paper N. 01-2020.

JENSEN J. Bradford, and KLETZER L. G. (2006), "Tradable Services: Understanding the Scope and Impact of Services Offshoring", in COLLINS S. M. and BRAINARD L. (Eds.) *Offshoring White-Collar Work,* Brookings Trade Forum 2005, p. 75-133.

KOUMENTA M., and PAGLIERO M. (2019), "Occupational Regulation in the European Union: Coverage and Wage Effects", *British Journal of Industrial Relations,* vol. 57, n° 4, p. 818-849.

KOX, H, and LEJOUR, A. (2005), *Regulatory heterogeneity as obstacle for international services trade*, CPB Discussion Paper no. 49, 2005.

KOX, H, and LEJOUR, A. (2006), "The effects of the services Directive on intra-EU trade and FDI", *Revue Economique, 57(4)*, 747 – 769, 2006.

KOX, H, and NORDÅS, H. (2007), *Services trade and domestic regulation*, OECD Trade Policy Working Paper no. 49, 2007.

LEJOUR, A, and SMITH, P. M. (2008) "International Trade in Services—Editorial Introduction", *Journal of Industry, Competition and Trade, 8(3-4)*, 169–180.

NEVILLE, S. (2021), *Outflow of 'undervalued' nurses risks worsening NHS staff shortage*, Financial Times, 16/06/2021.

MUSTILLI, F., and PELKMANS, J. (2013), *Access Barriers to Services Markets*, CEPS Special Report No. 77 / June 2013.

NICOLETTI, G., SCARPETTA, S., and BOYLAUD, O. (2000), *Summary Indicators of Product Market Regulation with an extension to Employment Protection Legislation*, Economics Department Working Papers No. 226.

NORDÅS, H., and KIM, Y. (2013), *The Role of Services for Competitiveness in Manufacturing*, OECD Trade Policy Papers, No. 148.

PELKMANS, J. (2006), *European Integration Methods and Economic Analysis*, Third Edition Prentice Hall, 2006.

PIPPENGER, J. (2016), "Arbitrage and the law of one price: setting the record straight", *Theoretical Economics Letters, 6*, 1017-1033.

PLIMMER, G. (2021), "Builders raise alarm after EU labour flight", Financial Times, 15/06/2021.

PORTES, J. (2020), *Between the Lines: Immigration to the UK between the Referendum and Brexit*, DCU Brexit Institute Working Paper 12-2020.

SAPIR, A. (2011), "European Integration at the Crossroads: A Review Essay on the 50th Anniversary of Bela Balassa's Theory of Economic Integration", *Journal of Economic Literature, XLIX:4*, 1200–1229.

SLEUWAEGEN, L., and SMITH, P. M. (2021), "Service characteristics and the choice between exports and FDI: Evidence from Belgian firms", *International Economics*, vol. 168, December, p. 115-131.

SLEUWAEGEN, L., and SMITH, P. M. (2020), "Who purchases cross-border? Individual and country level determinants of the decision to purchase cross-border in the European Single Market", *Electronic Commerce Research*, https://doi.org/10.1007/s10660-020-09440-1.

SMITH, P. M. (2015), "Does integration of services differ from integration of goods?", *The Service Industries Journal 35(4)*, 217–235.

SMITH, P. M. (2017), "Trade costs and services", *European Review of Service Economics and Management, 4(2) 2*, 129-162.

TINBERGEN, J. (1954), *International Economic Integration*, Amsterdam, Elsevier.

UNCTAD, *World Development Report 2011*.

ANNEXE

TABLE A1 INTRA-EU TRADE BY DETAILED SERVICE, 2017

		Share Intra-EU Imports	Share Intra-EU Sales of Foreign Affiliates
Total non-financial services		57%	57%
Utililities, Construction & Distribution	Electricity, gas, steam supply	93%	82%
	Waste treatment and de-pollution	90%	53%
	Construction	77%	81%
	Distribution	58%	52%
Transport	Land transport and transport via pipelines	85%	78%
	Water transport	44%	48%
	Air transport	51%	76%
	Warehousing and support activities for transportation	50%	54%
	Postal and courier activities	55%	65%
Information & Communication	Audiovisual services	61%	49%
	Telecommunications	63%	77%
	Computer programming, consultancy and related activities	64%	33%
	Information service activities	63%	41%

Professional, Technical & Other Business Services	Legal and accounting activities	62%	76%
	Activities of head offices; management consultancy activities	64%	49%
	Architectural and engineering activities; technical testing and analysis	59%	49%
	Scientific research and development	32%	24%
	Advertising and market research	66%	43%
	Other business services	51%	55%
	Rental and leasing activities	66%	70%

TABLE A2 BALANCE OF UK CROSS-BORDER TRADE FOR A SELECTION OF SERVICES WITH EU MEMBER STATES, AVERAGE 2016-2019 £ MILLIONS

	Non Financial Services	Transport-ation	Travel	Construction	Telecommun-ications, computer and information services	Professional services	Technical, trade-related and other business services	Audiovisual and related services
Austria	-278	277	-1302	-13	455	323	-74	10
Belgium	5354	563	51	162	791	1402	343	20
Bulgaria	-1048	-361	-577	0	121	55	-96	-11
Croatia	-1720	-19	-1733	0	32	0	0	0
Cyprus	26	999	-1719	68	279	397	98	12

Czech Republic	596	-43	34	24	194	429	-93	-13
Denmark	6439	198	1179	73	1115	245	1534	-64
Estonia	47	8	14	1	26	16	9	-2
Finland	621	-182	80	-75	328	632	205	34
France	-2337	2394	-11600	-261	6088	5848	-4017	394
Germany	12305	-1378	3048	-381	7114	5302	-2739	411
Greece	-5095	1643	-7527	-17	389	396	113	6
Hungary	-3933	-3698	-357	9	215	129	-263	-3
Ireland	-537	-22312	233	637	1832	5264	16008	1
Italy	9903	4189	2717	-50	1021	2255	296	345
Latvia	-54	-26	-84	22	71	-12	13	4
Lithuania	-92	32	24	-39	36	5	-72	1
Luxembourg	2946	25	170	67	-1149	2936	-173	34
Malta	-379	135	-1334	0	185	238	213	11
Netherlands	19614	605	674	163	5280	7874	1828	44
Poland	-4755	-3413	-1431	-112	874	452	-348	-128
Portugal	-4133	1244	-6335	179	472	97	41	0
Romania	-2718	-2466	-157	-10	162	-41	-154	-4
Slovak Republic	-10	-320	-49	15	137	292	-110	0
Slovenia	124	11	38	-4	84	0	0	-5
Spain	-22993	9254	-35368	-340	1500	2897	222	-5
Sweden	6106	-576	2502	-3	2017	2417	109	98
EU Institutions	186	0	0	0	-4	50	0	0
Total EU28	-8120	-16219	-58809	-375	16769	36782	12025	920

COVID-19 PANDEMIC AND LECTURERS INTENTION TO USE LEARNING MANAGEMENT SYSTEM (LMS)

Singha Chaveesuk[a1]
Paweensuda Dechaprasert[a2]
[a]KMITL Business School, Bangkok, Thailand

INTRODUCTION

The COVID-19 pandemic emerged as 2019 dawned, in the Chinese province of Wuhan, and was quickly identified as a deadly disease, and, because it is highly contagious, soon spread across the world (Raza et al., 2021); in 2020, the World Health Organization reported that COVID-19 had spread to more than 130 countries. In a bid to combat this pandemic, nation states promoted social distancing, quarantine, and isolation, forcing people to stay in their homes. This new reality has seriously affected student access to education; to protect populations from the disease, governments around the globe have imposed policies of social distancing, isolation, necessary mask-wearing, hand sanitization, and self-quarantine (Anderson et al., 2020). The crisis has also severely affected the financial and psychosocial conditions of nations all over the globe; fully-fledged lockdowns were also imposed, and educational institutions suspended their physical educational activities (Raza et al., 2021). Technological advances provided opportunities for

1   singha@it.kmitl.ac.th
2   paweensuda.de@kmitl.ac.th

online education (Raza et al., 2021), and e-learning facilitated learning during periods of lockdown (Zwain, 2019). During COVID crises, universities around the world moved towards e-learning (Ali, 2020) and certain recent studies have reported on the significance of e-learning in HE (Wang et al., 2020; Raza et al., 2021; Kerres, 2020; Mailizar et al., 2020). E-learning tech (also known as Learning Management Systems - LMS), is defined by Alias and Zainuddin (2005) as web-based technology that facilitates the online learning process by implementing Information Technology (IT) at educational institutions. LMS enables students and lecturers to interact and share course materials and content online, allowing synchronous or asynchronous learning (Al-Busaidi and Al-Shihi, 2010).

Educational institutions currently use such LMS technologies as Desire2Learn, WebCT, Moodle, Blackboard, etc. (Waheed et al., 2016; Iqbal, 2011). LMS technology offers many supporting features and requires huge investment from universities, even though these features are not fully utilised by faculty members (Raza et al., 2020; Dahlstrom, et al., 2014). Jaschik and Lederman (2014) conducted a survey on lecturer attitudes towards technology, revealing that only 20% of faculty members use LMS to record lectures and post course materials. Further, Dahlstrom et al. (2014) posited that though 99% of HE establishments have LMS installed, only half of the faculty members use it on a regular basis, with most faculty members not using the benefits of LMS technology to improve their teaching practice. These results indicate a gap in factors affecting lecturer use of LMS for teaching purposes. Past studies have focused on student intention to use technology for learning in HE. Ali's 2020 study on online learning emphasised the importance of lecturer readiness to use online technology for teaching purposes. This study seeks to fill this gap in the literature by assessing lecturer intention to use LMS for teaching purposes in Thailand during COVID-19. Few studies have focused on the significance of Perceived Interaction and User-Interface Design as it affects technology use for teaching (Liu et al., 2010; Fathema et al., 2015; Liu et al., 2020). A recent study by Ali (2020) reveals that staff readiness is one important component of the online and remote learning process. Therefore, analysing the significant antecedents affecting those Thai lecturers using LMS technology would help us understand lecturer intention to use technology in times of crisis, such as COVID-19. Further, previous studies had applied the original TAM model using different perspectives, adding only studied variables (Fathema et al., 2015; Falode, 2018; Herrenkind et al., 2019; Muangmee et al., 2021; Khalid, Chaveesuk, et al., 2021; Khalid, Lis, et al., 2021). This study therefore builds on the foundations of the theoretical TAM framework by adding novel constructs (such as Perceived Interaction and User-Interface Design) to predict faculty intention to use LMS technology.

The current study focuses on HE lecturers' intention to use LMS for teaching purposes; its purpose is to identify the impact of factors affecting lecturer intention to use LMS technology for teaching and assess the causal relationship between the constructs. The current study, then, uses Davis' (1989) Technology Acceptance Model (TAM) to predict lecturer intention to use LMS for teaching purposes. By incorporating three additional factors – namely Perceived Self-Efficacy, User-Interface Design, and Perceived Interaction into TAM to predict lecturer intention to use LMS, this study extends TAM.

1. LITERATURE REVIEW AND MODEL DEVELOPMENT

1.1. THEORETICAL BACKGROUND AND HYPOTHESES DEVELOPMENT

ICT development has enabled the development of online learning systems (Ali, 2020), and there are now several online courses and LMS that allow institutions to facilitate student learning processes outside of class time and at students' own pace, 24/24, regardless of physical location, contingent only on reliable internet access. A review of recent literature shows that many studies have been conducted within the context of e-learning technologies (Raza et al., 2021; Fathema et al., 2015); COVID-19 has accelerated use of ICT technology in most professional activities as a way of maintaining social distancing and thence, the safety of economic agents. There has been dramatic change in emerging countries, where technology adoption was relatively new, and where a lack of adequate ICT infrastructure is prevalent. Despite its shortcomings, ICT adoption in general and e-learning management systems in emerging countries has been phenomenal. However, the factors affecting uptake by instructors in emerging countries may well be different from those operating in developed countries.

According to Davis (1989), perceived ease of use and perceived usefulness are two important constructs in technology acceptance. This study developed an extended model of the TAM by adding three independent variables (Perceived Self-Efficacy, User-Interface Design, and Perceived Interaction) to the classic model, which already included perceived usefulness (PU), perceived ease of use (PEOU) and intention to use. The original TAM model was designed to capture general information regarding the acceptance of technology. The extended TAM theory, with the new variables, might better reflect LMS in emerging countries. The study by Sukendro et al. (2020) on acceptance of technology by Indonesian science students has added facilitating conditions as additional variables into the TAM model. Pal and Vanijja (2020) added perceived usability and system usability into the original TAM model, from the perspective of an online learning platform in India. Fauzi et al. (2021) used an extended TAM model to explore student acceptance of Google Classroom in Indonesia, including price value and facilitating conditions as additional constructs to the TAM model. Similarly, Hong et al. (2021) extended the TAM model, including job relevance and computer self-efficacy, in their assessment of acceptance of technology by preschool lecturers during COVID-19 in China. Prasetyo (2021) identified the factors affecting e-learning adoption during the COVID-19 pandemic, extending the TAM model by incorporating external variables such as information quality, system quality, and user-interface. More specifically, Chayomchai (2020) applied an extended TAM model and analysed Generation-Z acceptance of online technology in Thailand, adding performance expectancy, effort expectancy, and trust as additional constructs to the original TAM model. This study, then, extends the TAM model by adding three additional constructs – Perceived Interaction, user-interface, and Perceived Self-Efficacy – to predict lecturer use of LMS technology during COVD-19 in Thailand.

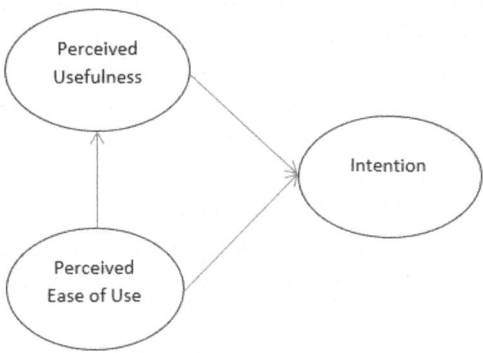

FIG. 1 – Original TAM (Technology Acceptance Model), (Davis, 1989).

1.2. PERCEIVED EASE OF USE AND PERCEIVED USEFULNESS

In the TAM, behavioural intention is affected by two factors: Perceived Ease Of Use (PEOU) and PU. TAM posits that PEOU will affect PU; if users feel the system is easy to use and useful, they will adopt the technology. Past studies have proved the causal relationship between PEOU and PU, indicating that ease of use does affect perceived usefulness (Davis, 1989; Hwa et al., 2015; Jabeur et al., 2013; Venkatesh and Davis, 1996). For example, in the online shopping context, researchers found that site interface, layout, checkout procedures, and other variables were the important system features affecting online shopping adoption (Palmer, 2002). Liu et al. (2010) posited that PEOU has a significant positive impact on the PU of the online learning community.

PU is also an important aspect of the TAM model; it refers to system usefulness in performance and accomplishment (Herrenkind et al., 2019). According to researchers, PU is a major construct of the TAM model and leads to behavioural intention (Falode, 2018; Juhary, 2014). Fathema et al. (2015) argue that both PEOU and PU have significant positive impact on lecturer intention to use LMS technology at HE establishments. This study has therefore chosen TAM because of its high predictive power in terms of technology acceptance (Venkatesh & Davis, 2000). This study focused on external factors affecting lecturer use of LMS at HE establishments. The wider use of LMS to deliver teaching services to students is less familiar to faculty members in emerging countries (Raza et al., 2021), although a relative ease of use and PU can enhance their use of LMS. The authors highlight the fact that users will adopt a technology if they find it easy to use and are able to perform tasks (Falode, 2018; Hwa et al., 2015). Research has shown that when users perceive technology as easy to use, intention to use the technology will also rise, showing a positive relationship between the two variables (Sukendr et al., 2020; Falode, 2018; Hwa et al., 2015). On the basis of these arguments, we assume PEOU and PU to be vital constructs of LMS adoption among university lecturers. We therefore suggest that:

H1: Perceived ease of use has a significant positive impact on the perceived usefulness of LMS

H2: Perceived ease of use has a significant positive impact on lecturer intention to use LMS

As past studies (Prasetyoet al., 2021; Chayomchai, 2020; Falode, 2018; Juhary, 2014) have found, users who find the technology useful will have a stronger intention to adopt it. Users who both find the technology useful and perceive the technology as easy to use will have an even stronger intention to adopt the technology (Wang et al., 2020; Juhary, 2014). At the same time, those who both consider themselves competent users and consider the technology useful will be more inclined to have the intention to use online technology during COVID-19 (Fauzi et al., 2021). Scholars have indicated that perceived ease significantly affects user intention to use technology during COVID-19 (Hong et al., 2021; Sukendro et al., 2020). The extant studies from the perspective of COVID-19 have revealed a significant effect of PU on technology adoption (Hong et al., 2021; Fauzi, 2021; Chayomchai, 2020), and researchers have also identified the fact that PU mediates the relationship between Perceived Self-Efficacy and intention to use a technology (Hwa et al., 2015; Juhary, 2014). Therefore, we assume that both PEOU and PU will affect intention to use LMS. Further, PU will mediate the positive relationship between Perceived Self-Efficacy and intention to use LMS. Hence, we suggest that:

H3: Perceived usefulness has a significant positive impact on lecturer intention to use LMS

H4: Perceived usefulness mediates the positive relationship between perceived ease of use and intention to use LMS

H5: Perceived usefulness mediates the positive relationship between perceived self-efficacy and intention to use LMS

In developing countries, technology users are relatively new users of LMS (Chayomchai, 2020). PEOU will influence them positively towards an intention to use that technology. Studies on the positive relationship between Perceived Self-Efficacy and intention to use technology have highlighted how PEOU mediates the two variables (Ong & Lai, 2006; Compeau et al., 1999). An easy and methodical user-interface can convince users to use new technology and become familiar with it. Mediation (by PEOU) of the positive relationship between User-Interface Design and intention to use was broadly discussed in Liu et al. (2010). Based on this discussion on the interconnectedness of Perceived Self-efficacy (PSE), User-Interface Design (UID), and PEOU with the intention to use LMS, we can suggest the following hypotheses:

H6: Perceived ease of use mediates the positive relationship between perceived self-efficacy and intention to use LMS

H7: Perceived ease of use mediates the positive relationship between user-interface design and intention to use LMS

1.3 PERCEIVED INTERACTION

Learning through ICT has been popular for a long time now, and has gained momentum due to developments in electronic media (Liu et al., 2010). Improvements in technology have seen such teaching evolve from a one-way model to two-way interaction, through online learning. Nonaka and Nishiguchi (2001) described the online learning method as a series of processes that facilitate knowledge sharing and interaction. Similarly, Cantoni et al. (2004) argued that discussion boards, games, quizzes, email, instant messaging, and chatrooms improve interaction between learners during online learning sessions. Further, Liu et al. (2020) found that Perceived Interaction positively affects intention to use the online learning community. Based on these arguments, we assume that Perceived Interaction on LMS will enhance lecturers' ability to deliver online lectures. Studies have highlighted the positive influence of Perceived Interaction on intention to use LMS (Cantoni et al. 2004; Liu et al., 2020); the interactive nature of a learning platform will increase intention to use it. The literature has also adequately discussed the relationship in which Perceived Interaction mediates the positive relationship between UID and intention to use (Cantoni et al. 2004; Liu et al., 2020). We therefore suggest that:

H8: Perceived interaction has a significant positive impact on lecturer intention to use LMS

H9: Perceived interaction mediates the positive relationship between user-interface design and intention to use LMS

1.4 PERCEIVED SELF-EFFICACY (PSE)

PSE refers to the individual behaviours that help achieve the desired goals. It has in general been observed that PSE increases both the individual PEOU and the PU of accepting the technology. On the other hand, if people feel that they are unable to operate LMS, then they perceive it as ineffective and difficult to use. Past studies show that users' PSE has a positive impact on both the PEOU and the PU of advanced technology (Fathema et al., 2015; Fathema & Sutton, 2013). If individuals feel they are unable to operate the learning system with optimal results, this may affect adoption of the technology (Compeau et al., 1999; Fathema et al., 2015; Fathema and Sutton, 2013).

Furthermore, researchers indicate that PSE has a significant impact on the PU of using various technologies, such as e-learning and computing technologies (Ong and Lai, 2006; Compeau et al., 1999). On the basis of these arguments, we assume that PSE will positively impact both the PEOU and the PU of using LMS. Studies have outlined the positive influence of PSE on PU, especially in terms of the application of an LMS (Fathema et al., 2015; Ong and Lai, 2006). Rizun and Strzelecki (2020) found individual self-efficacy to be an important factor affecting the adoption of online education. With particular reference to the adoption of online technology, Hong et al. (2021) found that self-efficacy affects PEOU. Similarly, arguing on the effectiveness of the e-learning platform during the COVID-19 pandemic, Malureanu et al. (2021) found that self-efficacy positively affects both the PEOU and the PU of the e-Learning platform. It is therefore appropriate to consider PSE to be a significant predictor of both the PEOU and the PU of the LMS during the COVID-19 pandemic. We therefore suggest that:

H10: Perceived self-efficacy has a positive impact on the PEOU of using LMS
H11: Perceived self-efficacy has a positive impact on the PU of using LMS

1.5 USER-INTERFACE DESIGN (UID)

UID is one of the most important factors determining software quality. McKnight et al. (1996) have highlighted the importance of user-centric design in technology systems, and a User-Interface Design both helps users operate the system easily and reduces mental load (Martin-Michiellot and Mendelsohn, 2000). Based in Gestalt theory, Leflore (2000) suggested UID guidelines for online instructions, arguing that information should be arranged in a systematic way, depicting text and figures succinctly while providing a clear message to students. In a web-based learning system, a well-designed user-interface provides support to students (Evans and Edwards, 1999). Liu et al. (2010) observed that UID has a positive influence on both PEOU and Perceived Interaction (PI) in terms of intention to use the online learning community. A systemically-arranged user-interface can ensure congruence between UID and PEOU (Liu et al., 2010; Martin-Michiellot & Mendelsohn, 2000). UID creates likeability for the technology and, in the process, positively influences PI (Evans and Edwards, 1999; Liu et al., 2010). Prasetyo et al. (2021) posited that UID enables two-way communication, which is an essential feature of online education. Because this is such an effective means of communication, students prefer to use online platforms for learning (Hart et al., 2019). Mohammadi (2015) has asserted that UID makes it easier for the lecturer to control the system during communication. System features were also found to influence user experience of online technology (Prasetyo et al., 2021).

H12. User-interface design has a positive impact on the PEOU of using LMS
H13. User-interface design has a positive impact on the PI of using LMS

1.6 CONCEPTUAL MODEL DEVELOPMENT

Based on the literature review, we have built the following conceptual model:

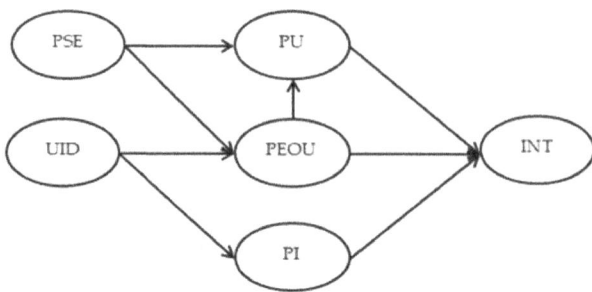

FIG. 2 – The proposed conceptual model for lecturer acceptance of LMS.

Note: INT = Intention to use LMS; PEOU = Perceived Ease Of Use; PU = Perceived Usefulness;
PI = Perceived Interaction; PSE = Perceived Self-Efficacy; UID = User-Interface Design.

2. METHODOLOGY

2.1 DATA COLLECTION AND INSTRUMENTATION

The study was an online survey of lecturers from ten universities in Thailand. Teachers at each university were approached using convenience sampling. The researcher began by visiting the websites of universities of all sizes. Next, academic university staff were included in the sampling framework, irrespective of gender, faculty, or department. The lecturers selected were sent a link to the survey after their email addresses (numbering 874) were retrieved from various university websites, and after a week, three reminder messages were sent to those who had not responded, at one-week intervals. Our survey ran from August–December 2020, and by the end of it, we had received 396 responses – a response rate of 45.3%. In terms of the development of measurement scales, each was adapted from previous studies. The scale of intention to use LMS was adapted from Venkatesh et al. (2003) and Raza et al. (2021). The scales for the measurement of PEOU and PU were adapted from the studies of Rizun and Strzelecki (2020) and Ratna and Mehra (2015). The scale for the measurement of PSE was adapted from a study by Fathema et al. (2015). The scales for the measurement of PI and UID were adapted from a study by Liu et al. (2010). The survey was checked for both content validity and face validity, and was assessed by three academic experts from the fields of Management and Computer Sciences. These experts suggested minor changes relating to content, layout, and sentence/question formulation. After incorporating the suggested changes, the questionnaire was pre-tested on a sample of 55 lecturers. The result of the pre-test was satisfactory as all factors met the recommended thresholds.

2.2 DEMOGRAPHICS

Our analysis of participant profiles is presented in Table 1. In terms of sex distribution, the majority (55.1 %) of participants were male, and in terms of age distribution, the majority (65.2 %) of participants were aged 29–33. In terms of teaching experience, the majority of participants (51.8%) had between 8 and 14 years of teaching experience. And in terms of academic posts, the majority of participants (34.8%) were senior lecturers.

TAB. 1 – Participant profile.

		Frequency	Percentage
Sex	Male	218	55.1
	Female	178	44.9
Age	24-28	73	18.4
	29-33	258	65.2
	34-38	58	14.6
	39 and over	07	1.8
Teaching experience	1 to 7 years	120	30.3
	8 to 14 years	205	51.8
	15 to 21 years	45	11.4
	More than 21 years	26	6.6
Academic Positions	Lecturer	81	20.5
	Senior Lecturer	138	34.8

	Assistant Professor	114	28.8
	Associate Professor	57	14.4
	Professor	06	1.5

3. RESULTS

The Partial Least Square Structural Equation Model (PLS-SEM) was employed in this study; its use offers certain advantages (e.g. the avoidance of factor indeterminacy, theory development) and also does not require data normality (Hair et al., 2021: Fornell and Bookstein, 1982). The criterion suggested by Ringle et al. (2015) was used to test the proposed hypotheses. We therefore followed the 5000-subsampling bootstrapping method to determine significance level in the current study. The PLS-SEM is a two-step process; measurement model followed by analysis of the structural model. In the first step, we assessed the construct reliability, the Convergent Validity and the discriminant validity. In the second step, we assessed the structural model to determine the level of significance among constructs. In order to determine the path coefficient and assess R^2 a variance-based structural equation model was applied (Ringle et al., 2015).

3.1 MEASUREMENT MODEL

The measurement model assessed Reliability, Composite Reliability (CR), Convergent Validity, and Average Variance Extracted (AVE). Scale reliability is determined using Cronbach's alpha values, presented in Table 2. Where the outer loading of all factors was above 0.70, this indicates good reliability of the constructs (Hair et al., 2020). According to Churchill (1979), a scale is reliable if the value of Cronbach's alpha is greater than 0.70 since, in this study, all Cronbach's alpha values are above 0.55; scale reliability is thus established. Next, we determined

CR. Straub (1989) posited that the CR value should be greater than 0.70. CR values above 0.70 and AVE above 0.50 determine the presence of Convergent Validity (Gefen, Straub, and Boudreau, 2000). Table 2 shows the results of the measurement model, including the presence of Convergent Validity. Figure 2 (below) presents the measurement model.

TAB. 2 – Measurement model outer loadings.

	Intention To Use LMS	Perceived Ease Of Use	Perceived Interaction	Perceived Self-Efficacy	Perceived Usefulness	User-Interface Design
INT1	0.888	0.495	0.547	0.400	0.559	0.619
INT2	0.912	0.526	0.562	0.405	0.593	0.638
INT3	0.821	0.532	0.529	0.439	0.517	0.637
INT4	0.871	0.537	0.597	0.402	0.585	0.669
PEOU1	0.559	0.938	0.453	0.596	0.473	0.541
PEOU2	0.565	0.938	0.478	0.609	0.514	0.550
PEOU3	0.515	0.819	0.420	0.541	0.450	0.495
PEOU4	0.534	0.930	0.439	0.634	0.493	0.541
PI1	0.546	0.390	0.930	0.415	0.588	0.591
PI2	0.620	0.483	0.872	0.404	0.616	0.617
PI3	0.583	0.499	0.863	0.452	0.577	0.617
PI4	0.539	0.387	0.917	0.391	0.571	0.591
PSE1	0.494	0.660	0.467	0.952	0.462	0.453
PSE2	0.443	0.627	0.444	0.943	0.444	0.413
PSE3	0.362	0.532	0.377	0.890	0.369	0.337
PU1	0.467	0.363	0.497	0.296	0.752	0.514
PU2	0.582	0.503	0.586	0.451	0.848	0.613
PU3	0.465	0.423	0.431	0.351	0.748	0.451
PU4	0.510	0.372	0.550	0.335	0.800	0.544
UID1	0.628	0.533	0.558	0.382	0.580	0.883
UID2	0.658	0.511	0.634	0.384	0.606	0.903
UID3	0.669	0.518	0.605	0.394	0.616	0.877

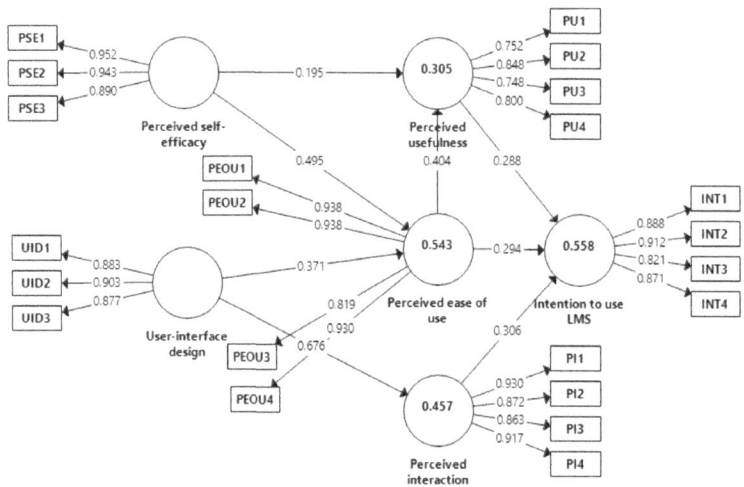

FIG. 3 – Measurement model.

Scale Reliability, Composite Reliability (CR), and Average Variance Extracted (AVE) are presented in Table 3.

TAB. 3 – Reliability and Convergent Validity Analysis.

Constructs	Items	Loading	Cronbach's alpha	CR	AVE
Intention	INT1	0.888	0.896	0.928	0.763
	INT2	0.912			
	INT3	0.821			
	INT4	0.871			
Perceived Ease Of Use	PEOU1	0.938	0.927	0.949	0.824
	PEOU2	0.938			
	PEOU3	0.819			
	PEOU4	0.930			
Perceived Usefulness	PU1	0.752	0.796	0.867	0.621
	PU2	0.848			

	PU3	0.748			
	PU4	0.800			
Perceived Interaction	PI1	0.930	0.918	0.942	0.803
	PI2	0.872			
	PI3	0.863			
	PI4	0.917			
Perceived Self-Efficacy	PSE1	0.952	0.920	0.950	0.863
	PSE2	0.943			
	PSE3	0.890			
User-Interface Design	UID1	0.883	0.865	0.918	0.788
	UID2	0.903			
	UID3	0.877			

We also measured discriminant validity (the extent to which one construct is unrelated to other constructs). In this study, discriminant validity was assessed using two methods: Fornell and Larcker's (1981) Criterion and Heterotrait-Monotrait Ratio (HTMT), which states that the AVE of the square root should be greater than the correlation among variables in the study. Table 4 confirms that the square root of AVE is greater than the correlation among the variables, and Table 5 shows that HTMT values are below 0.85, thus confirming the presence of discriminant validity among the variables (Henseler et al., 2015).

TAB. 4 – Fornell and Larcker's criterion.

Latent variables	1	2	3	4	5	6
Intention	0.874					
Perceived Ease Of Use	0.599	0.907				
Perceived Interaction	0.641	0.494	0.896			
Perceived Self-Efficacy	0.470	0.657	0.465	0.929		
Perceived Usefulness	0.646	0.532	0.658	0.460	0.788	
User-Interface Design	0.734	0.587	0.676	0.436	0.677	0.888

Notes: The bold diagonal values represent the square root of the AVE. The corresponding values are correlations among the constructs.

TAB. 5 – Heterotrait-Monotrait Ratio (HTMT) criterion.

Latent variables	1	2	3	4	5	6
Intention						
Perceived Ease Of Use	0.658					
Perceived Interaction	0.704	0.533				
Perceived Self-Efficacy	0.514	0.707	0.502			
Perceived Usefulness	0.760	0.614	0.765	0.527		
User-Interface Design	0.834	0.656	0.756	0.484	0.811	

3.2 STRUCTURAL MODEL

A bootstrapping of 10000 subsamplings was used to test the proposed hypotheses. A path coefficient value of close to +1 represents a strong correlation, while a value of close to -1 indicates a weak, inverse relationship. In PLS-SEM, two methods are used to assess the goodness-of-fit measure. First is the value of R^2, which is the predictive power of the model, and second is the Q^2 which reflects the predictive relevance of the model. R^2 explains the variance in the dependent constructs explained by the independent constructs. The value of R^2 is 55.8% which reflects the model's high predictive power. Further, the value of Q^2 was assessed in order to determine the predictive relevance of the model in this study; it was obtained using the blindfolding method. In this study, the value of Q^2 for the dependent variable intention to use LMS was 41.9%, which defines high predictive relevance.

Table 5 shows the hypotheses summary for the direct causal relationships between the variables. There were eight hypotheses on causal relationships. H1 and H2, which propose a positive impact of PEOU on both PU and intention to use LMS technology were accepted (β = 0.404, p < 0.000; β = 0.294, p < 0.000). H3 proposes a positive impact of PU on intention to use LMS technology, which was accepted (β = 0.288, p < 0.000). H8 related to the positive impact of PI on intention to use LMS technology, and was also accepted (β = 0.306, p < 0.000). H10 and H11 related to the positive impact of PSE on PU and PEOU, and were accepted (β = 0.195, p < 0.002; β = 0.495, p < 0.000). H12 and H13 related to the positive impact of UID on PEOU and PI, and were accepted (β = 0.371, p < 0.000; β = 0.676, p < 0.000).

Furthermore, the mediation analysis was assessed through Preacher and Hayes' (2008) criterion; they suggested that mediation exists if the indirect relationship between the constructs has been confirmed. Following this assessment, we tested mediation analysis and assessed the indirect impact of PEOU on intention to use LMS through PU. The results of the indirect relationship show that PU mediates the positive relationship between PEOU and intention to use LMS. Furthermore, PSE also has an indirect effect on intention to use LMS, through PU. H4 and H5 are thus also accepted. The results also show that PEOU mediated the positive relationship between PSE and intention to use LMS, and UID and intention to use LMS. H6 and H7 are therefore accepted. Lastly, the indirect effect of user-interface on intention to use LMS through PI was proved; hypothesis H9 is thus accepted. The mediation analysis results are shown in Table 6.

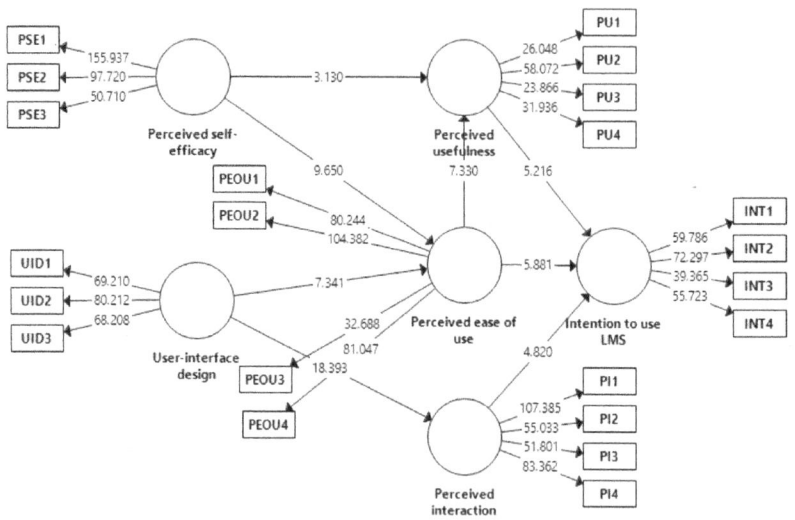

FIG. 4 – Structural model.

TAB. 6 – Hypotheses Assessment Summary.

Hypotheses	Beta	SE	p-values	t-values	Decision	R2	Q2
PEOU PU	0.404	0.405	0.000	7.286	Supported	55.8 %	41.9 %
PEOU INT	0.294	0.294	0.000	5.9949	Supported		
PU INT	0.288	0.289	0.000	5.197	Supported		
PI INT	0.306	0.306	0.000	4.910	Supported		
PSE PU	0.195	0.195	0.002	3.131	Supported		
PSE PEOU	0.495	0.497	0.000	9.907	Supported		
UID PEOU	0.371	0.370	0.000	7.58	Supported		
UID PI	0.676	0.675	0.000	18.482	Supported		

Note: Relationships are significant at p < 0.05*.

Tab. 7 – Mediation Analysis Results.

Hypotheses	Path coefficient	C.I	p-values	t-values	Decision
PEOU PU INT	0.116	0.066, 0.178	0.000	4.021	Mediation
PSE PEOU INT	0.146	0.096, 0.206	0.000	5.236	Mediation
UID PEOU INT	0.109	0.022, 0.075	0.000	4.161	Mediation
PSE PU INT	0.056	0.022, 0.101	0.000	2.787	Mediation
UID PI INT	0.207	0.116, 0.309	0.000	4.161	Mediation

4. DISCUSSION

The COVID-19 pandemic has brought about many changes in people's lives as a result of the government's lockdowns and isolation policies. During this pandemic, educational institutions worldwide have adopted distance learning and the role of LMS has been vital to providing students with relevant materials and delivering lectures. Past studies have focused mainly on student intention to use e-learning technologies for learning, although, to the best knowledge of the authors, very few studies have focused on lecturer intention to use technology to deliver lectures. LMS has provided a platform through which lecturers and students can interact and manage course-related activities. This study, based on the extended TAM model, sought to evaluate lecturer intention to use LMS in HE establishments. The extended TAM model includes three constructs, namely: Perceived Self-Efficacy, User-Interface Design, and Perceived Interaction. In addition, we have also studied the indirect effect of PSE and UID on intention to use LMS.

The direct path analysis results show that PEOU has a significant positive impact both on PU and on HE lecturer intention to use LMS. These findings are consistent with the work of Davis (1986) and Venkatesh and Davis (1996). Lecturers feel LMS ease of use and usefulness in the learning process, and do intend to use LMS. Our results also validate the findings of Fathema et al. (2015) and Liu et al. (2010) regarding the positive and significant impact of PU lecturer intention to use LMS. We discovered that PSE has a positive and significant impact on both PEOU and PU, and this is consistent with the findings of previous researchers (Hong et al., 2021; Rizun and Strzelecki, 2020; Fathema et al., 2015). Lecturers having high self-efficacy, then, tend to perform their duties and deliver lectures through LMS. During COVID-19, the delivery of physical lectures was impossible; therefore, if a lecturer was able to deliver lectures through LMS, student needs were fulfilled.

Scholars have argued that UID is the most important factor of PEOU. Similarly, where technology is easy to use, then users will easily adapt it – as previous researchers have found (Prasetyo et al., 2021; Hart et al., 2019; Fathema et al., 2015). Likewise, our results show that UID is also an important factor affecting the ease of performing duties through LMS. In times of COVID-19, the need for a well-developed support system serves to facilitate users of technology. The results of this study reveal that lecturers feel that LMS technology features are both supportive and user-friendly when used to deliver lectures during COVID-19. Moreover, its indirect effects were considered to further the understanding of related constructs in the model. Our findings prove that PEOU, PU, and PI are significant mediators in the extended TAM model. These findings are consistent with the work of previous researchers having proved the significant indirect effects of PEOU, PU, and PI on intention to use technology (Venkatesh & Davis, 1996; Fathema et al., 2015). The idea that (in addition to being important variables in the extended TAM model) PEOU, PU, and PI act as mediating constructs in lecturer intention to use LMS in HE establishments, is validated.

CONCLUSION

There are several theoretical and policy implications of our findings. The first theoretical implication is the extension of the TAM to the current COVID-19 situation, and its application within educational establishments as a way of understanding the likelihood of lecturers using

LMS. The second is the inclusion of PI as a mediating variable in the extended TAM model, which is vital because both lecturer and student interactions are important in attaining desired outcomes; earlier studies conducted using the TAM model had not included PI. Its addition is instrumental because, during COVID19, the faculty-student interaction has had to happen through LMS technology. This model represents the unique combination of PSE and user-interface with PEOU and PU regarding LMS use in HE during COVID-19 in Thailand. The third theoretical implication, then, is that this relationship can enrich the TAM literature, helping explain the relationships between the variables. Study results also show that UID is strongly associated with PI and intention to use LMS, signifying the importance of interface design in online teaching during COVID-19 in Thailand.

This is the first study of HE lecturer intention to use LMS undertaken during the Covid-19 pandemic in Thailand, and in terms of practical implications, the current situation demands a thorough analysis of those factors affecting the adoption of technology in the preparation of course materials and the delivery of lectures. Universities in Thailand should focus on improving interface design, as this will enhance the delivery of lectures. Earlier studies revealed the importance of UID to effective operation of the system (Prasetyo et al., 2021; Hart et al., 2019; Mohammadi, 2015), and these results show that during this crisis, an effective, user-friendly system has proved vital to the delivery of lectures and the performance of the educational duties. Because the pandemic has generated fear around the globe, people were rarely able to focus on physical duties. A substitute online system was what was needed in that moment in order to offer students educational services and compensate for their educational losses. As lecturers' teaching efficiency increased, they were motivated to deliver lectures using LMS technology. It was easy for tech-confident lecturers to facilitate student understanding. High self-efficacy is a personality attribute capable of keeping work moving forward, especially in terms of the performance of educational services during such a period. Furthermore, improvements to LMS ensure success, because lecturers feel that the LMS technology is beneficial, efficient, and easy to use. When lockdowns are lifted, and classes resume, lecturers can adapt aspects of online teaching alongside with traditional classroom methods and lectures. This will both increase university revenue and provide flexibility. There should also be an emphasis on lecturer training, aimed at building their confidence in online teaching and making them more effective. Ultimately, it would be good to establish an efficient and robust online system capable of facilitating lecturer and student interaction while enhancing student learning and retention, and without presenting any obstacles.

In conclusion, we acknowledge certain limitations to this study, though these do not invalidate our findings. This study has extended the TAM model and explained high variance among many other constructs, and has shown how this could affect lecturer intention to use LMS, though individual personality traits and social influences are also important constructs that can potentially have significant impact on intention to use LMS. Future researchers will be able to include these constructs and expand the theoretical contributions.

A further limitation is related to the population of the study, since it has included only data from HE lecturers. Future researchers can extend the scope of the research and achieve a holistic understanding by including teachers at colleges and high schools. Researchers can also conduct in-depth interviews with lecturers, to explore new constructs that may also be barriers to the adoption of LMS technology.

REFERENCES

AL-BUSAIDI, K. A., AL-SHIHI, H. (2010), "Instructors' acceptance of learning management systems: A theoretical framework" *Communications of the IBIMA*, 2010(2010), p. 1–10.

ALI W. (2020), "Online and remote learning in higher education institutes: A necessity in light of COVID-19 pandemic", *Higher education studies*, vol. 10, n° 3, 16-25.

ALIAS N. A., ZAINUDDIN, A. M. (2005), "Innovation for better teaching and learning: Adopting the learning management system", *Malaysian Online Journal of Instructional Technology*, vol. 2, n° 2, p. 27–40.

CANTONI V., CELLARIO M., PORTA M. (2004), "Perspectives and challenges in e-learning: towards natural interaction paradigms", *Journal of Visual Languages & Computing*, vol. 15, n° 5, p. 333-345.

CHAYOMCHAI A. (2020), "The Online Technology Acceptance Model of Generation-Z People in Thailand during COVID-19 Crisis", *Management & Marketing*, vol. 15, n° 1, p. 496-512.

CHURCHILL JR G. A. (1979), "A paradigm for developing better measures of marketing constructs", *Journal of marketing research*, vol. 16, n° 1, p. 64-73.

COMPEAU D., HIGGINS C. A., HUFF S. (1999), "Social cognitive theory and individual reactions to computing technology: A longitudinal study", *MIS quarterly*, vol. 23, n° 2, p. 145-158.

DAHLSTROM E., BROOKS D. C., BICHSEL J. (2014), *The current ecosystem of learning management systems in higher education: Student, faculty, and IT perspectives*, Research Report, Louisville, CO: ECAR, September.

DAVIS F. D. (1986), *Technology acceptance model for empirically testing new end-user information systems: Theory and results*, MA, USA: Massachusetts Institute of Technology.

DAVIS F. D. (1989), "Perceived usefulness, perceived ease of use, and user acceptance of information technology", *MIS quarterly*, vol. 13, n° 3, 319-340.

EVANS C., EDWARDS M. (1999), "Navigational interface design for multimedia courseware", *Journal of Educational Multimedia and Hypermedia*, vol. 8, n° 2, p. 151-174.

FALODE O. C. (2018), "Pre-service Teachers' Perceived Ease of Use, Perceived Usefulness, Attitude and Intentions Towards Virtual Laboratory Package Utilization in Teaching and Learning of Physics", *Malaysian Online Journal of Educational Technology*, vol. 6, n° 3, p. 63-72.

FATHEMA N., SUTTON K. L. (2013), "Factors influencing faculty members' Learning Management Systems adoption behavior: An analysis using the Technology Acceptance Model", *International Journal of Trends in Economics Management & Technology*, vol. 2, n° 6, p. 20-28.

FATHEMA N., SHANNON D., ROSS, M. (2015), "Expanding the Technology Acceptance Model (TAM) to examine faculty use of Learning Management Systems (LMSs) in HE establishments", *Journal of Online Learning & Teaching*, vol. 11, n° 2, p. 210-232.

FAUZI A., WANDIRA R., SEPRI D., HAFID A. (2021), "Exploring Students' Acceptance of Google Classroom during the Covid-19 Pandemic by Using the Technology Acceptance Model in West Sumatera Universities", *Electronic Journal of e-Learning*, vol. 19, n° 4, p. 233-240.

FORNELL, C., BOOKSTEIN F. L. (1982), "Two structural equation models: LISREL and PLS applied to consumer exit-voice theory", *Journal of Marketing research*, vol. 19, n° 4, p. 440-452.

FORNELL C., LARCKER D. F. (1981), "Evaluating structural equation models with unobservable variables and measurement error", *Journal of marketing research*, vol. 18, n° 1, p. 39-50.

GEFEN D., STRAUB D., BOUDREAU M. C. (2000), "Structural equation modeling and regression: Guidelines for research practice", *Communications of the association for information systems*, vol. 4, n° 7, p. 1-79.

HAIR J. F., HOWARD M. C., NITZL C. (2020), "Assessing measurement model quality in PLS-SEM using confirmatory composite analysis", *Journal of Business Research*, vol. 109, n° C, p. 101–110.

HAIR J., HULT G.., RINGLE C., S. (2021), *A primer on partial least squares structural equation modeling*, Thousand Oaks: SAGE, 3rd edition.

HART T., BIRD D., FARMER R. (2019), "Using blackboard collaborate, a digital web conference tool, to support nursing student's placement learning: A pilot study exploring its impact", *Nurse education in practice*, vol. 38, July, p. 72-78.

HENSELER J., RINGLE C. M., SARSTEDT M. (2015), "A new criterion for assessing discriminant validity in variance-based structural equation modeling", *Journal of the academy of marketing science*, vol. 43, n° 1, p. 115-135.

HERRENKIND B., BRENDEL A. B., NASTJUK I., GREVE M., KOLBE L. M. (2019), "Investigating end-user acceptance of autonomous electric buses to accelerate diffusion", *Transportation Research Part D: Transport and Environment*, 74, p. 255-276.

HONG X., ZHANG M., LIU Q. (2021), "Preschool Teachers' Technology Acceptance During the COVID-19: An Adapted Technology Acceptance Model", *Frontiers in Psychology*, vol. 12:691492.

Hwa S. P., Hwei O.S., Peck W. K. (2015), "Perceived Usefulness, Perceived Ease of Use and Behavioural Intention to Use a Learning Management System among Students in a Malaysian University", *International Journal of Conceptions on Management and Social Sciences*, vol. 3, n° 4, p. 29-35.

Iqbal S. (2011), "Learning management systems (LMS): Inside matters", *Information Management and Business Review*, vol. 3, n° 4, p. 206–216.

Jabeur F., Mohiuddin M., Karuranga E. (2013), Timeline of initial perceptions and adoption of e-business among Quebec forestry sector SMEs. *Communications of the IIMA*, vol. 13, n° 3. https://scholarworks.lib.csusb.edu/ciima/vol13/iss3/1

Jaschik S., Lederman D. (2014), *The 2014 Inside Higher Ed Survey of faculty Attitudes on Technology: A Study by Gallup and Inside Higher Ed. Washington, DC* https://www.insidehighered.com/news/survey/online-ed-skepticism-and-self-sufficiency-surveyfaculty-views-technology. Retrieved September 23, 2021.

Juhari J. (2014), "Perceived Usefulness and Ease of Use of the Learning Management System as a Learning Tool", *International Education Studies*, vol. 7, n° 8, p. 23-33.

Kasraie, N., Kasraie E. (2010), "Economies of elearning in the 21st century", *Contemporary Issues in Education Research (CIER)*, vol. 3, n° 10, p. 57-62.

Khalid B., Chaveesuk S., Chaiyasoonthorn W. (2021), "MOOCs Adoption in Higher Education: A Management Perspective", *Polish Journal of Management Studies*, vol. 23, n° 1, p. 239–256.

Khalid B., Lis M., Chaiyasoonthorn W., Chaveesuk S. (2021), "Factors influencing behavioural intention to use MOOCs", *Engineering Management in Production and Services*, vol. 13, n° 2, p. 83–95.

Leflore D. (2000), "Theory supporting design guidelines for web-based instruction", in Beverley A. (Ed), *Instructional and cognitive impacts of web-based education*, IGI Global, p. 102-117.

Liu I. F., Chen M. C., Sun Y. S., Wible D., Kuo C. H. (2010), "Extending the TAM model to explore the factors that affect intention to use an online learning community", *Computers & education*, vol. 54, n° 2, p. 600-610.

Mailizar M., Almanthari A., Maulina S., Bruce S. (2020), "Secondary school mathematics lecturers' views on e-learning implementation barriers during the COVID-19 pandemic: The case of Indonesia", *Eurasia Journal of Mathematics, Science and Technology Education*, vol. 16, n° 7, https://doi.org/10.29333/ejmste/8240. Retrieved April 23, 2021.

Malureanu A., Panisoara G., Lazar I. (2021), "The Relationship between Self-Confidence, Self-Efficacy, Grit, Usefulness, and Ease of Use of eLearning Platforms in Corporate Training during the COVID-19 Pandemic" *Sustainability*, vol. 13, n° 12, 6633.

MARTIN-MICHIELLOT S., & MENDELSOHN P. (2000), "Cognitive load while learning with a graphical computer interface", *Journal of computer assisted learning*, vol. 16, n° 4, p. 284-293.

MCKNIGHT C., DILLON A., RICHARDSON J. (1996), *User centered design of hypertext and hypermedia for education*, New York: Macmillan.

MOHAMMADI H. (2015), "Investigating users' perspectives on e-learning: An integration of TAM and IS success model", *Computers in human behavior*, 45, p. 359-374.

MUANGMEE C., KOT S., MEEKAEWKUNCHORN N., KASSAKORN N., TIRANAWATANANUN S., KHALID B. (2021), "Students use behavior towards eLearning tools during COVID-19 pandemics: Case study of higher educational institutions of Thailand", *International Journal of Evaluation and Research in Education*, 10 (4). https://doi.org/10.11591/ijere.v10i4.21821. Retrieved September 23, 2021.

NONAKA I., NISHIGUCHI T. (2001), "Social, technical, and evolutionary dimensions of knowledge creation, in Nonaka, I., Nishiguchi, T." (Eds), *Knowledge emergence: Social, technical, and evolutionary dimensions of knowledge creation*, Oxford, Oxford University Press, p. 286-289.

ONG C. S., LAI J. Y. (2006), "Gender differences in perceptions and relationships among dominants of e-learning acceptance", *Computers in human behavior*, vol. 22, n° 5, p. 816-829.

PALMER, J. W. (2002), "Web site usability, design, and performance metrics", *Information systems research*, vol. 13, n° 2, p. 151-167.

PRASETYO Y. T., ONG A. K. S., CONCEPCION G. K. F., NAVATA F. M. B., ROBLES R. A. V., TOMAGOS I. J. T., YOUNG M.N., DIAZ, J.F.T., NADLIFATIN R., REDI A. A. N. P. (2021), "Determining Factors Affecting Acceptance of E-Learning Platforms during the COVID-19 Pandemic: Integrating Extended Technology Acceptance Model and DeLone & McLean IS Success Model", *Sustainability*, vol. 13, n° 15, 8365.

PREACHER K. J., HAYES A. F. (2008), "Asymptotic and resampling strategies for assessing and comparing indirect effects in multiple mediator models", *Behavior research methods*, vol. 40, n° 3, p. 879-891.

RATNA P. A., MEHRA S. (2015), "Exploring the acceptance for e–learning using technology acceptance model among university students in India", *International Journal of Process Management and Benchmarking*, vol. 5, n° 2, p. 194-210.

RAZA S. A., QAZI W., KHAN K. A., SALAM J. (2021), "Social Isolation and Acceptance of the Learning Management System (LMS) in the time of COVID-19 Pandemic: An Expansion of the UTAUT Model", *Journal of Educational Computing Research*, vol. 59, n° 2, p. 183-208.

RINGLE C., DA SILVA D., BIDO D. (2015), "Structural equation modeling with the SmartPLS", *Brazilian Journal of Marketing*, vol. 13, n° 2, p. 56-73.

RIZUN M., STRZELECKI A. (2020), "Students' acceptance of the Covid-19 impact on shifting higher education to distance learning in Poland", *International Journal of Environmental Research and Public Health*, vol. 17, n° 18, 6468.

STRAUB D. W. (1989), "Validating instruments in MIS research", *MIS quarterly*, vol. 13, n° 2, p. 147-169.

STRZELECKI A., RIZUN M. (2020), *Infodemiological study using Google Trends on coronavirus epidemic in Wuhan, China*. Retrieved April 23, 2021 from https://www.learntechlib.org/p/217957/.

SUKENDRO S., HABIBI A., KHAERUDDIN K., INDRAYANA B., SYAHRUDDIN S., MAKADADA F. A., HAKIM H. (2020), "Using an extended Technology Acceptance Model to understand students' use of e-learning during Covid-19: Indonesian sport science education context", *Heliyon*, vol. 6, n° 11, e05410.

VENKATESH V., DAVIS F.D. (2000), "A theoretical extension of the technology acceptance model: four longitudinal field studies", *Management Science*, vol. 46, n° 2, p. 186–204.

VENKATESH,V., DAVIS F. D. (1996), "A model of the antecedents of perceived ease of use: Development and test", *Decision Sciences*, vol. 27, n° 3, p. 451–481.

WAHEED M., KAUR K., AIN N., HUSSAIN N. (2016), "Perceived learning outcomes from Moodle: An empirical study of intrinsic and extrinsic motivating factors", *Information Development*, vol. 32, n° 4, p. 1001–1013.

WANG C. J., NG C. Y., BROOK R. H. (2020), "Response to COVID-19 in Taiwan: big data analytics, new technology, and proactive testing", *Jama*, vol. 323, n° 14, p. 1341-1342.

WORLD HEALTH ORGANIZATION (2020), *Coronavirus disease 2019 (COVID-19): Situation report*, n° 51, World Health Organization.

ZWAIN A. A. A. (2019), "Technological innovativeness and information quality as neoteric predictors of users' acceptance of learning management system: An expansion of UTAUT2", *Interactive Technology and Smart Education*, vol. 16, n° 3, p. 239–254.

LA QUÊTE DU SERVICE IDÉAL
PAR L'INNOVATION COLLABORATIVE
DANS UN BUSINESS MODEL PUBLIC
AVEC L'INTENDANCE DES CLIENTS

Le cas d'un hôpital universitaire ivoirien

Dagou Hermann-Wenceslas Dagou[1]
Université Félix Houphouët-Boigny

INTRODUCTION

Au cours des dernières décennies, le mode traditionnel de prestation de services publics a été remis en question par un certain nombre de turbulences qui ont été parfois imposées et parfois initiées et bien accueillies par les dirigeants politiques (Demircioglu et Audretsch, 2017 ; Torfing, 2019 ; Steen et Brandsen, 2020). La proposition de services publics peut être considérée comme le fruit d'une collaboration intersectorielle impliquant un mélange de prestataires publics, privés et à but non lucratif (Conner, 2015), par le biais d'une variété d'arrangements contractuels. Certaines des plus grandes innovations ont été réalisées en privatisant certaines organisations du secteur public, en franchisant d'autres, en sous-traitant des services aux secteurs privés et sans but lucratif ; et en introduisant une concurrence pour les programmes visant à soutenir et à améliorer les services publics. Le paradigme émergeant de la nouvelle gouvernance publique offre une vision différente de l'innovation (Sørensen et Torfing, 2012). Selon ce paradigme, le secteur public jouit

---

1   ddhgeek@gmail.com, hermann.dagou@univ-fhb.edu.ci

déjà d'une bonne capacité à innover et celle-ci pourrait être favorisée par l'application de formes collaboratives de gestion. Ainsi, une stratégie d'innovation dans le secteur public devrait viser l'amélioration de la capacité de ce secteur à engendrer des collaborations. Plusieurs auteurs suggèrent s'intéresser davantage à la question des liens entre la collaboration et l'innovation dans les services publics (Bommert, 2010 ; Sørensen et Torfing, 2012 ; Hartley *et al.*, 2013 ; Desmarchelier et al., 2019, 2020). Ces auteurs partent de l'hypothèse de l'existence d'un potentiel d'innovation collaborative, car la collaboration peut apporter une plus-value à différents niveaux. Grönroos (2017) fait référence à « un processus de résolution créatif de problèmes par le biais duquel des acteurs pertinents et concernés travaillent à travers les frontières institutionnelles formelles pour développer et mettre en œuvre des solutions innovantes à des problèmes urgents ». Ainsi, l'innovation collaborative implique l'inclusion d'un certain nombre d'acteurs différents et l'exploitation de leur potentiel (par exemple, connaissances, compétences et ressources) dans le but de trouver une solution aux problèmes de société et de créer de la valeur publique (Agger et Lund, 2017).

Dans la gestion publique, la collaboration recouvre à la fois l'efficacité de la prestation de services publics et le rôle des services publics dans la réalisation d'autres objectifs sociétaux, tels que l'engagement des citoyens. La littérature a souvent envisagé la coproduction de services publics comme substrat de la collaboration (Hartley *et al.*, 2013). Elle est une variante du modèle traditionnel de prestation de services publics dans lequel les agents publics sont exclusivement chargés de la conception et de la fourniture de services aux citoyens, qui à leur tour ne font que les demander, les consommer et les évaluer (Vigoda-Gadot et Meisler, 2010 ; Kim et Holzer, 2016). Ainsi, elle rend compte des moyens par lesquels la participation des utilisateurs peut être « ajoutée » au processus opérationnel de prestation de services. Une telle conception de la coproduction provient d'une logique dans laquelle la servuction et la consommation sont séparées en tant que processus discrets. Dans ce cadre, les services publics sont conceptualisés comme devant être conçus et produits par les décideurs publics et les professionnels des services et consommés passivement par les utilisateurs du service (Meyer et Leonard, 2014). En revanche, une approche axée sur l'innovation offre une perspective très différente de la coproduction (Seow et al., 2011 ;

Denhardt et Denhardt, 2015). En effet, la coproduction est un élément central du processus essentiel et intrinsèque d'interaction entre toute organisation de service et ses clients/usagers, au point de livraison d'un service (Grönroos, 2018). Dans une approche axée sur les services, il n'y a aucun moyen d'éviter la coproduction de services publics, car il s'agit d'un élément inaliénable de ces services.

La conceptualisation de la coproduction en tant que caractéristique fondamentale de la prestation de services publics met en exergue, à la fois le processus de prestation de services et le rôle de la gestion publique dans l'atteinte des résultats des services (Steen et Brandsen, 2020). Un élément central d'une approche de coproduction axée sur les services est qu'elle cherche à libérer les connaissances tacites que possèdent les utilisateurs de services afin d'améliorer les services existants ou de développer de nouveaux services. Imbert et Chauvet (2013) résument cette coproduction comme le moment de vérité de la prestation de services où les promesses de réalisation d'un certain processus ou d'une certaine expérience se « matérialisent ». Toutefois, Loock et Hacklin (2015) soulignent qu'une logique métier clairement articulée est l'une des conditions préalables à la coproduction axée sur les services. Par ailleurs, la dominance du service dans les prestations publiques, qui place l'utilisateur plutôt que le décideur ou le professionnel au cœur de ce processus, est caractérisée par l'innovation dans le modèle d'affaires de l'organisation publique (Osborne, 2018). L'innovation collaborative implique également une tendance inhérente à perturber les pratiques établies et la pensée conventionnelle dans un domaine particulier (Seow et al., 2011). La force de la collaboration réside dans sa capacité à induire une intendance, centrée sur les relations et orientée vers les autres, avec pour but ultime de promouvoir et de protéger leur bien-être à long terme. En effet, contrairement à la relation d'agence qui met l'accent sur la rationalité économique, l'intendance capture d'autres comportements pro-sociaux (à visée non nécessairement économiques), qui se trouvent au cœur de la manière de générer de la valeur pour les différentes parties prenantes à la coproduction. Parmi les interprétations du rôle et de la fonction des modèles d'affaires en général (Aversa *et al.*, 2015), l'une porte sur les schémas cognitifs et linguistiques en tant que manifestations observables. Le modèle d'affaires est vu par Doz et Kosonen (2010), comme un schéma mental implicite dont les unités d'analyse appropriées sont les esprits et discours individuels et collectifs qui servent à façonner la reconnaissance des opportunités et l'identité partagée. Cela implique une obligation pour les employés envers le modèle d'affaires et un engagement à promouvoir la capacité de l'organisation.

Pour la théorie de l'intendance, la coproduction reflète, par conséquent, un sens continu de l'obligation envers les autres, basé sur l'intention de maintenir la relation d'alliance à long terme (Davis et al., 1997 ; Segal et Lehrer, 2012). Comme l'explique Hernandez (2012), ce sens de l'obligation repose sur deux éléments psychologiques, à savoir le cognitif et l'affectif. La dimension cognitive décrit la volonté d'un manager d'assujettir ses intérêts personnels à la protection du bien-être à long terme des autres. La composante affective quant à elle représente les éléments émotionnels, qui lient les managers aux autres parties prenantes, et qui font qu'ils sont prêts à maintenir ce comportement d'abnégation. L'innovation collaborative peut donc être comprise à travers les lentilles du modèle d'affaires, qui informe les parties prenantes à la coproduction des intendances nécessaires menant aux objectifs organisationnels (Sørensen et Torfing, 2012). À une époque de responsabilité et de gestion axées sur les résultats, le recours à l'intendance peut ne pas satisfaire ceux qui recherchent des preuves d'une prestation de services efficace. En effet, la gestion des organisations publiques est imprégnée de contrôles bureaucratiques, tels que les audits et les inspections (Van Slyke, 2007 ; Demircioglu et Audretsch, 2017). Le modèle d'affaires public devra donc souligner la nécessité des contrôles externes, mais aussi rappeler les irréductibles dimensions cognitives et affectives dans le service aux clients/patients (Dagou, 2021). Pour Simpkins et al., (2021), ce cadre simultané des demandes concurrentes remet en question la confiance, l'autonomie et la motivation intrinsèque pour plus d'intendance. Cette dernière se concentre sur le contenu des valeurs culturelles qui conduisent à l'efficacité organisationnelle, comme l'analyse Denison et Mishra (1995). Suivant leurs logiques, la coproduction sera d'autant plus efficace que l'intendance du modèle d'affaires public permettra de proposer aux clients/patients des services en amélioration continue. La coproduction, forme concrète d'innovation collaborative qui vise à susciter « de nouvelles façons de créer et de fournir des services publics » (Agger et Lund, 2017, p. 17), suppose l'inclusion de clients pour une efficacité culturelle dans le modèle d'affaires. En effet, ces clients manipulent les aspects de la culture du service dont ils ont l'usage, ce qui permet de passer de l'efficacité organisationnelle à l'efficacité culturelle. Cette dernière est la valeur qui traduit des résultats organisationnels satisfaisant, sachant que ces résultats ne peuvent être obtenus sans la participation du client/patient. Le service idéal est alors perçu comme la conformité des besoins à un standard de perfection construit ensemble. Adoptant une perspective cognitive, la question est de savoir comment un service idéal dans un modèle d'affaires peut-il être envisagé par l'efficacité culturelle.

L'article est organisé en cinq sections. Dans les deux premières sections, une revue de la littérature présente le modèle d'affaires dans les services publics (section 1) et les adaptations par intendance nécessaires pour un service de qualité idéal (section 2). La section 3 est consacrée à la méthodologie de recherche. L'article s'appuie sur une enquête auprès des patients du Centre Hospitalier Universitaire d'Angré en Côte d'Ivoire. Celle-ci est centrée sur les clients en situation de collaboration et elle adopte une analyse qui « coche tout ce qui s'applique ». Dans les sections 4 et 5, les résultats sont présentés puis discutés.

1. LE MODÈLE D'AFFAIRES DANS L'UNIVERS PUBLIC, UNE APPROCHE COGNITIVE

De plus en plus, les organisations du secteur public adoptent de nouveaux modèles commerciaux pour mieux collaborer avec les clients et ainsi réduire les obstacles à l'innovation. Les modèles d'affaires peuvent encourager une plus grande importance accordée aux avantages tangibles et aux améliorations pour les citoyens et déplacer l'équilibre des pouvoirs vers la première ligne, où les services sont fournis. La théorie de l'intendance considère les agences du service public comme, davantage axées sur des objectifs collectifs plutôt que sur une somme d'objectifs individuels (Segal et Lehrer, 2012). Si les services d'un hôpital, par exemple, n'agissent pas de manière opportuniste, mais partagent les mêmes objectifs que le ministère de la Santé, il n'y aura aucune raison pour le supérieur de ne pas croire que l'exécutant accomplira une tâche déléguée sans dérive bureaucratique (Van Slyke, 2007). Favoriser une collaboration à ces efforts d'intendance injecte de nouvelles compétences et de nouvelles idées dans les services et peut aider à surmonter la résistance et l'aversion au risque (Larson et al., 2019). Compte tenu de sa nature intrinsèquement complexe et dynamique, l'innovation collaborative du modèle d'affaires public nécessite non seulement de la créativité dans la collaboration, mais aussi une structure et des conseils pour encadrer et focaliser la pensée (Eppler et Hoffmann, 2013). En réalité, la coproduction de services publics est plus un continuum qu'un état stationnaire. Les services publics tels que les soins et l'éducation sont clairement des cas où la coproduction est élevée, du fait que la consommation et la production ont lieu au même moment et avec un contact direct entre l'utilisateur et le fournisseur de services. Furnari (2015) suggère qu'en raison de leur caractère prospectif, les récits du modèle d'affaires jouent un rôle important en suscitant des attentes parmi les parties intéressées par l'avenir du service public offert. Les récits du modèle d'affaires peuvent être construits par les gestionnaires et les entrepreneurs et utilisés non seulement pour simplifier la cognition, mais aussi comme un moyen de communication qui pourrait permettre d'atteindre divers objectifs, tels que persuader des publics externes, renforcer le sentiment de légitimité. Le modèle d'affaires est donc conceptualisé comme le reflet de structures cognitives (Doz et Kosonen, 2010), des schémas managériaux (Martins et al., 2015) ou un instrument cognitif (Aversa et al., 2015).

À l'image de cette diversité, la définition d'un modèle d'affaires fait intervenir un ensemble structuré de rapports opérationnels interdépendants entre une organisation et ses partenaires dépositaires d'enjeux. On est passé d'un système d'activités fonctionnant comme une représentation subjective de ces parties prenantes (Doz et Kosonen, 2010, p. 371), à une articulation de logiques qui supporte une proposition de service pour le client, et une structure viable de coûts/revenus pour l'organisation (Furnari, 2015). Alors que différents courants ne sont pas en accord sur le concept de modèle d'affaires, faisant référence à quelque chose de réel (Casadesus-Masanell et Ricart, 2010 ; Zott et al., 2011), ou représentant uniquement les modèles cognitifs des décideurs (Zott et al., 2011), l'importance de la cognition managériale dans la conception et l'innovation des modèles d'affaires est reconnue (Aversa et al., 2015). En représentant un modèle d'affaires comme une carte cognitive, Furnari (2015) espère mieux apprécier les aspects autrement implicites ou cachés de l'articulation de logiques et approfondir les liens, améliorant ainsi leur compréhension. Les bouleversements induits par l'innovation ont engendré des inquiétudes sur l'avenir, provoquant toutes sortes de politiques publiques pour y faire face. À cet effet, une part importante des innovations est réalisée, grâce aux usagers ou clients « disrupteurs » qui repensent significatives les services existants, car l'apprentissage par la pratique (*learning by doing*) fait toujours émerger des problèmes inattendus (Kim et Holzer, 2016). Par conséquent, l'intérêt est d' « expliquer les processus par lesquels la logique cognitive peut être modifiée pour créer et concevoir de nouveaux services du modèle d'affaires en leur présence » (Martins et al., 2015, p. 100). La prestation de services publics et la création de valeur pour les clients sont un seul processus interactif, collaboratif, fait de dialogue (Bommert, 2010). En particulier, la démarche qualité certifiante ISO 9001 représente une approche de modèle d'affaires qui préside à une activité d'innovation par la possibilité d'engager un processus de création de valeur plus adapté aux besoins du client (Lim et al., 2019 ; Ikram et al., 2020). Van Kemenade et Hardjono (2019) y identifient un aspect technique, faisant référence aux outils et pratiques de gestion, consistant en des méthodes claires et bien documentées, et un aspect philosophique, associé aux concepts et principes de gestion, composant toute sa théorie, combinant son arrière-plan et ses éléments cognitifs. Ce dernier aspect évoque un attachement aux valeurs du service (Torfing, 2019) et de service public ou comme le formulent Antonsen et Jorgensen (1997) de « *publicness as organizational attachment to public sector values: for example due process, accountability, and welfare provision* ». Cet attachement du modèle d'affaires aux valeurs du secteur public constitue une condition sine qua non pour la performance du service (Parrado *et al.*, 2020).

2. LES ADAPTATIONS À UN SERVICE IDÉAL PAR INTENDANCE

Les organisations du secteur privé comme du secteur public cherchent à être des organisations axées sur le client pour mener à bien leurs opérations dans un environnement concurrentiel. Par conséquent, pour être compétitifs en tant qu'organisation orientée client, il est nécessaire d'offrir aux clients des services de qualité avec leur participation (Imbert et Chauvet, 2013). En supposant que les clients peuvent tirer une utilité à agir de manière égoïste ou opportuniste aussi bien que de manière altruiste ou intendante, ils réévaluent périodiquement, et même inconsciemment, les avantages et les inconvénients d'un tel comportement. Dès lors, il est difficile de définir la qualité du service qui prend sa source dans une attitude du client vis-à-vis des résultats de comparaisons entre les attentes de service et ses perceptions. Chercher les conditions d'une bonne participation mobilise la théorie de l'intendance. Cette théorie permet de comprendre les processus cognitifs et les modèles mentaux qui façonnent la conception du modèle d'affaires. Raasch et Von Hippel (2013) suggèrent que les utilisateurs innovateurs ont généralement des motivations intrinsèques importantes qui font qu'ils retirent des bénéfices non seulement de l'usage, mais également du fait de participer en raison du divertissement et de l'apprentissage que procure la participation.

Selon Chaniotakis et Lymperopoulos (2009), dans un environnement de santé compétitif, les hôpitaux sont obligés d'évaluer à la fois la performance financière et non-financière de leur modèle d'affaires. Lorsque des services médicaux sont fournis à un client/patient, celui-ci compare l'expérience avec ses attentes. Grönroos (2017) explique ainsi que la qualité technique implique ce qui est fourni eu égard aux attentes des clients/patients et que la qualité de l'usage tient compte de la manière dont le service s'ajuste avec leurs perceptions. Samat *et al.* (2006) indiquent que la qualité d'usage compensera les problèmes temporaires de qualité technique, mais ne compensera pas un niveau de qualité globalement inférieur. Dans une situation de coproduction ou une partie de la responsabilité de servuction est déléguée aux clients, une intendance bonne et loyale se crée à leur niveau, qui placera les objectifs de l'organisation au-dessus de leurs intérêts personnels.

L'intendance publique ou « publicness » (Antonsen et Jorgensen, 1997 ; Andrews et al., 2011) se concentre sur la conduite prudente et responsable des valeurs publiques pour l'alignement et la congruence des intérêts, au service d'objectifs collectifs et sociaux, en particulier, d'un service de qualité. La théorie de l'intendance cherche à comprendre les conditions dans lesquelles les agents sont moins susceptibles de fonder leurs actions sur l'intérêt personnel et de prendre plaisir à servir des objectifs collectifs ou à agir en tant qu'intendants des intérêts des mandants. Hernandez (2012) décrit la théorie de l'intendance comme étant soucieuse d'encourager les acteurs à se gouverner pour créer un fort sentiment d'autonomie et de responsabilité pour les résultats. Ainsi, les organisations publiques qui utilisent la collaboration pour fournir des services (comme c'est le cas des hôpitaux) ont besoin d'encourager l'intendance chez l'ensemble des acteurs (Simpkins et al., 2021; Yilmaz, 2021). Le lien entre la valeur qui est souhaitable et l'intendance publique est que la vision de l'intendance postule un acteur expert dont le comportement est collectif par nature, en mettant l'accent sur la création de scénarios gagnant-gagnant. En substance, le sentiment pour le client que quelque chose d'une partie de l'organisation est à lui, facilite l'alignement des valeurs publiques avec ses propres intérêts. Par conséquent, la protection des intérêts du service psychologiquement détenu devient l'une des préoccupations des clients/patients. La mise en œuvre d'un service idéal se déroulera grâce aux comportements d'intendance réels ou prévus en tant que résultat de l'appropriation psychologique. En ce sens, l'intendance devient un facteur de décision critique qui assure, que la gestion des ressources publiques se fera avec prudence et probité. Le service idéal par intendance devra tendre vers un équilibre intégré des dimensions de l'efficacité culturelle de Denison et Mishra (1995).

3. LA MÉTHODOLOGIE DE LA RECHERCHE

3.1. LE CONTEXTE DE LA RECHERCHE

Le rapport d'activité sanitaire du Ministère ivoirien de la santé et de l'hygiène publique (MSHP, 2017b) estime les capacités de pilotage des établissements de santé comme actuellement insuffisantes tant dans le secteur public que privé. Ce rapport relève également que les préoccupations managériales et les résultats en termes de bien-être des populations sont relégués au second rang. Les managers des organisations de santé, à l'écoute des réalités des professionnels, se rendent compte que les solutions imposées par les politiciens ou conçues par les technocrates ont souvent des effets négatifs et non-contextuels. En l'occurrence, la moyenne de conformité pour le développement de la qualité des soins et services de santé est insuffisante et représente environ 50,2 % (PNAQS, 2016). En effet, bien que devenue une priorité révélée par des faits (grève, insécurité sanitaire, sélections adverses des assureurs, doute sur l'efficacité thérapeutique, etc.) et inscrite comme telle dans le Plan National de Développement Sanitaire 2016-2020, l'amélioration de la qualité des soins et des services de santé n'est pas guidée par des orientations stratégiques nationales devant être opérationnalisées au niveau décentralisé du ministère en charge de la santé. Ensuite, l'insuffisance du personnel maîtrisant les outils de la gestion par la qualité et la faiblesse des moyens logistiques et des ressources financières (RASS, 2018), laissent présager que les objectifs qualité ne seront pas atteints. De plus, les textes dans le domaine de la qualité des soins et des services hospitaliers sont insuffisamment vulgarisés, suivis ou ne sont plus d'actualité face aux évolutions constatées dans le secteur. Comment peut-on alors dans ces conditions demander au professionnel de santé de faire des efforts alors même que les buts à atteindre sont irréalisables ? Pour faire face à ces problèmes, le projet Leadership, Management et Gouvernance (LMG) lancé en 2011, avait pour objectif de renforcer les capacités du personnel de santé à tous les niveaux du système de santé. Cette approche mise en œuvre par l'Organisation Management Sciences for Health (MSH) dans plusieurs régions de Côte d'Ivoire, a conduit les managers des organisations de santé à se tourner vers une plus grande coopération entre acteurs des domaines cliniques, administratifs et politiques. L'un des axes principaux utilisés par l'approche LMG, est le Programme de Développement du Leadership ciblant les acteurs en instance de diriger et de gouverner des programmes, relever des défis et obtenir des résultats mesurables.

Dans la phase d'achèvement de ce projet, est inauguré le 15 décembre 2017, le Centre Hospitalier Universitaire d'Angré. La vision de la Direction du CHU est de le hisser au premier rang des hôpitaux publics de référence dans la sous-région Ouest-africaine avec un pôle d'excellence de radiodiagnostic et d'exploration fonctionnelle. Pour ce faire, et en accord avec le plan national de développement sanitaire de (MSHP, 2017a), la direction œuvre à la mise en place d'une démarche qualité certifiante qui s'appuie sur la norme ISO 9001 : 2015. À partir de 2020, la direction souhaite s'attaquer à trois défis à savoir, l'ennui émotionnel, la déshumanisation des relations et la diminution de l'accomplissement personnel (PNDS, 2015 ; RASS, 2018).

Le premier défi, l'ennui organisationnel, qui peut avoir des conséquences psychologiques internes ou externes, est la situation dans laquelle le professionnel de santé cherche à trouver une occupation. Intérieurement, le professionnel va ressentir cet ennui sous la forme du sentiment d'une errance affective au travail, d'une difficulté à être en relation avec les émotions de l'autre. C'est comme s'il n'avait pas suffisamment de travail pour remplir la journée et n'était plus capable de faire face aux sollicitations des clients/patients. Extérieurement, on observe des explosions émotionnelles comme des crises de larmes ou de colère, mais aussi des refus d'agir ou de répondre à une demande, même anodine. Cet état, associé à la déshumanisation de la relation à l'autre, aboutit à la situation ou le soignant, devenu impassible est capable d'assumer et d'affronter toutes les souffrances humaines sans ciller.

Le second défi, la déshumanisation de la relation à l'autre est, marqué par un détachement et une sécheresse relationnelle. Le malade est plus considéré comme un cas, un numéro de chambre, une chose plus qu'une personne. Il s'agit là d'une mise à distance de l'autre qui va être illustrée par de petits signes langagiers qui souvent n'apparaissent qu'à un observateur étranger à la situation ou externe au service. C'est parfois une description tellement scientifique du corps malade que l'analyse des différents organes malades ne rend plus compte de l'état de santé de la personne.

Conséquence des deux autres défis, le troisième à savoir la diminution de l'accomplissement personnel s'exprime par le sentiment de ne pas être efficace, de ne plus savoir aider les gens, d'être frustré dans son travail, en un mot de ne plus faire du bon travail. En effet, la relation à l'autre est le fondement du travail de soignant et la motivation principale de ce choix professionnel. Le professionnel commence à douter de lui et de ses capacités d'aller vers l'autre. Ainsi apparaissent la dévalorisation de soi, la culpabilité, la démotivation. Les conséquences de ces difficultés sont souvent l'absentéisme motivé ou non, l'abandon de travail, le manque de rigueur ou les erreurs professionnelles.

3.2. LA MÉTHODE DE COLLECTE DES DONNÉES

Le pilotage du système de santé insiste sur la nécessité de prêter attention au dialogue entre expériences clients/patients et professionnels pour transformer les systèmes de santé en questionnant la prise en compte de la subjectivité des bénéficiaires (Larson et al., 2019). Ainsi, le slogan de l'établissement « Nos clients, c'est vous les patients et les parents des patients. Vous êtes au cœur de nos actions », exprime l'intention de questionner les pratiques des professionnels par ce qu'en disent les clients/patients. Avec la nécessité reconnue du rôle actif des clients/patients pour améliorer à la fois la qualité et l'efficacité des soins de santé, la méthodologie utilisée est centrée sur les personnes (Woo et al., 2018). En particulier, elle s'adresse aux patients devenus clients, plus représentatifs du marché, plutôt qu'à des personnels hospitaliers. Comme le résument Eklund et al. (2019), la perspective centrée sur le patient exige qu'un soignant tienne compte de manière holistique de ce que l'on sait sur le client et le comprenne comme un être spécifique avant de poser le diagnostic de la maladie. Dans une perspective centrée sur les personnes, la théorie de l'intendance pour un soignant peut être caractérisée par la motivation intrinsèque de celui-ci, son appartenance à l'organisation, son usage des formes de pouvoir, son aptitude aux partages, sa faible distance hiérarchique et son orientation vers l'engagement (Davis et al., 1997 ; Van Slyke, 2007 ; Hernandez, 2012). Selon l'analyse d'Eklund et al. (2019), les soins centrés sur la personne impliquent l'empathie, le respect, l'engagement, la relation, la communication, la prise de décision partagée, l'orientation holistique, l'orientation individualisée et la coordination. Cependant, la méthodologie centrée sur les personnes tient compte directement des aspects des cultures qui semblent influencer l'efficacité organisationnelle (Denison et Mishra, 1995). Elle met l'accent sur les traits de participation, de cohérence, d'adaptabilité et de mission.

L'instrument de collecte est un questionnaire avec une définition des attributs au sens de Denison et Mishra (1995), que sont la responsabilité, l'équipe, la capacitation, la valeur, la coordination, l'intégration, le changement, le client, l'apprentissage, le but et la vision. Les pôles concernés au CHU d'Angré sont le pôle femme - mère enfant, le pôle médecine et spécialités médicales et le pôle chirurgie et spécialités.

Chaque client d'un pôle a reçu le questionnaire contenant des attributs appliqués à plusieurs services. Pour chaque service qu'il aura une fois sollicité, il coche les attributs qui, selon lui, s'appliquent ou ne les cochent pas dans le cas contraire. Ensuite, il note les services réels et un service idéal au travers des scores d'appréciation de ces attributs. La base de sondage est constituée de cinq services réunissant 134 clients issus du registre de consultation du premier trimestre 2021 au service d'informations médicales. Les clients ont été ensuite contactés par ce service de façon à garder leur anonymat. Les critères d'inclusion étaient le niveau de fréquentation et la possibilité puis la volonté de donner un avis pour améliorer les services fréquentés au CHU d'Angré. Le questionnaire, déposé au service communication et relations publiques, a été auto-administré et collecté par le service qualité, avec plusieurs relances. Les trois pôles concernés ont collaboré à l'enquête surtout parce qu'elle comblait le point « 4. Contexte de l'organisation » des exigences de la norme ISO 9001:2015. L'enquête par services, excluant les informations médicales, donne les taux de réponse respectifs dans l'annexe 1. On observe une dominance des femmes (57 %) et de la tranche d'âge de 25 à 45 ans. L'échantillon présente une situation matrimoniale avec très peu de veuf (ve) ayant une fréquentation régulière (34,627 %) et forte (29,851 %) du CHU. Les niveaux d'étude montrent des personnes en majorité instruites. La situation professionnelle suggère des enquêtés exerçant une activité, donc en mesure de payer des services de soin.

La méthode d'analyse « cocher tout ce qui s'applique » ou « check-all-that-apply » (CATA) préconise que le client marque son intérêt, avec l'hypothèse implicite que les éléments cochés sont un « oui » et les éléments non cochés sont un « non » (Meyners et al., 2013 ; Callegaro et al., 2015). La première série de résultats correspond aux tests Q de Cochran effectués sur un tableau attributs x services issus des données brutes. Il est suivi de comparaisons multiples basées sur l'approche de Marascuilo (1970). Ces comparaisons multiples identifient les services responsables du rejet de l'hypothèse nulle d'égalité des services. La seconde étape est une analyse factorielle des correspondances sur un plan des services et du service idéal. Ceci permet d'étudier le positionnement relatif des services les uns par rapport aux autres. L'analyse peut être basée sur la distance du Khi-deux ou la distance de Hellinger, dans le cas où certains attributs sont peu sélectionnés (Meyners et al., 2013; Callegaro et al., 2015). La troisième étape est l'analyse de pénalités qui recherche les caractéristiques susceptibles de pénaliser l'intendance des patients pour un service donné. Elle vise à identifier les attributs cochés entraînant une mauvaise intendance, une absence d'intendance ou une meilleure intendance. La pénalité est basée sur les écarts entre les services réels et l'idéal, et l'impact sur l'appréciation des scores afin d'identifier des axes d'amélioration possibles pour des services.

4. RÉSULTATS DE LA RECHERCHE

4.1. LES ATTRIBUTS NÉCESSAIRES ET LE POSITIONNEMENT DES SERVICES

Les deux premiers tableaux ne prennent en compte que les données des attributs portant sur les services réels. Le tableau de contingence correspond à une somme des tableaux d'attributs, client par client.

Tab. 1 – Matrice de contingence créé à partir des données CATA.

Attributs	Chirurgie	Consultation	Maternité	Médecine	Urgence	Idéal
Responsabilité	91	23	87	88	25	105
Équipe	101	63	62	83	70	125
Capacitation	53	81	8	39	42	103
Valeurs	25	15	30	13	12	7
Coordination	17	5	105	71	12	28
Intégration	74	15	62	85	21	83
Changement	58	39	34	55	33	102
Client	6	42	11	7	28	14
Apprentissage	4	61	4	5	67	9
But	20	23	17	10	42	6
Vision	1	78	4	4	52	10

La colonne chirurgie représente le nombre de fois que chaque client marque son intérêt pour ce service. En principe, si tous les clients manifestent un intérêt pour la chirurgie, la somme sera de 670 (134 x 5) points au lieu de 450. Ainsi, les clients accordent 91 points sur 134 à l'attribut « responsabilité ». À la suite du tableau 1, des tests Q de Cochran sont effectués (*cf.* tableau 2).

TAB. 2 – Test de Cochran pour chaque attribut.

Attributs	p-values	Chirurgie	Consultation	Maternité	Médecine	Urgence
Responsabilité	0,000	0,679 (b)	0,172 (a)	0,649 (b)	0,657 (b)	0,187 (a)
Équipe	0,000	0,754 (b)	0,470 (a)	0,463 (a)	0,619 (ab)	0,522 (a)
Capacitation	0,000	0,396 (b)	0,604 (c)	0,060 (a)	0,291 (b)	0,313 (b)
Valeurs	0,001	0,187 (ab)	0,112 (ab)	0,224 (b)	0,097 (a)	0,090 (a)
Accord	0,212	0,075 (a)	0,097 (a)	0,112 (a)	0,142 (a)	0,075 (a)
Coordination	0,000	0,127 (a)	0,037 (a)	0,784 (c)	0,530 (b)	0,090 (a)
Intégration	0,000	0,552 (bc)	0,112 (a)	0,463 (b)	0,634 (c)	0,157 (a)
Changement	0,001	0,433 (c)	0,291 (abc)	0,254 (ab)	0,410 (bc)	0,246 (a)
Client	0,000	0,045 (a)	0,313 (b)	0,082 (a)	0,052 (a)	0,209 (b)
Apprentissage	0,000	0,030 (a)	0,455 (b)	0,030 (a)	0,037 (a)	0,500 (b)
Orientation	0,192	0,216 (a)	0,179 (a)	0,187 (a)	0,157 (a)	0,254 (a)
But	0,000	0,149 (a)	0,172 (a)	0,127 (a)	0,075 (a)	0,313 (b)
Vision	0,000	0,007 (a)	0,582 (c)	0,030 (a)	0,030 (a)	0,388 (b)

La première colonne contient les p-values associées aux tests Q de Cochran qui comparent les services indépendamment et permet de tester l'effet d'un service sur la validation ou non de chaque attribut. Une p-value se trouvant en-dessous du seuil de significativité indique que les services sont significativement différents les uns des autres. Les autres colonnes contiennent les proportions de « 1 » choisi par les clients pour chaque combinaison de services et d'attributs. Ces comparaisons multiples sont basées sur l'approche de Marascuilo indiquant qu'une proportion élevée signifie que l'attribut est souvent coché par les clients pour le service considéré. Si tel est le cas, les comparaisons multiples par paires représentées par les petites lettres à l'intérieur des cellules du tableau 2. Deux services partageant la (les) même(s) lettre(s) ne sont pas significativement différents contrairement à ceux qui ne partagent aucune lettre.

À l'exception des attributs « accord » et « orientation », tous les attributs sont associés à des p-values significatives. Par exemple, si on considère l'attribut « changement », le service médecine est plus enclin au changement. Cependant, il n'est pas significativement plus changeant que la consultation. De même, la médecine est plus intégrative, mais pas plus significativement que la chirurgie. A contrario, sur le travail en équipe, ce service en demande plus que la médecine, mais de façon moins significative. Les services chirurgie, maternité et médecine ont les attributs « client », « apprentissage », « but » et « vision » qui sont moins mis en exergue et ne sont pas significativement différents l'un de l'autre.

Le tableau 2 est utilisé pour effectuer une analyse factorielle des correspondances (AFC). Le test d'indépendance entre les lignes et les colonnes, utilise la distance de Hellinger, adaptée à certains attributs peu sélectionnés comme « vision », « but » et « apprentissage ». La p-value étant inférieure au niveau de signification (0,05), il y a une forte probabilité pour que de vraies différences existent entre les services. La table des valeurs propres montre 93,07 % d'inertie expliquée sur les deux premières dimensions. La Figure 1 permet de vérifier la qualité de l'analyse.

Dans le contexte local, la Figure 1 peut-être mise en relation avec les points révélés par le RASS (2018). L'ennui organisationnel conduit le professionnel à vouloir s'occuper en ressentant une errance affective au travail quand les malades se présentent aux urgences. N'étant plus capable d'en accueillir, on observe des refus de répondre aux demandes anodines au service consultation. Pour cela, les clients proposent de se recentrer sur le but et la vision, l'apprentissage et les clients. Le second critère de déshumanisation de la relation à l'autre est marqué par un détachement bien décrit par une mise à distance des clients, observable en médecine et une sécheresse relationnelle surtout avec les accouchés ou dans les complications liées aux accouchements. Ils proposent de rappeler les valeurs et la coordination. La diminution de l'accomplissement personnel qui se traduit par ne plus faire du bon travail, vécu en chirurgie est un point sensible d'autant que le CHU d'Angré envisage de devenir un pôle d'excellence de radiodiagnostic et d'exploration fonctionnelle. Pour ce faire, le changement, l'équipe, la responsabilité et l'intégration sont envisageables. Selon le plan de projection, un service idéal doit être relativement apte à changer, faire en équipe, être capacitant, intégrateur et responsabilisant. Par ailleurs, le service de chirurgie semble se rapprocher le plus du produit idéal, alors que la maternité, et dans une moindre mesure les urgences et la consultation en sont loin. La médecine et la consultation sont également relativement éloignées du service idéal.

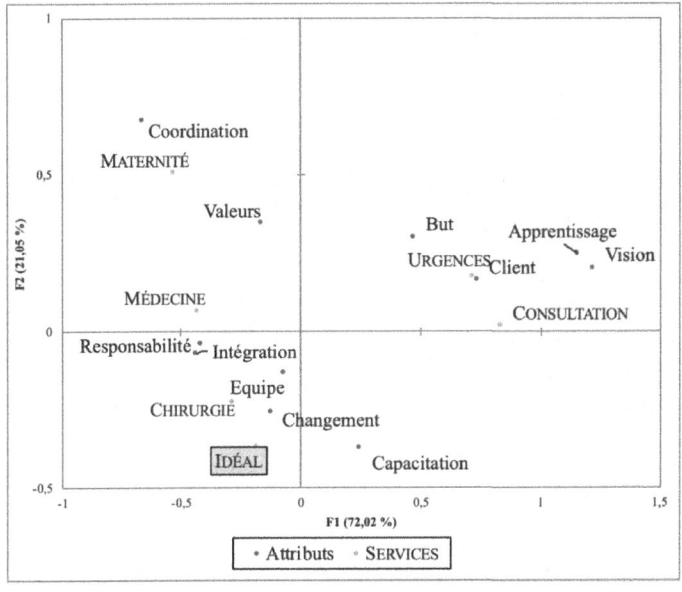

FIG. 1 – Analyse factorielle des correspondances (axes F1 et F2 : 93,07 %).

Ayant des services pour lesquels on dispose d'une matrice de proximité avec le service idéal et de la distance de Hellinger, les corrélations bisérielles entre chaque attribut et les données de préférence sont calculées par une Analyse en Coordonnées Principales. L'objectif est de représenter des ressemblances décrites par une matrice carrée contenant des corrélations. Les résultats sont représentés sur un plan de projection (Figure 2). La qualité de l'analyse est acceptable avec une variabilité cumulée (F1=38 208 % et F2= 20 592 %) de 58,80 %. Sur la figure 2, la note d'appréciation d'ensemble met en exergue les regroupements possibles des attributs. À cet effet, l'équipe et le changement sont nécessaires ainsi que l'intégration et la responsabilité en opposition aux attributs de vision et d'apprentissage puis de coordination et de valeur. Le clivage par la diagonale met les attributs nécessaires proches de la « Note » d'appréciation des services réels. Enfin, on peut relever que ce résultat confirme la congruence avec celui de l'AFC quant au fait que les clients/patients ont un service idéal décrit par des attributs proches.

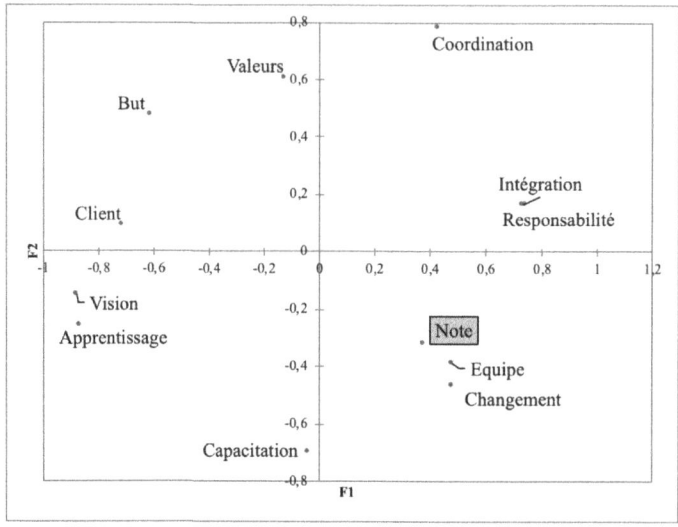

FIG. 2 – Analyse en Coordonnées Principales (axes F1 et F2).

4.2. LES AMÉLIORATIONS POSSIBLES
DU SERVICE RÉEL VERS LE SERVICE IDÉAL

Puisque les données d'appréciation sont disponibles, il est possible d'identifier des axes d'améliorations possibles pour les cinq services grâce à une analyse de pénalités. La méthode consiste à identifier, en utilisant des ANOVA pour chacun des services étudiés, si à une différence de notation des attributs est associée une différence significative au niveau des données globales de préférence. Avec les données de préférence et l'évaluation du service idéal, une analyse est effectuée, pour les attributs nécessaires (P (Non)|(Oui) et P (Oui)|(Oui)) et un autre les attributs négatifs (P(Oui)|(Non) et P (Non)|(Non)).

Une première analyse basée sur les incongruences pour lesquelles l'attribut est coché pour le service idéal, mais pas pour le produit réel permet d'identifier les attributs nécessaires. Un tableau de comparaison contient les fréquences d'apparition de P (Non)|(Oui) et P (Oui)|(Oui) pour chaque attribut. Le tableau 3 permet de visualiser ces fréquences ainsi que les pourcentages d'occurrence de ces deux situations. Les différences de moyenne d'appréciation entre les deux situations sont présentées pour chaque attribut et leur significativité est testée. L'effet sur la moyenne montre combien de points de préférence sont perdus lorsque le service est jugé idéal par un client. La statistique de pénalité montre combien de points de préférence sont perdus lorsque le service ne correspond pas à l'attente du client.

Par exemple, l'attribut « Responsabilité » implique une augmentation de 1,54 point d'appréciation entre les services réels et le service idéal. Cette augmentation est significative à 0,05 (p < 0,000 1).

TAB. 3 – Comparaison des attributs nécessaires.

Variable	Niveau	%	Moyenne (Note)	Effets sur la moyenne	p-value	Pénalités
Responsabilité	P (Non)I(Oui)	38,36 %	5 537	1,549	< 0,000 1	
	P (Oui)I(Oui)	40,00 %	7 086			1,310
Équipe	P (Non) I (Oui)	39,40 %	5 027	2 145	< 0,000 1	
	P (Oui) I (Oui)	53,88 %	7 172			1,890
Capacitation	P (Non) I (Oui)	48,66 %	5 525	1,899	< 0,000 1	
	P (Oui) I (Oui)	28,21 %	7 423			1,565
Valeurs	P (Non) I (Oui)	2,99 %	5 700	1,033		
	P (Oui) I (Oui)	2,24 %	6 733			0,443
Coordination	P (Non) I (Oui)	12,24 %	5 793	1,207	0,010	
	P (Oui) I (Oui)	8,66 %	7 000			0,766
Intégration	P (Non) I (Oui)	32,99 %	5 620	1,571	< 0,000 1	
	P (Oui) I (Oui)	28,96 %	7 191			1,254
Changement	P (Non) I (Oui)	48,36 %	5 448	2 337	< 0,000 1	
	P (Oui) I (Oui)	27,76 %	7 785			2 056
Client	P (Non) I (Oui)	7,01 %	7 128	-1,258		
	P (Oui) I (Oui)	3,43 %	5 870			-0,446
Apprentissage	P (Non) I (Oui)	4,63 %	5 097	2 618		
	P (Oui) I (Oui)	2,09 %	7 714			1,444
But	P (Non) I (Oui)	1,94 %	7 308	-0,896		
	P (Oui) I (Oui)	2,54 %	6 412			0,115
Vision	P (Non) I (Oui)	5,52 %	7 135	-0,981		
	P (Oui) I (Oui)	1,94 %	6 154			-0,149

En somme, le changement et le travail d'équipe, puis la capacitation, la responsabilité et l'intégration, et enfin la coordination sont nécessaires pour promouvoir le service réel. Cela correspond à une situation où l'attribut décrit bien le service idéal, mais est relativement peu ressenti dans les services réels.

Une deuxième analyse, similaire à la première, mais basée sur les incongruences pour lesquelles l'attribut est coché pour le produit réel, mais pas pour le produit idéal permet d'identifier les attributs intéressants. Le tableau de comparaison (Tableau 4) contient les fréquences d'apparition (P [Oui]|[Non] et P [Non]|[Non]) pour chaque attribut. Cela correspond à une situation où l'attribut décrit bien les services réels, mais est relativement peu coché pour le service idéal.

Tab. 4 – Comparaison des attributs négatifs.

Variable	Niveau	%	Moyenne (Note)	Effets sur la moyenne	p-value	Pénalités
Responsabilité	P (Non) I (Non)	14,78 %	6 030			-0,316
	P (Oui) I (Non)	6,87 %	6 565	0,535		
Équipe	P (Non) I (Non)	4,03 %	6 185			-0,120
	P (Oui) I (Non)	2,69 %	7 667	1,481		
Capacitation	P (Non) I (Non)	18,06 %	6 380			0,098
	P (Oui) I (Non)	5,07 %	7 206	0,826		
Valeurs	P (Non) I (Non)	82,84 %	6 407			0,625
	P (Oui) I (Non)	11,94 %	5 625	-0,782	0,006	
Coordination	P (Non) I (Non)	56,42 %	6 558			0,592
	P (Oui) I (Non)	22,69 %	5 664	-0,894	0,000	
Intégration	P (Non) I (Non)	28,66 %	6 047			-0,355
	P (Oui) I (Non)	9,40 %	6 714	0,667		
Changement	P (Non) I (Non)	18,96 %	5 835			-0,574
	P (Oui) I (Non)	4,93 %	8 091	2 256		
Client	P (Non) I (Non)	78,96 %	6 490			0,901
	P (Oui) I (Non)	10,60 %	4 479	-2 011	< 0,0001	
Apprentissage	P (Non) I (Non)	74,33 %	6 629			1,280
	P (Oui) I (Non)	18,96 %	5 150	-1,479	< 0,0001	
But	P (Non) I (Non)	81,34 %	6 639			1,815
	P (Oui) I (Non)	14,18 %	4 200	-2 439	< 0,0001	
Vision	P (Non) I (Non)	73,73 %	6 591			1,108
	P (Oui) I (Non)	18,81 %	4 929	-1,663	< 0,0001	

Les clients estiment que par rapport à leur représentation d'un service idéal, les valeurs, la coordination, le client, l'apprentissage, le but et la vision sont acceptables. Les tableaux 4 et 5 montrent plus globalement que les missions, l'adaptation et la cohérence des services sont des valeurs qui conduisent à l'efficacité. Ici encore, la responsabilité, l'équipe, la capacitation, l'intégration et le changement apparaissent comme nécessaires, tandis que les attributs comme la coordination, le client, l'apprentissage, le but et la vision sont négatifs. Dans la théorie de l'intendance, l'employé attache une plus grande importance aux comportements collectifs, centrés sur l'organisation plutôt que sur l'intérêt personnel. Le tableau 4 montre que les services ont un sens clair de la direction qui définit les buts organisationnels et les objectifs stratégiques et exprime une vision de ce que l'organisation ressemblera à l'avenir. Ces deux attributs, liés à la mission, fournissent un but et un sens en définissant le rôle social et des objectifs externes pour l'organisation. Le sens de la mission permet de façonner le comportement actuel en envisageant un état futur souhaité. Les services actuels offrent un ensemble clair de buts et d'objectifs lié à la mission, à la vision et à la stratégie, qui servent à définir un plan d'actions approprié. Les clients/patients incarnent les valeurs fondamentales et captent le cœur et l'esprit des hospitaliers, tout en fournissant des conseils et une orientation. Être capable de s'intérioriser et de s'identifier à la mission d'une organisation contribue à un engagement à court et à long terme de l'organisation.

Selon Van Slyke (2007), le comportement sur lequel repose la théorie de l'intendance comprend un comportement collectif pro-organisationnel. Ce dernier peut être perçu, comme identitaire pour Conner (2015), dans la vision, le but, les valeurs qui mettent l'accent sur la convergence des objectifs plutôt que sur l'intérêt personnel. Cependant, Hartley et al. (2013) et Van Slyke (2007), supposent qu'au sens de la théorie de l'intendance, les relations de long terme entre l'organisation et le client sont basées sur la confiance, les objectifs collectifs et l'implication.

5. DISCUSSION

Les résultats montrent que l'atteinte du service idéal responsabilise et engage les clients/patients, se construit autour d'équipes (agents hospitaliers et clients/patients) et développe les capacités humaines à tous les niveaux. Les agents hospitaliers sont engagés dans la servuction et ressentent un fort sentiment d'appartenance. Les clients/patients ont le sentiment qu'ils ont au moins une certaine influence sur les décisions qui affecteront le modèle d'affaires et que celui-ci est directement lié aux objectifs d'un service idéal. Pour Kim et Holzer (2016), ce sentiment permet une forte implication dans le modèle d'affaires aux moyens de participations informelles, volontaires et implicites. La démarche qualité fait une référence explicite au besoin de placer le client au centre du dispositif (van Kemenade et Hardjono, 2019; Ikram et al., 2020), celui-ci étant considéré comme un acteur actif de ses soins. La personne soignée est alors perçue comme un acteur au même titre que les autres intervenants du système de soins pour promouvoir la qualité des soins. Ainsi, la poursuite du service idéal du modèle d'affaires appelle l'autorité, l'initiative et la capacité des patients à construire un sentiment d'appartenance et de responsabilité. Ce faisant, la valeur est accordée au travail coopératif vers des objectifs communs (Grönroos, 2018), pour lesquels des capacitations sont développées afin que le CHU reste compétitif et anticipe les besoins des clients/patients. Le modèle d'affaires est ainsi conforté non pas comme un système d'activité (Casadesus-Masanell et Ricart, 2010; Zott et al., 2011), mais avant tout comme une représentation cognitive de ce qui peut être fait avec les clients/patients (Dagou, 2021). La quête du service idéal est enracinée dans une culture de l'efficacité où l'ensemble de valeurs fondamentales pour les dirigeants et les clients, permettent de parvenir à un accord et d'intégrer divers points de vue pour tendre vers le service idéal (Simpkins et al., 2021). Cela nécessite d'investir continuellement dans le développement des compétences. Ces résultats confirment, ce que Samat et al. (2006) avaient déjà souligné que la cohérence développe un état d'esprit et créée des systèmes organisationnels qui construisent un système interne de gouvernance basé sur un soutien consensuel. Ainsi, on peut dire que le service idéal du modèle d'affaires existe en tant que représentations mentales dans l'esprit des hospitaliers et des clients/patients qui le conçoive et le mette en œuvre. Comme le confirme Yilmaz (2021), ces systèmes de maîtrise implicites peuvent être un moyen plus efficace de parvenir à la coordination et à l'intégration que les systèmes de contrôle externe qui reposent sur des règles et réglementations explicites. Ces représentations cognitives sont généralement encodées dans les discours et les objets visuels ou physiques utilisés par les intendants (hospitaliers et clients/patients) pour articuler le modèle d'affaires (Imbert et Chauvet, 2013). Ce dernier, grâce à la démarche qualité, est caractérisé par des employés très engagés, une méthode distincte axée sur les processus, une tendance à promouvoir de l'intérieur et un ensemble clair de « choses à faire » et à « ne pas faire ». Ce qui confirme au final les attributs techniques (négatifs) de la démarche qualité. Du point de vue de l'intendance, on peut parler de quasi-intendance ou d'intendance partielle, puisque le succès du modèle d'affaires et particulièrement du service réel, est un accomplissement et un encouragement malgré le manque d'incitation financière ou utilitaire individuelle.

Malgré certains avantages, les organisations bien intégrées peuvent aussi être les moins adaptatives et les plus difficiles à changer. Le thème des soins adaptatifs signifie la coordination dans l'ensemble du système de santé, de la collaboration interprofessionnelle et de la coordination dans le temps (Vigoda-Gadot et Meisler, 2010). Meyer et Leonard (2014) estiment que, en fournissant de la valeur aux clients, le système de normes et de croyances qui soutiennent cette capacité peut nuire à l'apprentissage et au changement par la tendance à routinier les pratiques. En particulier, le traitement habituel des réclamations clients ou le jeu du bouc émissaire (Van Slyke, 2007), expriment de façon contre-intuitive dans quelle mesure l'organisation est motivée par le souci de satisfaire ses clients. L'intendance devrait aligner les objectifs des hospitaliers sur ceux de l'organisation et de ses parties prenantes, qu'il s'agisse des objectifs financiers tels que la croissance des ventes, l'innovation et la rentabilité ou des objectifs non-financiers au sens d'Andrews et al. (2011) et Antonsen et Jorgensen (1997). De plus, l'utilité que l'intendant gagne à travers des comportements pro-organisationnels est supérieure à celle obtenue à travers des comportements individualistes et égoïstes (Simpkins et al., 2021). Ainsi, lors du développement d'un nouveau service, la recherche confirme, ce que soulignait Parrado et al. (2020), à savoir qu'il faut prêter une attention non seulement à la conception des caractéristiques et des attributs de base du service, mais également aux participations (intégration et équipe) et aux responsabilités qui augmentent la valeur pour les consommateurs. De leur côté, Von Hippel (1986) et Denhardt et Denhardt (2015) soulignent que les clients retirent des bénéfices non seulement de l'usage de leurs innovations, mais également de leur participation au processus d'innovation qui engendre du divertissement et de l'apprentissage. En effet, c'est pendant la fourniture des services que des opportunités de collaboration se présentent, donnant aux employés et aux clients, la chance d'apprendre, d'innover et de co-créer de la valeur (Steen et Brandsen, 2020). En s'intéressant à la démarche qualité, Lim *et al.* (2019) et Chaniotakis et Lymperopoulos (2009), quant à eux, mettent l'accent sur une valeur basée sur les services, créée par l'intégration de ressources et de capacités intangibles dans la collaboration avec les clients. En devenant intendants comme les hospitaliers, les clients reconnaissent qu'offrir un service idéal requiert l'apprentissage du modèle d'affaires, l'alignement des objectifs hospitaliers-clients, et la réciprocité relationnelle en particulier par les aspects philosophiques de la démarche qualité.

CONCLUSION

Selon Loock et Hacklin (2015), plutôt que de se concentrer sur les similitudes entre clients, les fournisseurs de services peuvent exploiter les différences, en recherchant des idées et des intrants pour l'innovation de service. Les clients qui contribuent au processus de conception et de prestation de services étendent la notion de coproduction à la co-création de services (Osborne, 2018). Alors que l'objectif du modèle d'affaires passe de l'échange de propriété transactionnel au service relationnel, les organisations cherchent à impliquer le client dans les processus, avant, pendant et après la prestation de services, et à prolonger le temps que le client passe à chaque rencontre. Selon Raasch et Von Hippel (2013), lorsque les pratiques des clients interviennent, les défis cognitifs se répartissent entre la complexité de la tâche, la logique dominante existante et les connaissances requises. Cette implication des clients permet aux organisations de mieux répondre aux changements de comportement de ceux-ci avec des services innovants. Au-delà de ces défis cognitifs pour réussir une coproduction, il existe d'autres questions délicates pour les services publics et en particulier pour le CHU. L'une concerne le changement des rôles, droits et responsabilités de la direction, des professionnels et des clients/patients dans le processus d'innovation collaborative. L'identification d'un modèle d'affaires pour la conception de services ne parvient pas à identifier les éléments et attributs de service clés. Dans le passé, la conception du modèle d'affaires « hospitalier » n'a pas tenu compte de la qualité telle que définie par le client (Grönroos, 2018), ce qui a entraîné une mauvaise conception, l'insatisfaction des utilisateurs, de faibles taux d'adoption et de faibles niveaux d'utilisation. Cette insuffisance renforce l'appel à apprendre des clients et des situations de co-conception, et ainsi à améliorer la délivrance des services et l'expérience utilisateur.

Pour ce type d'initiative ascendante, il faut en premier lieu souligner l'importance d'un cadre institutionnel qui permette aux initiatives de coproduction d'avoir lieu et de se poursuivre. La création de ce cadre pour une coproduction durable permet l'infusion par les clients/patients de valeurs au-delà des exigences techniques de l'exécution du service. Cette infusion augmente le besoin de règles afin de déterminer les limites des responsabilités des clients/patients qui fournissent un soutien. En second lieu, la contribution des coproducteurs, professionnels et clients, doit être complémentaire plutôt que simplement substitutive. Si chacun a quelque chose dont l'autre a besoin, chacun apportant ses compétences, son temps et sa perspective, il y a possibilité d'innovation collaborative. Il faut revoir cette complémentarité et sa reconnaissance par les hospitaliers, après un an ou deux d'expérimentation sous forme de projet pilote (Eppler et Hoffmann, 2013). En effet, une organisation n'est institutionnalisée que dans la mesure où elle devient le vecteur par lequel les hospitaliers et le clients/patients poursuivent leurs aspirations et leurs idéaux. En troisième lieu, enfin, la transformation de l'assemblage, cadre institutionnel et contribution des coproducteurs, en un organisme social nécessite de la part du CHU des incitations monétaires (primes à la réalisation individuelle de performance absolue, bonus associés à des objectifs de performance relative) et non-monétaires (récompenses sous la forme d'objets ou de services, variété des tâches, autonomie et horaires flexibles, écoute et valorisation des opinions, reconnaissance du travail accompli, attitude favorisant l'estime de soi de chacun). Ces incitations sont destinées à la fois aux professionnels et aux clients pour encourager et soutenir la coproduction. Un engagement mutuel est également nécessaire, afin que les coproducteurs puissent avoir confiance que s'ils continuent ou même augmentent leur contribution, l'autre partie fera de même. Plus globalement, ces trois dimensions renvoient à la question des composantes du processus d'institutionnalisation (Tolbert et Zucker, 1996, p. 182) de ce type d'initiative ascendante. En regard à l'habituation pour le renforcement des capacités, à l'objectivation pour la contribution des coproducteurs et à la sédimentation pour les incitations, Martins et al. (2015) soulignent la nécessité de maintenir la capacité, la motivation et les opportunités des coproducteurs. Ce contexte s'inscrit dans le cadre du travail institutionnel mené « autant par des acteurs avec les ressources et compétences … que par les personnes jouant le rôle de support ou de facilitateur des objectifs de l'entrepreneur » (Lawrence et Suddaby, 2006, p. 217). Ainsi, la poursuite de cette recherche pourrait explorer le processus d'institutionnalisation de l'innovation collaborative dans les services publics hospitaliers par le biais de la coproduction pour tendre vers une gouvernance collaborative avec les coproducteurs.

RÉFÉRENCES

AGGER A., LUND D. H. (2017), "Collaborative Innovation in the Public Sector–new perspectives on the role of citizens?", *Scandinavian Journal of Public Administration*, vol. 21, n° 3, p. 17-38.

ANDREWS R., BOYNE G. A., WALKER R. M. (2011), "Dimensions of publicness and organizational performance: A review of the evidence", *Journal of public administration research and theory*, vol. 21, n° suppl_3, p. i301-i319.

ANTONSEN M., JORGENSEN T. (1997), "The "Publicness" of Public Organizations", *Public Administration*, vol. 75, p. 337-357.

AVERSA P., HAEFLIGER S., ROSSI A., BADEN-FULLER C. (2015), "From Business Model to Business Modelling: Modularity and Manipulation", in C. BADEN-FULLER and V. MANGEMATIN (Eds.), *Business Models and Modelling (Advances in Strategic Management)*, UK: Emerald Group Publishing Limited, p. 151-185

BOMMERT B. (2010), "Collaborative Innovation in the Public Sector", *International Public Management Review*, vol. 11, n° 1, p. 15-33.

CALLEGARO M., MURAKAMI M. H., TEPMAN Z., HENDERSON V. (2015), "Yes–no Answers versus Check-all in Self-Administered Modes: A Systematic Review and Analyses", *International Journal of Market Research*, vol. 57, n° 2, p. 203-224.

CASADESUS-MASANELL R., RICART J. E. (2010), "From Strategy to Business Models and onto Tactics", *Long Range Planning*, vol. 43, n° 2–3, p. 195-215.

CHANIOTAKIS I. E., LYMPEROPOULOS C. (2009), "Service quality effect on satisfaction and word of mouth in the health care industry", *Managing Service Quality: An International Journal*, vol. 19, n° 2, p. 229-242.

CONNER T. (2015), "Representation and Collaboration: Exploring the Role of Shared Identity in the Collaborative Process", *Public Administration Review*, vol. 76, n° 2, p. 288-301.

DAGOU D. H.-W. (2021), « La reconfiguration d'un modèle d'affaires : une analyse de la hiérarchisation des composantes dans une organisation publique certifiée ISO 9001 », *Gestion et management public*, Vol. 9, n° 1, p. 59-77.

DAVIS J. H., SCHOORMAN F. D., DONALDSON L. (1997), "Toward a stewardship theory of management", *Academy of Management Review*, vol. 22, n° 1, p. 20-47.

DEMIRCIOGLU M. A., AUDRETSCH D. B. (2017), "Conditions for innovation in public sector organizations", *Research Policy*, vol. 46, n° 9, p. 1681-1691.

DENHARDT J., DENHARDT R. (2015), "The New Public Service Revisited", *Public Administration Review*, vol. 75, n° 5, p. 664-672.

DENISON D., MISHRA A. (1995), "Toward a theory of organizational culture and effectiveness", *Organization science*, vol. 6, n° 2, p. 204-223.

DESMARCHELIER B., DJELLAL F., GALLOUJ F. (2019), "Innovation in public services in the light of public administration paradigms and service innovation perspectives", *European Review of Services Economics and Management*, vol. 2019-2, n° 8, p. 91-120.

DESMARCHELIER B., DJELLAL F., GALLOUJ F. (2020), "Public service innovation networks (PSINs): an instrument for collaborative innovation and value co-creation in public service(s)", *European Review of Service Economics and Management*, vol. 2020-2, n° 10, p. 133-169.

DOZ Y. L., KOSONEN M. (2010), "Embedding Strategic Agility: A Leadership Agenda for Accelerating Business Model Renewal", *Long Range Planning*, vol. 43, n° 2–3, p. 370-382.

EKLUND J. H., HOLMSTRÖM I. K., KUMLIN T., KAMINSKY E., SKOGLUND K., HÖGLANDER J.,... MERANIUS M. S. (2019), "'Same same or different?' A review of reviews of person-centered and patient-centered care", *Patient Education and Counseling*, vol. 102, n° 1, p. 3-11.

EPPLER M. J., HOFFMANN F. (2013), "Strategies for business model innovation: challenges and visual solutions for strategic business model innovation", in PFEFFERMANN N., MINSHALL T. MORTARA L. (Eds.), *Strategy and Communication for Innovation*, Suisse, Springer, p. 3-14

FURNARI S. (2015), "A Cognitive Mapping Approach to Business Models: Representing Causal Structures and Mechanisms", in C. BADEN-FULLER and V. MANGEMATIN (Eds.), *Business Models and Modelling (Advances in Strategic Management)*, UK, Emerald Group Publishing Limited, p. 207-239

GRÖNROOS C. (2017), "On value and value creation in service: a management perspective", *Journal of Creating Value*, vol. 3, n° 2, p. 125-141.

GRÖNROOS C. (2018), "Reforming public services: does service logic have anything to offer?", *Public Management Review*, vol. 9, n° 4, p. 1-14.

HARTLEY J., SØRENSEN E., TORFING J. (2013), "Collaborative Innovation: A Viable Alternative to Market Competition and Organizational Entrepreneurship", *Public Administration Review*, vol. 73, n° 6, p. 821-830.

HERNANDEZ M. (2012), "Toward an understanding of the psychology of stewardship", *Academy of Management Review*, vol. 37, n° 2, p. 172-193.

IKRAM M., ZHANG Q., SROUFE R. (2020), "Future of quality management system (ISO 9001) certification: novel grey forecasting approach", *Total Quality Management & Business Excellence*, vol. 15, n° 2, p. 1-28.

IMBERT G., CHAUVET V. (2013), « Faire coproduire le client en conception innovante. Les quatre processus mobilisés par les sociétés de conseil en innovation », *Revue Française de Gestion*, vol. 234, n° 5, p. 167-183.

KIM T., HOLZER M. (2016), "Public employees and performance appraisal: A study of antecedents to employees' perception of the process", *Review of Public Personnel Administration*, vol. 36, n° 1, p. 31-56.

LARSON E., SHARMA J., BOHREN M., TUNÇALP Ö. (2019), "When the patient is the expert: measuring patient experience and satisfaction with care", *Bulletin of the World Health Organization*, vol. 97, n° 8, p. 563–569.

LAWRENCE T., SUDDABY R. (2006), "Institutions and Institutional Work", in CLEGG, S. R., HARDY C., LAWRENCE T. B. NORD W. R. (Eds.), *The SAGE Handbook of Organization Studies*, London, Sage, p. 215-254

LIM A.-F., NAIR R. K., FOO P.-Y. (2019), "TQM and organisational innovation: a systematic review and research framework", *International Journal of Innovation and Learning*, vol. 26, n° 3, p. 273-300.

LOOCK M., HACKLIN F. (2015), "Business Modelling as Configuring Heuristics", in BADEN-FULLER C. MANGEMATIN V. (Eds.), *Business Models and Modelling (Advances in Strategic Management)*, UK: Emerald Group Publishing Limited, p. 187-205

MARASCUILO L. A. (1970), "Extensions of the significance test for one-parameter signal detection hypotheses", *Psychometrika*, vol. 35, n° 2, p. 237-243.

MARTINS L. L., RINDOVA V. P., GREENBAUM B. E. (2015), "Unlocking the hidden value of concepts: a cognitive approach to business model innovation", *Strategic Entrepreneurship Journal*, vol. 9, n° 1, p. 99-117.

MEYER A., LEONARD A. (2014), "Are we there yet? En route to professionalism", *Public Relations Review*, vol. 40, n° 2, p. 375-386.

MEYNERS M., CASTURA J. C., CARR B. T. (2013), "Existing and new approaches for the analysis of CATA data", *Food Quality and Preference*, vol. 30, n° 2, p. 309-319.

MSHP (2017a), *Plan National de Développement Sanitaire 2016-2020*, Abidjan, Côte d'ivoire, Ministère de la Santé et de l'Hygiène Publique.

MSHP (2017b), *Rapport annuel sur la situation d'activité sanitaire 2016*, Abidjan, Ministère de la Santé et de l'Hygiène Publique.

OSBORNE S. (2018), "From public service-dominant logic to public service logic: are public service organizations capable of co-production and value co-creation?" *Public Management Review*, vol. 20, n° 2, p. 1-7.

PARRADO S., REYNAERS A.-M., RAMA J. (2020), "The impact of publicness on the performance of professional services: Do private sector organizations perform better?", *Public policy and administration, https://doi. org/10.1177/0952076720977616*. Consulté le 23 septembre 2021.

PNAQS. (2016), *Politique nationale d'amélioration de la qualité des soins et des services de santé en Côte d'Ivoire*, Abidjan, Ministère de la Santé et de l'Hygiène Publique (MSHP).

PNDS (2015), *Plan National de Développement Sanitaire 2016-2020*, Abidjan, Ministère de la santé et de l'Hygiène Publique.

RAASCH C., VON HIPPEL E. (2013), "Innovation process benefits: the journey as reward", *MIT Sloan Management Review*, vol. 55, n° 1, p. 33-39.

RASS. (2018), *Rapport Annuel sur la situation Sanitaire 2017*, Abidjan, Ministère de la Santé et de l'Hygiène Publique (MSHP).

SAMAT N., RAMAYAH T., SAAD N. M. (2006), "TQM practices, service quality, and market orientation: Some empirical evidence from a developing country", *Management Research News*, vol. 29, n° 11, p. 713-728.

SEGAL L., LEHRER M. (2012), "The institutionalization of stewardship: Theory, propositions, and insights from change in the Edmonton public schools", *Organization Studies*, vol. 33, n° 2, p. 169-201.

SEOW C., WISNIEWSKI M., JÄÄSKELÄINEN A., LÖNNQVIST A. (2011), "Public service productivity: how to capture outputs?", *International Journal of Public Sector Management*, vol. 24, n° 4, p. 289-302.

SIMPKINS L., BEAUDRY M., LEMYRE L. (2021), "Can we better define stewardship for public sector executives? A research agenda", *Canadian Public Administration*, vol. 64, n° 1, p. 143-159.

SØRENSEN E., TORFING J. (2012), "Introduction: Collaborative innovation in the public sector", *Innovation Journal*, vol. 17, n° 1, p. 1-14.

STEEN T., BRANDSEN T. (2020), "Coproduction during and after the COVID-19 Pandemic: Will It Last?", *Public Administration Review*, vol. 80, n° 5, p. 851-855.

TOLBERT P., ZUCKER L. (1996), "The institutionalization of institutional theory", in CLEGG S., HARDY C., W. NORD S. (Eds.), *Handbook of Organisation Studies*, London, Sage, p. 179-193

TORFING J. (2019), "Collaborative innovation in the public sector: the argument", *Public Management Review*, vol. 21, n° 1, p. 1-11.

VAN KEMENADE E., HARDJONO T. W. (2019), "Twenty-first century Total Quality Management: the Emergence Paradigm", *The TQM Journal*, vol. 31, n° 2, p. 150-166.

VAN SLYKE D. (2007), "Agents or stewards: Using theory to understand the government-nonprofit social service contracting relationship", *Journal of public administration research and theory*, vol. 17, n° 2, p. 157-187.

VIGODA-GADOT E., MEISLER G. (2010), "Emotions in Management and the Management of Emotions: The Impact of Emotional Intelligence and Organizational Politics on Public Sector Employees", *Public Administration Review*, vol. 70, n° 1, p. 72-86.

WOO S. E., JEBB A. T., TAY L., PARRIGON S. (2018), "Putting the "person" in the center: Review and synthesis of person-centered approaches and methods in organizational science", *Organizational Research Methods*, vol. 21, n° 4, p. 814-845.

YILMAZ V. (2021), "Exploring patient experiences of the internal market for healthcare provision in Turkey: Publicness under pressure", *Journal of Social Policy*, vol. 50, n° 3, p. 588-605.

ZOTT C., AMIT R., MASSA L. (2011), "The Business Model: Recent Developments and Future Research", *Journal of management*, vol. 37, n° 4, p. 1019-1042.

ANNEXE 1
Statistiques descriptives de l'échantillon

Variable \ Statistique	Somme des poids	Modalités	Fréquence par modalité (%)
Genre	134	Féminin	56,72
		Masculin	43,28
Age	129	[0-25[	06,28
		[25-35[	26,27
		[35-45[	30,24
		[45-55[	17,83
		sup 55	19,38
Situation matrimoniale	132	Célibataire	34,24
		Divorcé(e)	26,52
		Marié(e)	31,52
		Veuf(ve)	05,72
Niveau de Fréquentation	134	Exception	06,42
		Faible	11,94
		Moyen	17,16
		Régulier	34,63
		Fort	29,85
Niveau d'étude	130	BT, BEPC, classe de Lycée	18,46
		Baccalauréat	20,00
		BTS, DEUG, Licence	11,54
		Ingénieur, Maîtrise	27,69
		Doctorat, Master	6,92
		Sans diplôme, CEP, CAP	15,39
Situation professionnelle	133	Activité libérale	36,84
		Employé(e)	15,04
		Retraité(e) / préretraité(e)	18,05
		Étudiant(e) salarié(e)	30,07

RÔLE DES TENSIONS DE NORMES

chez les soignants dans la configuration des pratiques
de soins avec les patients âgés vulnérables[1]

Abdelmajid Amine[a]
Audrey Bonnemaizon[a]
Margaret Josion-Portail[a]
[a]Institut de Recherche en Gestion
(IRG), Université Paris-Est Créteil

INTRODUCTION

Le vieillissement de la population est devenu un phénomène mondial sans précédent, impactant la plupart des pays à travers le monde. En France, les seniors de 65 ans et plus représentaient 20 % de la population en 2018 et deviendront le groupe d'âge le plus important en 2070, pesant près de 30 % de la population totale (Insee 2018). Cette avancée en âge massive augmente le risque de perte d'autonomie des personnes qui découle principalement d'une dégradation de leur état de santé physique et mentale générant des limitations fonctionnelles, des restrictions d'activité et une nécessaire prise en charge. Cette tendance a un fort impact sur la gestion des hôpitaux publics et des institutions d'accueil des personnes âgées, qui sont confrontés à la prise en charge médicale et sociale croissante de ce public vulnérable.

La relation de soins est une relation de service particulière qui se nourrit de la mobilisation des ressources respectives des deux parties

---

1   Cette recherche a été financée par une subvention du « Projet Exploratoire Premier Soutien PEPS, UPE-CNRS ».

prenantes que sont le patient et le soignant. Si cette mobilisation de ressources est équilibrée dans le cadre d'une relation dite « normale », celle-ci prend une autre tournure lorsqu'il s'agit d'une relation qui concerne des publics vulnérables. En effet, dans ce dernier cas, les deux parties prenantes semblent à première vue s'inscrire dans un rapport asymétrique au profit de l'organisation (ici l'établissement de santé) et de ses agents (personnel de soins) qui peuvent se prévaloir d'une légitimité dans l'administration des soins fondée sur leurs compétences. Cette asymétrie est amenée à se refléter dans les pratiques d'administration des soins qui vont se (re)configurer tout au long des expériences de service avec les patients. Comme les patients âgés hospitalisés sont considérés comme des sujets fragiles confrontés à une altération de leurs ressources physiques et cognitives, les prestataires de soins ont une tendance naturelle à prendre l'ascendant dans la relation de service de soins.

Par ailleurs, en matière de santé et d'administration de soins, la logique gestionnaire qui tend à prévaloir actuellement dans les établissements de santé répond à un objectif affiché de performance économique risquant paradoxalement d'engendrer des externalités négatives sur le bien-être des malades, en raison notamment des tensions vécues par les personnels dans l'administration des soins. En effet, le champ de l'administration des soins peut être considéré comme un lieu d'expression de différentes formes de « dominations ordinaires » du côté du prestataire (l'établissement de soins et/ou de ses agents/personnels). Ces dernières peuvent susciter des formes de critiques ou d'opposition à la fois de la part des personnels de ces organisations lorsque leurs propres valeurs sont en tension avec les normes organisationnelles/institutionnelles établies et de la part des patients sur qui s'exerce *in fine* cette relation asymétrique de pouvoir.

Si l'étude de ces tensions a déjà fait l'objet de quelques rares travaux en sciences de gestion (Rivière *et al.*, 2013), leur nature, leurs conséquences en matière de relation de service aux patients, et les potentielles actions d'ajustement qu'elles peuvent générer, en l'occurrence chez les personnels soignants, n'ont pas encore reçu l'attention qu'elles méritent de la part des chercheurs en marketing. Cette question est pourtant centrale, à la fois pour améliorer la prise en charge des patients, et notamment des plus âgés, qui font l'objet d'une attention croissante des pouvoirs publics au nom du principe de respect du pouvoir d'agir du patient[2], et pour questionner l'invisibilisation d'un pan utile du travail des soignants. Cette double préoccupation rejoint par ailleurs la logique des tenants du courant de la Transformative Consumer Research (Mick *et al.*, 2012) qui défend une vision capacitante/habilitante des acteurs internes et externes de l'organisation et tend à promouvoir l'amélioration de leur bien-être.

Cette recherche a pour objectif de combler ce manque, au travers d'une étude qualitative explorant les pratiques de relations de soins par le personnel de santé aux patients âgés dans un contexte hospitalier de plus en plus normé. La suite de l'article se structure comme suit : dans un premier temps nous convoquons le cadre théorique de la vulnérabilité en santé pour éclairer la compréhension des ressorts de la fragilité des personnes âgées et leur rôle dans l'alimentation des tensions de normes vécues par les soignants, ainsi que les dispositifs de négociation et de contournement des normes mis en place pour résoudre ces tensions dans le but d'accomplir leur mission de dispense des soins. Ensuite nous présentons la méthodologie engagée pour collecter les données auprès des personnels soignants en charge des patients âgés avant de décliner et de discuter les principaux résultats obtenus. Nous concluons avec les implications de la recherche sur les plans théorique et managérial et proposons quelques pistes pour de futures recherches.

1. LA VULNÉRABILITÉ DES PATIENTS ÂGÉS, UN CATALYSEUR DES TENSIONS DE NORMES VÉCUES PAR LES SOIGNANTS

Le cadre conceptuel de la vulnérabilité a été initialement mobilisé en marketing dans des contextes de consommation, en vue de traduire l'idée de domination et de soumission de l'individu vulnérable à des facteurs extérieurs défavorables capables d'altérer les conditions de vie, l'intégrité et le bien-être de ce dernier comme le restitue la définition consensuelle de Baker *et al.* (2005), qui considère que « *la vulnérabilité du consommateur est un état d'impuissance provenant soit d'un déséquilibre dans*

---

2   La loi relative à l'adaptation de la société au vieillissement a été adoptée par le Parlement le 14 décembre 2015 et est entrée en vigueur au 1er janvier 2016 (www.social-sante.gouv.fr).

les interactions avec le marché ou avec la consommation des messages marketing et des produits ». L'extension de ce cadre au champ de la santé permet de caractériser la situation des patients dans les relations de service de soins avec l'organisation hospitalière et ses agents. Dans cette recherche, la vulnérabilité permet singulièrement de mettre en exergue les tensions vécues par le personnel soignant au contact des patients âgés, dont la prise en charge nécessite une allocation de ressources temporelles, techniques et humaines dont sont démunis les soignants, raison de la rationalisation des moyens et de la standardisation des protocoles de dispense des soins en vigueur à l'hôpital.

Plus que les autres patients, les patients âgés de plus de 75 ans accueillis dans les services de gériatrie aiguë sont confrontés à un cumul de vulnérabilités (Baker *et al.*, 2005), car ils souffrent de déficiences physiques et cognitives chroniques et de pluripathologies. Ces handicaps combinés augmentent la tendance à les percevoir comme des personnes fortement diminuées (Monod et Sautebin, 2009). La vulnérabilité peut ainsi être considérée comme le résultat de la combinaison de facteurs internes et externes affectant les patients âgés, le déclin de la santé étant un catalyseur central (Mason et Pavia, 2014 ; Pavia et Mason, 2014).

Outre les recherches de Pavia et Mason (2014) et Mason et Pavia (2014) qui visent à comprendre comment diverses déficiences d'ordre physique, cognitif et comportemental peuvent mener à la vulnérabilité, des travaux publiés sur le sujet dans le champ de la santé fournissent une définition de la vulnérabilité qui s'inscrit dans une perspective bioéthique. Ainsi, Kemp et al. (2000) conçoivent *« les personnes vulnérables comme celles dont l'autonomie, la dignité et l'intégrité sont menacées ».* Cette définition, assez ouverte au demeurant, permet de considérer les patients âgés comme des individus confrontés à la vulnérabilité parce qu'ils cristallisent des maladies chroniques, des pluripathologies, un déclin fonctionnel et une déchéance du rôle social (Monod et Sautebin, 2009). Parmi les facteurs de risque de vulnérabilité chez la personne âgée identifiés par ces auteurs, deux sont particulièrement éclairants dans le cadre de cette recherche portant sur des patients âgés hospitalisés en service de gériatrie aiguë : *la dépendance fonctionnelle*, qui exprime l'incapacité du patient âgé à réaliser des activités physiques ou mentales nécessaires à la vie quotidienne, ce qui le place dans une situation de dépendance vis-à-vis de tiers pour l'accomplissement de ces différentes tâches ; et *la perte d'autonomie*, qui consiste en l'incapacité de l'individu à faire des choix en toute autonomie. L'effet conjugué de ces deux types de dépendance alimente la tendance à percevoir ce dernier comme une personne vulnérable et porte les germes d'un risque d'atteinte au sentiment de dignité et d'intégrité de ces patients (Monod et Sautebin, 2009). Privé de la faculté d'agir par lui-même, et perdant le contrôle sur son propre destin, celui-ci devient tributaire des décisions prises par les autres (soignants, ayants droit) à sa place, ce qui accentue de fait sa vulnérabilité.

La conséquence de la prise en compte des facteurs de risque d'incapacité, de dépendance et de perte d'autonomie associés aux patients âgés, se traduit par la nécessité d'allouer davantage de temps, d'efforts et d'attention à leur prise en charge par le personnel soignant selon la singularité de chaque expérience de service de soins et la variabilité de l'état de santé de ces malades. Or, depuis l'instauration d'une logique gestionnaire par la réforme de l'hôpital, le protocole d'administration des soins est encadré, standardisé et cadencé, accentuant de fait les tensions chez les soignants qui vivent des conflits de valeurs, tiraillés entre le respect des normes organisationnelles les enjoignant de traiter indistinctement cette population et leur éthique personnelle en regard de la vulnérabilité des patients âgés, qui les incite à veiller à la préservation du pouvoir d'agir et de la dignité de ces derniers.

2. LOGIQUES DE NÉGOCIATION ET DE CONTOURNEMENT DES NORMES PAR LES SOIGNANTS

L'hégémonie culturelle à l'œuvre dans les organisations traduit une sorte d'autorité sociale qui impose le consentement des acteurs de manière à ce que le pouvoir puisse être naturellement et légitimement exercé (Clark *et al.*, 1976). La domination symbolique par la norme s'exprime au travers des idéologies enchâssées dans les discours organisationnels. Elle se manifeste aussi dans leur traduction, plus ou moins formalisée, dans les pratiques quotidiennes, qui ont pour effet de les imposer en tant qu'ensemble de valeurs acceptées comme « allant de soi ». En se naturalisant, ces idéologies deviennent partie intégrante de la vie quotidienne des acteurs, et imprègnent leurs comportements. Lorsque les membres du personnel s'écartent de ces pratiques, ils s'inscrivent dans une démarche qui tend à substituer aux pratiques dominantes des façons de faire personnelles nourries de normes et de valeurs individuelles. Ces logiques de négociation ou de contournement des normes organisationnelles et/ou professionnelles constituent ce que certains auteurs, à l'instar de Dobré (2002), Moisio et Askegaard (2002) et Sitz (2008), désignent par *résistance tacite ou ordinaire*. D'autres auteurs, à l'image de Lazarus (1966) et Folkman *et al.* (1986) les qualifient de stratégies de *coping*, permettant d'ajuster les comportements aux contraintes de la situation. Ces logiques ne consistent pas en une opposition franche ni en un rejet facial des normes mais se traduisent par le développement de micro-pratiques quotidiennes, qui dévient des règles et des codes formels *via* l'importation de normes et de pratiques exogènes plus à même d'être consonantes et efficientes par rapport au contexte d'usage ou d'action. La conception retenue de ces logiques d'adaptation renvoie aux pratiques quotidiennes en tant que réactions conscientes ou non, volontairement dirigées ou non à l'encontre de la suprématie des normes (professionnelles) prescrites, ou encore à l'encontre de la domination symbolique d'une norme (organisationnelle) ancrée dans les pratiques individuelles et collectives (Clark *et al.*, 1976 ; Hebdige, 1979).

Qu'il s'agisse de logiques de résistance ordinaire ou de schémas de coping, ces phénomènes se distillent de manière implicite, voire inconsciente, derrière les pratiques des acteurs au quotidien. Les individus sont amenés à remplacer progressivement les normes et schémas d'interprétation imposés par l'idéologie dominante par leurs propres valeurs ou normes socio-culturelles, et altèrent par conséquent le sens initial qui leur était donné. Ce faisant, ils défient discrètement l'hégémonie de la norme organisationnelle, et construisent au travers de leurs pratiques du sens culturel qu'ils entretiennent et reproduisent au quotidien. Ces pratiques quotidiennes deviennent symboliquement des micro-actes politiques (Bourdieu, 1979) de résistance tacite, dans la mesure où elles expriment implicitement un rejet du sens initial ancré dans les pratiques normées et leur remplacement par un sens alternatif appelé à se normaliser. Hebdige (1979) note à cet effet que le défi pour la suprématie de la culture dominante ne provient pas directement de l'individu mais davantage du sens connoté de son action qui percute la signification associée à la culture dominante édictée : le simple fait de discuter ou d'amender la norme revient intrinsèquement à la contester et à s'y opposer même si ce n'est pas forcément fait de manière explicite ou consciente. La résistance tacite et ordinaire et les stratégies de coping mobilisées s'expriment ainsi dans le contournement des codes et normes (Moisio et Askegaard, 2002) et dans la confection de solutions alternatives au quotidien.

Ce prisme de lecture éclaire opportunément l'étude des tensions en milieu hospitalier qui constitue un environnement fortement normé où des contraintes fortes s'exercent sur les soignants, sans que ceux-ci puissent contester ou s'extraire totalement des règles en vigueur dans l'organisation.

Cette recherche contribue au champ des relations de service de soins avec les publics vulnérables en apportant une compréhension fine des tensions de normes auxquelles sont confrontés les soignants dans la réalisation de leur mission de soins. Elle s'attèle aussi à explorer les stratégies de coping mobilisées au quotidien par les personnels de soin en vue de déjouer la suprématie des normes professionnelles et d'aligner leurs valeurs et éthique personnelles avec leurs pratiques de soins quitte à adapter, voire à déroger aux règles organisationnelles au gré des ressources physiques et cognitives dont disposent les patients âgés vulnérables dont ils ont la charge.

3. ÉLÉMENTS DE MÉTHODE

Cette recherche a été menée dans le cadre d'un projet portant sur la gestion des parcours de soins des patients âgés de 75 ans et plus entre leur domicile et l'hôpital. La collecte de données a été conduite auprès des professionnels de santé du service de Gériatrie Aiguë d'un groupe hospitalier d'Ile de France. La participation à l'étude s'est opérée sur la base du volontariat après que les chefs de service aient présenté le thème général de l'étude aux informants potentiels. Dix-huit entretiens semi-directifs ont été conduits avec différents types de professionnels de santé proches du corps des patients [personnels infirmiers (IDE) et aide-soignants (AS), diététiciens (DIET)], des deux sexes, avec une ancienneté allant de moins d'un an à plus de 30 ans (*cf.* tableau 1 des informants en annexe). Les entretiens (durée moyenne 50 mn) ont été menés sur le lieu de travail en service de jour comme de nuit, puis enregistrés et intégralement retranscrits avant de faire l'objet d'une analyse de contenu thématique.

Le codage s'est appuyé sur des allers-retours entre les données recueillies et les interprétations successives des chercheurs nourries par leurs lectures (Miles et Huberman, 1994). Les discours ont d'abord été réduits à un ensemble d'extraits pertinents au regard de notre problématique. Ensuite, les données ont été organisées en sous-catégories de sens au plus près du discours des répondants puis ces dernières ont été agrégées par proximité de sens en montant en abstraction/théorisation pour être structurées en catégories de sens. L'unité d'analyse retenue est l'interaction de service entre les soignants et les patients âgés. La pertinence de ce prisme d'analyse a été mise en évidence par Coulter (2012), qui conçoit cette unité d'analyse comme un niveau adéquat pour observer les manières dont les patients sont associés (ou non) à la prise de décision médicale et à leur parcours de soins. En termes d'interprétation des données, nous avons d'abord cherché à identifier et typer les sources de tensions et de dissonances vécues par les soignants lors de la dispense aux patients âgés des pratiques de soins engagées quotidiennement. Nous avons ensuite pu incarner ces pratiques de soins en les adossant aux stratégies de coping mobilisées pour résoudre ou absorber ces tensions de normes.

Afin de favoriser la fiabilité de nos résultats, les discours des répondants ont fait l'objet d'un double codage par les auteurs. Les divergences inter-codeurs ont été résolues au travers de discussions autour des motifs sous-jacents aux regroupements opérés, qui ont permis au final d'aboutir à une structuration consensuelle des résultats.

4. RÉSULTATS

L'analyse des discours montre que la polypathologie constitue une représentation consubstantiellement associée au patient âgé par tous les personnels soignants. Elle renvoie à la perception de l'altération du corps des patients âgés et de leurs troubles cognitifs, incarnés par leur incapacité à réaliser les tâches quotidiennes doublée de l'instabilité et de la variabilité de leur état de patients qui peut se dégrader très rapidement, mais aussi à la difficulté d'évaluer les effets secondaires des traitements administrés. Par conséquent, les pratiques de soins permettent d'incarner des stratégies d'adaptation déployées par les soignants confrontés à cette variabilité des situations des patients âgés en vue de leur dispenser opportunément des soins. Ces schémas de coping tendent à réduire/gérer les tensions vécues par le personnel soignant et s'incarnent dans les arbitrages qu'ils opèrent dans les micro-pratiques de soins dispensées aux patients âgés fragiles et dépendants. Ceux-ci les amènent à déroger aux normes professionnelles (lorsque le patient âgé est perçu comme limité dans ses ressources) ou à convoquer les ressources restantes de ce dernier afin de favoriser l'expression de son pouvoir d'agir.

Les discours des informants donnent à voir deux niveaux de tensions de normes qui traversent les pratiques de soins et la relation de service soignant-soigné, et deux stratégies d'ajustement mobilisées pour résorber ces tensions.

4.1 TENSIONS ENTRE LE TEMPS DU PATIENT ET LE TEMPS DE L'ORGANISATION

Les discours des acteurs donnent à voir tout d'abord des tensions entre des normes organisationnelles façonnées par une logique gestionnaire et des valeurs professionnelles plaçant le patient au cœur des dispositifs de soins et de prise en charge[3]. Les premières se diffusent dans l'organisation par le biais d'indicateurs de performance économique et soumettent les professionnels de soins à des cadences élevées, les obligeant à intégrer une culture de la rentabilité dans la réalisation de leurs tâches quotidiennes. Les secondes reposent sur « l'approche globale du patient âgé », très prégnante dans le service de Gériatrie Aiguë dans lequel cette étude a été menée, et nécessitent un temps long pour

---

3   Référence à la loi 2002-2 du 2 janvier 2002 qui fait de l'usager des dispositifs de l'action sociale et médico-sociale l'acteur central de son parcours de soins. Cette loi sollicite désormais sa participation la plus active possible aux décisions et mesures d'accompagnement et de prise en charge qui le concernent, sur lesquels il doit pouvoir, selon son état, exercer ses choix ou donner son consentement.

prendre en compte les particularités des patients âgés vulnérables qui cristallisent des maladies chroniques, des pluri-pathologies, un déclin fonctionnel et une déchéance du rôle social (Monod et Sautebin, 2009).

4.2 TENSIONS ENTRE PRESCRIPTION DU POUVOIR D'AGIR DES PATIENTS ET LEUR INCAPACITÉ PERÇUE

Un deuxième niveau de tension émerge de nos entretiens, entre la norme professionnelle prônant le respect du pouvoir d'agir des patients et la perception par les soignants des déficiences physiques et cognitives de ces derniers. L'altération progressive des capacités qui peut survenir au cours de l'hospitalisation des patients âgés questionne de manière pratique les ambitions de participation à la relation de soins qui leur est proposée. L'asymétrie des ressources disponibles chez les patients et les personnels soignants est clairement vécue par ces derniers. Elle s'accompagne de questionnements sur les façons les plus raisonnables de faire en tentant d'articuler des objectifs qui ne sont pas toujours conciliables, en l'occurrence « respecter les attentes des patients » sans pour autant les mettre en danger et « assurer leur confort » sans porter atteinte à leur autonomie.

Les stratégies de résolution des tensions par le personnel soignant reposent sur le registre du bricolage et celui de la ruse.

4.3 BRICOLER LES NORMES PROFESSIONNELLES AU NOM DU PRINCIPE DE RESPECT DU POUVOIR D'AGIR DU PATIENT

Les données recueillies révèlent que la validité de l'ordre dominant (normes professionnelles « gestionnaires ») n'est ni occultée, ni altérée, ni même visée ouvertement par le comportement non conforme des personnels de soins. Les acteurs ne manifestent pas de volonté d'échapper (de s'opposer) à ces normes, ou d'entrer en rébellion par rapport à l'ordre établi (Weber, 1978). En revanche, la pratique quotidienne des soins et la variété des contextes d'interaction avec des patients vus comme déficients sur le plan des ressources font apparaître des interstices dans lesquels la norme professionnelle ne s'applique pas pleinement, ouvrant un champ pour imaginer et bricoler d'autres façons de faire pour administrer les soins. Les pratiques sont hybridées, modifiées, amé-nagées par les soignants qui puisent dans leurs répertoires personnels et leurs valeurs culturelles les ressources nécessaires pour accomplir leurs missions de soins. Ils n'agissent ni *contre*, ni *par*, ni *sur*, mais *avec* la norme (Le Goff, 2013).

Les soignants doivent ainsi arbitrer entre l'obligation de respecter le pouvoir d'agir des patients et la perception de leurs déficiences physiques et cognitives. L'altération progressive des capacités des patients âgés, qui peut survenir lors d'une hospitalisation ou pendant leur séjour dans l'institution médicale, conduit à des questions pratiques sur la possibilité de les impliquer ou non dans la relation de soins. Elle soulève des interrogations sur la meilleure façon de le faire, en essayant d'articuler des objectifs qui ne sont pas toujours compatibles : « respecter la volonté des patients » sans les mettre réellement en danger et « leur prodiguer les soins de qualité nécessaires » sans porter atteinte à leur autonomie.

Ces pratiques de bricolage et d'adaptation auxquelles s'adonnent les soignants reflètent la perspective de Certeau (1980) qui s'inscrit à l'opposé d'une théorie du consentement des individus à leur domination, et qui suppose que les *usagers, ici les personnels de santé, "bricolent" avec et dans les normes qui sont censées les dominer pour qu'elle versent subrepticement dans le sens de leurs intérêts et de leurs règles propres.* Le « bricolage » utilisé ici peut être compris comme une métaphore pour désigner les reconstructions de sens que les personnes d'une culture donnée utilisent pour réorganiser leur vision du monde et des objets ainsi que leurs comportements sur la base de divers traits culturels, qui sont réunis et arrangés ensemble en vue de produire de nouvelles significations (Lévi-Strauss, 1960). Cette malléabilité des normes provoque l'émergence de comportements hybrides, tiraillés entre la nécessité de maintenir des liens avec les valeurs personnelles internalisées et l'application stricte des normes professionnelles qui peuvent être perçues comme des valeurs externes. Nous identifions six pratiques hybrides mises en œuvre par les soignants (Tableau 1) : *1. Ralentir le rythme des soins ; 2. S'adapter à l'individu ; 3. Prendre le temps d'expliquer et traduire pour le patient âgé ; 4. Réaménager l'ordre des tâches ; 5. Reporter, différer les tâches ; 6. Autoriser ce qui proscrit mais non dangereux.*

TAB. 1 – Bricolage des normes professionnelles au nom du principe du patient
« acteur de son parcours de soins ».

Pratiques de soins mobilisées par les soignants	Exemples de Verbatim
Ralentir le rythme des soins	« Un jour, il y a un médecin qui m'a dit : "tu as vu, tu prends deux heures pour faire ton tour". Je lui ai dit : "pas de problème. Après maintenant tu fais le tour avec moi et tu me dis où je suis lente et où…" Parce que prendre un médicament, le mettre là et lui dire : "vous prenez cela" et je m'en vais, cela je peux le faire. Cela je peux le faire et je vais gagner du temps. Mais au final, le médicament je ne sais pas s'il est pris » (IDE 3)
S'adapter à l'individu	« Voilà, une fois qu'ils ont goûté ils disent : "ah et bien non…je suis désolé, j'avais demandé un menu haché mais je n'en veux pas. Cela ne me plaît pas…changez." Des fois, cela arrive qu'on change et puis après on repasse derrière : "et pourquoi on lui a mis cela ? (…) on lui a mis cela parce qu'elle l'a demandé. C'est sa demande" » (AS 1)
Prendre le temps d'expliquer et traduire pour le patient âgé	« Le patient âgé, des fois, il ne comprend pas. Il…voilà, on réexplique, on reformule, on…voilà, on essaie de se mettre à sa hauteur » (IDE 3). « Ils déambulent bien, des fois cela nous pose problème mais, du coup, et bien il faut les accompagner en…en leur expliquant quoi faire, pourquoi. Toujours les…les rassurer. C'est plus du travail un petit peu psychique » (IDE 1)
Réaménager l'ordre des tâches	« Et les soins techniques en même temps. Tout en même temps en fait. Oui. Mais après, chacun gère…chaque infirmière gère comme elle peut. Moi, c'est comme cela que je gère. Je fais toujours la première approche avec les constantes. J'essaie de…j'essaie de les voir tous pour voir s'ils vont bien, comment ils sont avant de pouvoir faire les soins techniques » (IDE 6)
Reporter / différer les tâches	« Il y a des soins que…bon et bien je ne veux pas maintenant…je suis fatigué… » « Voilà, ce n'est pas grave. On continue. Enfin, on revient. (…) il y a des gens qui ne veulent pas être lavés tous les jours hein. Vous savez c'est…ce sont des gens qui sont…d'avant-guerre et…et…il faut prendre cette situation-là. » (AS 1)

| Autoriser ce qui proscrit mais non dangereux | « Et donc, théoriquement, [apporter de la nourriture] c'est interdit. (…) Le problème c'est que…enfin, après on sait… quand même que la nutrition (…) d'ici n'est quand même pas toujours très bonne et…pas facile à manger. Et surtout, nous on encourage le fait de…enfin de… – comment dire – d'augmenter les apports. Donc on…on tolère les…les apports extérieurs, alors de préférence tout ce qui est sec, qui ne se met pas au frigo, donc effectivement les gâteaux, les boissons » (DIET 1) |

IDE : Infirmier(e) Diplômé(e) d'État ; AS : Aide soignant(e) ; Diet : Dietéticien(ne)

4.4 RUSER POUR RÉHABILITER LA NORME DU POUVOIR D'AGIR DES PATIENTS EN VUE DE MAINTENIR L'IDÉAL-TYPE DU PATIENT AUTONOME

Au dispositif de *bricolage*, il est possible d'adjoindre celui de *ruse* comme stratégie de *coping* déployée par les soignants lorsqu'ils perçoivent chez les patients âgés des compétences restantes ou des capacités résiduelles, afin de préserver l'idéaltype de patients autonomes. Le dispositif de la ruse, emprunté au travail de Hennion et Vidal-Naquet (2012) sur les relations de soins à domicile, est imprégné des cadres de pensée d'Erving Goffman (en particulier de son usage de la fiction, 1973) et de Paul Ricœur sur le récit (1983). Les auteurs (p. 329) envisagent la scène du soin à domicile comme porteuse d'un *paradoxe fictionnel* : « *c'est justement pour préserver malgré tout une autonomie dont le sens même s'effrite et pour assurer une protection dont la personne ne voit plus forcément elle-même l'opportunité que, sur le tas, selon les problèmes concrets à résoudre en situation, il faut empiéter sur l'autonomie ou il faut accepter certaines prises de risque pour arriver à "sauver" l'essentiel, c'est-à-dire à maintenir une forme possible d'autonomie et de protection compte tenu de l'état des choses* ». Ces prises de risques, les auteurs leur donnent un nom contribuant à leur reconnaissance et leur valorisation : la ruse, « *vue non pas comme une tromperie, mais comme un art du faire faire* » (p. 326), voire du faire avec. C'est bien de cela qu'il s'agit dans le contexte de la relation de service de soins, où les pratiques de ruse déployées par les soignants s'expriment par la projection d'images positives et par l'activation d'attitudes favorables aux patients âgés qui se cristallisent dans les pratiques de soins.

Un ensemble de dix ruses logées dans des micro-pratiques de soins permettant de maintenir l'idéal-type du patient autonome en l'amenant à faire et à coopérer à la dispense des soins, ont été identifiées (Tableau 2) : *1. Stimuler les patients pour maintenir leurs capacités ; 2. Faire de l'humour pour instaurer un climat de confiance favorable à la coopération ; 3. Utiliser la communication non-verbale pour interagir avec les patients ; 4. Savoir lire entre les lignes grâce à l'observation pour favoriser le faire faire ; 5. Détourner les patients de leurs obsessions afin de parvenir à un échange « normal » ; 6. Faire intervenir la famille pour obtenir la coopération du patient ; 7. Avoir recours à la figure d'autorité du médecin pour contrer la famille au service des intérêts du patient ; 8. Argumenter vis-à-vis de la famille pour préserver la volonté du patient ; 9. Tempérer pour faciliter la coopération des patients ; 10. Surveiller / forcer pour sauver les capacités restantes et préserver la sécurité du personnel de soin.*

TAB. 2 – La ruse, levier de contournement des normes professionnelles pour maintenir l'idéal-type du patient autonome.

Pratiques de soins convoquées par les soignants	Exemples de Verbatim
Stimuler les patients pour maintenir leurs capacités	« Et puis, parfois, ils ne savent plus aussi qu'ils sont capables de faire. (…) Nous c'est ce qu'on faisait, c'était : "vous prenez la brosse et vous essayez de vous brosser les cheveux". Parce que c'est avec des petits riens qu'on recommence, en fait, à reprendre un petit peu…et bien sa vie en main en fait. (…) il y a des choses qu'ils peuvent continuer à faire hein. Brosser ses cheveux, on peut encore y arriver ! » (IDE 7)
Faire de l'humour pour instaurer un climat de confiance favorable à la coopération	« En rigolant avec eux, des fois… Des fois, même la plaisanterie cela…leur permet de…penser à autre chose que la maladie et ça c'est… (…) dès que cette personne elle arrive à…à sourire avec vous, elle commence à rentrer en confiance et… Une fois qu'on a la confiance de la personne, alors…on peut ouvrir pas mal de portes ». (AS 1). « Ou des fois, moi je chante. Je ne sais pas si vous connaissez cette petite chanson "le petit vin blanc" (…) et, lorsque je rentre, je dis toujours : "alors les jeunes !" et tout. Cela leur fait plaisir. » (AS 4)

Utiliser la communication non-verbale pour interagir avec les patients	« Vu qu'elle ne parlait pas français, moi je regardais. Je me suis mise à sa hauteur. Je l'ai regardée et je lui ai dit : "ne vous inquiétez pas. On n'est pas là pour vous faire du mal". Je lui ai dit cela, dans mes mots. J'ai essayé de lui transmettre cela dans mon regard…pour qu'elle essaie de se calmer » (AS 2). « Oui. On fait des gestes. Récemment – je crois qu'elle sort aujourd'hui – bon, la mise en place il fallait écrire parce que bon…très mignonne mais bon, elle ne nous entend pas. On ne s'entend pas, et bien on écrit » (IDE 6)
Savoir lire entre les lignes grâce à l'observation pour favoriser le faire faire	« Alors, c'est de…le laisser faire ce qu'il veut faire. Donc c'est prendre en compte, effectivement, ses capacités. C'est de lui laisser le temps de le faire. C'est de le motiver à faire aussi. Donc, cela veut dire quoi ? Que vous ayez ce temps d'observation. C'est-à-dire qu'il faut que vous sachiez ce qu'il fait ou ce qu'il peut faire. Mais tout cela, cela demande du temps. Et ce temps…et bien les gens courent après » (IDE 7)
Détourner les patients de leurs obsessions afin de parvenir à un échange « normal »	« L'objectif c'est de la…de l'amener à penser à autre chose pour qu'elle puisse ne pas s'angoisser. Parce que, parfois, ils…s'angoissent quand ils restent dans cette époque. Ils s'angoissent : "mais pourquoi ? Mais pourquoi ?" Donc du coup, on essaie de les occuper pour essayer que, ne serait-ce qu'un instant, qu'ils…qu'ils oublient. Et parfois, il…cela passe. Cela arrive qu'ils oublient et qu'ils…qu'ils…qu'ils se calment en fait. C'est…c'est comme cela que moi j'ai essayé de mettre en place. Après…comme je vous dis, ce n'est pas toujours facile d'une personne à l'autre. Cela a fonctionné pour une personne, comme cela n'a pas fonctionné pour une autre » (AS 2). « Mais après, c'est vrai qu'on…en soit, la conversation, les mots ne sont pas très…c'est juste en fait de se dire que, oui, on…ils ont parlé avec nous…l'échange en fait qui compte plus que, vrai-ment…le thème j'ai l'impression » (IDE 4)

Faire intervenir la famille pour obtenir la coopération du patient	« Alors là, cela a été sa fille…qui, finalement, a pris la relève en disant : "et bien, je vais la [*la toilette*] faire. Je vais l'emmener et puis ça s'est passé comme cela". Mais du coup, il a fallu lui prendre ses vêtements parce que les vêtements étaient complètement imbibés [*d'urines*]…voilà. Donc il a fallu mettre les vêtements. C'était la course aux vêtements après » (IDE 7)
Avoir recours à la figure d'autorité du médecin pour contrer la famille au service des intérêts du patient	« Si on peut, on parle devant le patient. Si c'est un petit peu plus compliqué, on les prend à part dans le couloir en leur disant : "voilà, on n'arrive pas là. Est-ce que vous pouvez nous aider à…" Voilà, le médecin aussi nous aide. On a une assistante sociale aussi. On a des médecins, on a des gériatres exceptionnels. Oui. (…) On a des gériatres exceptionnels, oui. » (IDE 3). « Quand il y a vraiment un gros souci et bien on va chercher le médecin (…) oui parce que la famille par rapport au médecin … le médecin a plus d'impact » (IDE 1).
Argumenter vis-à-vis de la famille pour préserver la volonté du patient	« Il y a des fois : "ne lui demandez pas à lui, moi je sais" (…) pour les régimes pas forcément dans ce service mais moi ça m'est arrivé … où la famille insiste pour avoir un régime casher pour le patient mais le patient lui-même nous confie : moi j'en ai marre de manger la même chose mettez-moi juste sans porc (…) donc on change et la famille le lendemain "ce n'est pas casher, ça ne va pas" » (IDE 1).
Tempérer pour faciliter la coopération des patients	« Moi j'essaie…et bien une prise de sang, un bilan sanguin le matin ou un aérosol, ou…bon. Je vais venir. La personne va me dire non. Je vais essayer de parlementer en expliquant pourquoi. Si au bout de 10 minutes elle dit non, je m'en vais. Je vais faire autre chose. Je reviens une demi-heure après et bien cela va mieux » (IDE 3). « Oui, voilà. Quand les…bon on recrache ou… Et puis, il faut dire que d'autres ont des troubles de déglutition. Donc il faut être présent. Ce n'est pas… Il faut vraiment être patient dans la prise des traitements sinon… on n'a pas de résultats. On ne pose pas et puis on s'en va, ça c'est impossible » (IDE 6)

Surveiller/forcer pour sauver les capacités restantes et préserver la sécurité du personnel de soin	« Alors…par exemple, s'il y a des patients, ici, qui sont violents et du coup ils sont…ils sont contentionnés des membres inférieurs et supérieurs, mais c'est sous prescription. C'est-à-dire que c'est le médecin qui décide de le faire. Donc, quand on est à deux soignants pour ce soin, on essaie de…détacher une, mais par exemple, pour laisser le champ libre. Mais…c'est…ce n'est pas de la violence. C'est juste de la…il faut vraiment avoir une maîtrise de soi parce que…parce que… le patient il va être violent et…on peut…voilà […] Cela fait un peu…cela fait un peu barbare mais… des fois on n'a pas le choix » (AS 2)

IDE : Infirmier(e) Diplômé(e) d'État ; AS : Aide-Soignant(e)

5. DISCUSSION DES RÉSULTATS ET IMPLICATIONS DE LA RECHERCHE

Ces résultats amènent d'une part à engager une discussion autour de plusieurs implications en marketing des services à destination des publics vulnérables afin de garantir leur bien-être, et d'autre part, à repenser la valorisation du travail invisible engagé par les personnels soignants en vue de leur dispenser les soins tout en préservant leur dignité. Nous identifions ainsi le rôle joué par un réseau d'acteurs de soins gériatriques à l'hôpital qui prennent en compte l'avancée en âge et la vulnérabilité des patients pour élaborer des stratégies d'adaptation tenant compte de ces caractéristiques et les déployer à travers leurs pratiques de soins durant les interactions de service.

Les stratégies de coping déployées par les soignants s'incarnent dans une variété de pratiques de soins allant de l'internalisation par les soignants de la (quasi)totalité des éléments du service de soins lorsqu'ils perçoivent le patient âgé comme un être démuni de ressources (corps et cognition en incapacité), jusqu'à des formes embryonnaires de co-production de soins lorsque le patient âgé est perçu comme doté de ressources résiduelles que les soignants vont chercher à activer pour le faire participer à son parcours de soins. En procédant ainsi à la torsion et au contournement des normes organisationnelles (exécution cadencée des tâches, temps compté, etc.) les soignants cherchent au travers de l'emploi du bricolage à « faire à la place » du patient en vue d'administrer les soins en temps et en heure, et au travers de la mobilisation de la ruse à « faire avec » le patient afin de préserver une forme possible d'autonomie des patients âgés contribuant à leur bien-être.

Nos résultats montrent ainsi une pluralité de pratiques de soins dispensées par les personnels soignants résultant de tensions entre des normes professionnelles façonnées par une logique gestionnaire et des normes éthiques plaçant le patient au cœur des dispositifs de soins et de prise en charge et nourrie par la vulnérabilité des sujets âgés. Par ailleurs, les stratégies de « bricolage » et de « ruse » sont mises en œuvre par les soignants qui internalisent des tâches additionnelles informelles sur leur temps de travail, voire de repos, souvent en dehors du protocole formalisé par l'organisation hospitalière. Ce faisant, le travail des soignants déborde du périmètre des missions et cadres préétablis par l'hôpital et inclut une part invisible qui reste non valorisée et non reconnue. Ce résultat renvoie à la notion de « réel du travail »[4] (Desjours, 2003). L'internalisation des tâches des patients âgés, favorisée par l'empathie envers ces publics vulnérables amène certains soignants à participer à un schéma de coping, sous forme d'alliance avec le patient, parfois contre l'organisation hospitalière ; les premiers aidant le second à contourner et déjouer les obstacles qu'ils jugent inacceptables et injustes, dressés par l'organisation à l'encontre de ces usagers vulnérables. Les implications de ce débordement du cadre prescrit afin d'assurer le service de soins adapté à chaque patient âgé sont palpables au regard des effets délétères générés sur la santé au travail des soignants (stress, anxiété, burnout, dissonance de valeurs) et qui impactent par ricochet le fonctionnement de l'organisation hospitalière au travers des absences, des arrêts maladies, voire des défections de membres du personnel de santé épuisés par le cumul des tâches et la non-reconnaissance des efforts consentis.

La pratique quotidienne des soins et la variété des contextes d'interaction avec les patients vulnérables dévoilent les limites de

---

4   Cela correspond à ce que font certains acteurs pour « combler l'écart entre le prescrit et l'effectif [...] ce que le sujet doit ajouter aux prescriptions pour pouvoir atteindre les objectifs qui lui sont assignés » (Desjours, 2003, p. 14)

l'application stricte de la norme professionnelle, incitant les soignants à imaginer et bricoler d'autres façons de faire. Ce faisant, l'implantation ou l'application d'une norme n'est pas réductible à son contenu manifeste, mais est croisée, hybridée, déviée par une diversité de sens possibles, créatifs, propres aux usagers qui en incarnent l'appropriation sous contraintes (Cingolani, 2022). Les pratiques sont par conséquent hybridées, modifiées, aménagées par les personnels de santé qui puisent dans leurs répertoires personnels et leurs valeurs culturelles et éthiques les ressources nécessaires pour accomplir leurs missions de soins. Ces pratiques hybridées tendent cependant à se normaliser, devenant au fil du temps comme « allant de soi » et se substituant naturellement aux normes professionnelles. Cette hybridation peut être comprise comme « une contribution à une sociologie de l'intermédiaire, une sociologie des interstices qui implique de fusionner les compréhensions endogènes et exogènes de la culture » (Pieterse, 1995). Le concept d'hybridation des pratiques permet ainsi d'explorer comment le sens des pratiques de soins est approprié et parfois reconfiguré de manière singulière, pour aider les acteurs de santé à négocier et légitimer leurs pratiques professionnelles, et à ajuster leurs relations de service à l'état des patients âgés.

Sur le plan des implications managériales, on peut imaginer en accord avec les principes de la TSR, que la mise en place de dispositifs habilitants de gestion des patients âgés vulnérables nécessite un travail auprès des personnels soignants sur la valorisation des « capacités restantes » des patients (Gzil et Hirsh, 2012). Cette approche contribue à préserver, même partiellement, l'autonomie des personnes âgées, en amenant les patients eux-mêmes à sortir de la posture de déprise (Caradec, 2008) dans laquelle ils s'enferment parfois en arrivant à l'hôpital. Ce travail permettrait d'éviter une déshumanisation des soins et une compromission de la relation thérapeutique avec le patient (Monod et Sautebin, 2009). Ce risque apparaît notamment lorsque les soignants, jugeant que les patients manquent de discernement, s'abstiennent de les informer et de les associer aux dispositifs de soins. Ce faisant, les patients âgés ressentent l'administration de soins dispensés sans concertation, ni prise en compte de la singularité de leur situation, comme une violence et une maltraitance exercées à leur endroit, entraînant un sentiment de perte de dignité et d'altération d'estime de soi chez ces patients.

Dans la même veine, des dispositifs d'informations et d'« éducation thérapeutique » pourraient notamment être développés en direction des familles, dont le rôle est présent dans les discours des soignants, comme facilitateur des soins ou comme source de tension autour et au nom du patient. Ils permettraient d'insister sur l'importance de véhiculer une image positive et habilitante des patients dans les interactions famille-patients âgés en vue de rehausser l'estime de soi de ces derniers et de leur redonner du pouvoir d'agir lorsque cela est possible, dans une perspective d'implication des aidants familiaux dans la co-production des soins.

Enfin, dans une perspective de revalorisation ces métiers du soin mais aussi du lien en prise avec les corps vulnérables et à la lumière de ces micro-pratiques de bricolage et de ruse, il conviendrait de changer de paradigme en matière de création de valeur à l'hôpital en ne la considérant pas seulement comme le fruit de l'augmentation de la productivité du personnel, de la satisfaction de l'usager au service de la performance économique de l'organisation mais davantage comme la somme de ces activités invisibles (Gomez, 2013) consistant à réduire les incapacités, progressives ou conjoncturelles, des patients au service de la préservation de leur bien-être et de leur (ré)inclusion dans la société. Cet objectif de réduction de la vulnérabilité nécessiterait des capacités d'adaptation et de mobilisation de ressources multiples non valorisées dans un hôpital géré par des instruments de mesure de la performance quantifiable et dont la crise sanitaire a révélé les limites. Il conviendrait de traduire cet investissement invisible en compétences, redéfinir les fiches de poste et les grilles de salaire associées. Ces compétences pourraient être aussi légitimées et institutionnalisées par des formations académiques.

Cette recherche exploratoire ouvre la voie à d'autres investigations afin de compléter notre compréhension de la production des services de soins avec les publics vulnérables. Cette étude ne s'appuie que sur les discours des personnels de santé et ne prend pas en considération la perception qu'ont les patients âgés de leur propre participation à la prestation des soins pour saisir l'entièreté du processus de production du service. Elle invite par ailleurs à étendre le périmètre de l'analyse à un échantillon plus large et diversifié de soignants pour affiner les résultats, en ana-lysant les corpus selon les profils (ancienneté, genre, âge) et les statuts des professionnels de santé (médecins figure d'autorité vs infirmiers et aides-soignants proches du corps des patients) qui ont une relation différente aux patients. Le but est d'explorer d'autres tensions qui pèseraient sur ces acteurs en vue de comparer les pratiques des différentes catégories de personnels en contact avec les patients âgés et de mieux comprendre comment se distribuent dans l'organisation les stratégies de gestion de ces conflits de normes vécus et leur incarnation dans les différentes pratiques de soins.

RÉFÉRENCES

BAKER S. M., GENTRY J. W. and RITTENBURG T. L. (2005), "Building Understanding of the Domain of Consumer Vulnerability", *Journal of Macromarketing*, vol. 25, n° 2, p. 128-139.

BOURDIEU P. (1979), *La distinction. Critique sociale du jugement*, Paris, éd. de Minuit, coll. Le Sens commun.

CARADEC V. (2008), « Vieillir au grand âge », *Recherches en soins infirmiers*, 2000/3, n° 94, p. 28-41.

CINGOLANI P. (2022), « Les proliférations du social. Michel de Certeau et le débat des usages », *Esprit*, janvier-février, n° 481-482, p. 71-81.

CLARK J., HALL S., JEFFERSON T. and ROBERTS B. (1976), "Subcultures, cultures and class: A theoretical overview", in HALL S. and JEFFERSON T. (Eds), *Resistance through rituals. Youth subcultures in post-war Britain*, London, Hutchinson University Library, p. 9-74.

COULTER A. (2012), "Patient engagement–What works?", *Journal of Ambulatory Care Management*, vol. 35, n° 2, p. 80-89.

DE CERTEAU M. (1980), *L'invention du quotidien. Tome I : Arts de faire*, Paris, Union générale d'Éditions.

DESJOURS C. (2003), *L'évaluation du travail à l'épreuve du réel. Critiques des fondements de l'évaluation*, Paris, Inra.

DOBRÉ M. (2002), *L'écologie du quotidien : Éléments pour une théorie sociologique de la résistance ordinaire*, Paris, L'Harmattan.

FOLKMAN S., LAZARUS R. S., DUNKEL-SCHETTER C., DELONGIS A. and GRUEN R. J. (1986), "Dynamics of a stressful encounter: cognitive appraisal, coping, and encounter outcomes", *Journal of Personality and Social Psychology*, vol. 50, n° 5, p. 992-1003.

GOFFMAN E. (1973), *La mise en scène de la vie quotidienne. Les relations en public*, Paris, éditions de Minuit, collection Le Sens commun.

GOMEZ P.-Y. (2013), *Le travail invisible : Enquête sur une disparition*, Les Pérégrines.

GZIL F. et HIRSH E. (2012), *Alzheimer, éthique et société*, Poche Espace Éthique, Érès.

HEBDIGE D. (1979), *Subculture. The Meaning of Style*, London, Routledge.

HENNION A., VIDAL-NAQUET P. GUICHET F. et HÉNAUT L. (2012), *Une ethnographie de la relation d'aide, de la ruse à la fiction ou comment concilier protection et autonomie*, Rapport de recherche pour la MiRe (DREES), Centre de sociologie de l'innovation, MinesParisTech Armines.

INSEE (2018), France. Portrait social édition 2018. Accessible à : https://www.insee.fr/fr/statistiques/3645986?sommaire=3646226. Consulté le 3 février 2022.

Kemp P., Rendtorff J. D. and Mattsson N. (2000), *Bioethics and biolaw*, Vol. 1/2. Copenhague, Rhodos.

Lazarus R. S. (1966), *Psychological Stress and the Coping Process*, New York, McGraw-Hill.

Le Goff J. (2013), Normes juridiques et règles du jeu stratégique, in Pezet E., Sénéchal J. (Eds), *Normes juridiques et normes managériales. Enjeux et méthode d'une nouvelle internormativité*, Paris, Librairie Générale du Droit et de la Jurisprudence, coll. « Droit et société », p. 137-152.

Lévi-Strauss C. (1960), *La pensée sauvage*, Paris, éditions Plon.

Mason M. and Pavia T. (2014), "Health Challenges and Consumer Vulnerability: Identity Dissolution and Resiliency Behaviors", in Cotte J. Wood S. (Eds), NA – *Advances in Consumer Research*, Duluth, MN: Association for Consumer Research, v. 42, p. 7-11.

Mick G. D., Pettigrew S., Pechmann C. and Ozanne J. L. (Eds) (2012), *Transformative Consumer Research. For personal and collective Well-Being*, New York, Routledge.

Miles M. and Huberman A. M. (1994), *Qualitative Data Analysis: An Expanded Sourcebook*, 2nd ed. Thousand Oaks, Sage.

Moisio R. J. and Askegaard S. (2002), "Fighting culture. Mobile phone consumption practices as means of consumer resistance", *Asia Pacific Advances in Consumer Research*, vol. 5, n° 1, p. 24-29.

Monod S. et Sautebin A. (2009), « Vieillir et devenir vulnérable », *Revue Médicale Suisse*, Novembre (5), n° 226, p. 2353-2357.

Pavia T. M. and Mason M. J. (2014), "Vulnerability and Physical, Cognitive, and Behavioral Impairment. Model Extensions and Open Questions", *Journal of Macromarketing*, vol. 34, n° 4, p. 471-485.

Pieterse J-N. (1995), "Globalization as hybridization", in Featherstone M., Lash S. and Robertson R. (Eds) *Global modernities*, London, Sage, p. 45-68.

Ricœur P. (1983), *Temps et récit. 1. L'intrigue et le récit historique*, Paris, Seuil.

Rivière A., Commeiras N. et Loubes A. (2013), « Tensions de rôle et stratégies d'ajustement : une étude auprès de cadres de santé à l'hôpital », *Journal de gestion et d'économie médicale*, vol. 31, n° 2, p. 142-162.

Sitz L. (2008), « La "résistance ordinaire" des consommateurs: étude exploratoire des discours résistants ordinaires », 13es Journées de Recherche en Marketing de Bourgogne, IAE de Dijon.

Weber M. (1978), *Economy and Society: An Outline of Interpretive Sociology*, University of California Press.

ANNEXE
Tableau des profils des informants (personnels soignants, n=18)

Codes	Fonction	Ancienneté (années)	Genre	Durée de l'interview (minutes)
IDE 1	Infirmière	>5	F	49
IDE 2	Infirmière	<1	F	42
IDE 3	Infirmière	>20	F	60
IDE 4	Infirmière	<1	F	44
IDE 5	Infirmier	>10	M	39
IDE 6	Infirmière	1	F	50
IDE 7	Infirmière	>10	F	78
IDE 8	Infirmière	<10	F	40
IDE 9	Infirmier	10	M	54
IDE 10	Infirmière	<10	F	33
AS 1	Aide soignant	>10	M	59
AS 2	Aide soignante	1	F	53
AS 3	Aide soignant	>10	M	48
AS 4	Aide soignante	>10	F	50
AS 5	Aide soignante	<10	F	33
AS 6	Aide soignante	<10	F	62
Diet 1	Dietéticien	<10	M	53
Diet 2	Dietéticienne	>10	F	46

DEBATES AND VIEWPOINTS

CREATIVE INNOVATION
IN GASTRONOMY SERVICES

Cheryl Marie CORDEIRO[a]
Jaap W. VAN HAL[b]
[a]Nofima,
The Norwegian Institute of Food,
Fisheries and Aquaculture Research
[b]TNO Energy Transition

1. CREATIVE INNOVATION

Creativity and innovation are influential elements in the development of gastronomy services. Gastronomy, the acts of preparing, presenting and the consuming of food, can be seen as a form of symbolic communication within a community, where local gastronomy services can bolster a destination's competitiveness and attractiveness for tourists (Andersson and Mossberg, 2017). In light of the global marketplace and increasing convergence of technology and science, scholars tend to view creativity and innovativeness as essentially synonyms (Amabile and Pratt, 2016; Woodman et al., 1993). Creativity and innovation are co-constructing material processes, particularly in the field of culinary research, where advancements in technology enable new food applications and culinary creations (Feuls, 2018; Schumpeter, 1947). The combined term "creative innovation" is used predominantly by scholars and practitioners at the intersection of the fields of international business, gastronomy services and culinary science (Mouritsen, 2012; Tohidi and Jabbari, 2012). In the past decade, creative innovation has been studied from various perspective including artistic value (Stierand and Lynch, 2008), its role in culinary science (Mouritsen, 2012), how its processes are managed (Feuls, 2018), and its role in haute cuisine (Messeni Petruzzelli and Savino, 2014). Creative innovation is considered the very ingredient needed for organization and enterprise success (Tohidi and Jabbari, 2012). Creative innovation has also been studied from various theoretical perspectives, such as enterprise or firm ambidexterity in the field of international business studies (Kurniawan et al., 2020), relational sociology in economic theory (Feuls, 2018), actor network theory (Voeten et al., 2015), and entrepreneurship theory in small social businesses (Messeni Petruzzelli and Savino, 2014).

For this article, we asked 25 elite Chefs how the processes of creative innovation influence the development of gastronomy services in a dining experience. The Chefs are mostly from the Nordic countries of Sweden, Norway, and Denmark. They all have a minimum of three years working experience in gastronomy services in the HoReCa (hotels, restaurants, cafés) industry. They were approached for an interview and for their opinions during a phycogastronomy trade conference held in Norway, in which they were themselves presenters and participants of the trade conference program. They ranged in age between early 20s to late 40s. All respondents were familiar with current Nordic cuisine trends, and Nordic holistic food and lifestyle philosophy. Sustainable food consumption and ecologically produced future foods are important to them, as well as the need to continuously develop new and meaningful dining experiences for their customers.

The interviews were transcribed in accordance to the Gothenburg Transcription Standard (GTS) 6.4 (Nivre et al., 2004), using Modified Standard Orthography version 6 (MSO6) that reflects standard spoken language. The interview transcripts were labelled Transcript 1 to Transcript 25, with each transcript belonging to a single Chef respondent. The transcribed texts were compiled into a small, topic focused corpus that consists of 82 427 word tokens. The text examples shown in this study are written in GTS 6.4 MSO6.

2. CREATIVITY

Creative processes were viewed as being both structured and unstructured. When working in a HoReCa environment that includes fast paced services, creative processes need to be structured in a way that they can be managed efficiently, and in a systematic manner. A good understanding of culinary science, such as the study of ingredients for their properties, the documenting of results from different cooking techniques and planning plating designs for presentation at the table are important steps of the creative process. From Transcript 13, for example, the respondent has eight structural elements in his creative processes that he pays attention to:

> unique / pure / texture / memory / salt / south / artisan / terroir // these are the eight most important words in < name of restaurant > / they are the backbone of everything that is created at < name of restaurant > / from a single dish to the restaurant's overall philosophy / [it is] our method of encouraging and managing the creative process / and a principle to live by

The act of creating is also associated with the capacity of creating and utilising a new language, which translates to new gastronomical services. Like the forming of new language and new words, innovative services are created out of the ability to express these new ideas, thoughts and concepts.

The availability of new culinary technology also helps in the creative process. From Transcript 11, creating novel cuisine with new cooking techniques is likened to the creation of a new language:

> if you have an alphabet you can then create words / with these words you then create sentences / with these sentences you can then create poems / article / text whatever you want / in cuisine and in with regards to many other disciplines / the way we would see this alphabet in our case / it would be new products / new techniques / new elaborations / new concepts and a new philosophy // i'm going to try to show you what a new language means / ... i have a very pragmatic approach to creativity // let's see whether it's a language that you can relate to and connect to / it's a new concept called natura and these dishes were inspired by nature they're all desserts

Because language is social, it is important that it has a shared meaning within a community of users in order to be meaningful and useful. Gastronomical services are acts of this social language that can be shared meaningfully. In this context, the element of familiarity is also present, even in the event of creating a new language and a new dining experience. With Latin etymology, the word "natura" can be broadly understood in most modern Indo-European languages such as Dutch, French, Spanish, Italian, Portuguese and Romanian. From Transcript 11, the respondent also says "I have a very pragmatic approach to creativity", which further supports this idea of familiarity and accessibility of the gastronomical service and experience. For this respondent, gastronomical services is a co-development between the Chef, the HoReCa team and the customers. Democratising gastronomy services so that anyone and everyone can take part in this creative innovation process is important, and it should not only be reserved for elite Chefs experimenting with rarely used ingredients and novel cooking techniques.

3. KNOWLEDGE

Innovative ideas are generally developed through a concerted effort of refining existing concepts and testing novel applications from an existing body of knowledge and practices. While Chefs might come across as creative geniuses and one with great expert knowledge in kitchens, serving dishes in a way that is unexpected by the customers will lead to that unforgettable dining experience. To embody a sense of curiosity and continuous learning and exploration is key for this Chef in Transcript 10:

> i'm sick of know-it-alls / i know nothing i'm here to learn / i'm just sharing my experience [of] the things that have happened to me

A similarly expressed thought about "knowing" is found in Transcript 13, where the respondent associates the unknown with the perception of what is unique:

[to be] unique / [it is] things that we know yet we don't know / ... it is about something that appears at the right environment [at the] right timing / nothing is really unique or not unique

And from Transcript 22:

i remember the first time i saw the [name of] restaurant website / i was astonished / it was my first glimpse of food that had been prepared and presented in a range of ways / which i had never seen before and could barely comprehend / it was all so simple and understated / yet even as a novice cook at the time / i could tell that the complexity of preparing such dishes must be immense / but how was it all done and more importantly how could i do it / this triggered a desire to learn more about this new / exotic form of cuisine / and my research into a field i came to know as molecular gastronomy / this journey for knowledge opened up my culinary eyes / and introduced me to a whole host of new names and faces i would otherwise have been ignorant of

These text examples illustrate how "knowing" includes knowing one's own limitations and boundaries, i.e., knowing what you don't know. To understand how "knowing" and "knowledge" contributes to the creative innovation process and towards the discovery of new gastronomical experiences.

4. DECONSTRUCTING

Creative innovation and new gastronomy services are developed through taking a familiar ingredient and extending its context of use. An example of taking a familiar ingredient such as salt, and working with existing consumer knowledge, expectation, and experience with the ingredient, one Chef decided to deconstruct the facets of 'saltiness' to create novel gastronomy experiences. From Transcript 13:

[salt is] the first seasoning that we know-- so salt has been very important / for me / we are always thinking that can we have a flavour that everybody understands / whether it's lemongrass / or it's chili / or it's curry-- / I don't know-- a cheese // somehow it's trapped in a certain boundary / but can we have one dish that everybody understands / so i was thinking salt / it's not

just the physical salt / but the depth of saltiness / what i mean is for example /
soy sauce / fish sauce / ham / anchovy / and sea water or seaweed / they are
all different depths of saltiness

This respondent used the various depths of flavours of salt to create
new dishes. He could now, for example, incorporate a relatively novel
ingredient such as seaweed as part of his culinary and gastronomy philosophy for sustainable future foods consumption. Phycogastronomy or
seaweed consumption is an emerging gastronomy service in the Nordic
culinary scene, where new products such as seaweed salt are produced
and sold in artisanal shops and restaurants that specialize in serving
seafood in the Nordic countries.

5. GASTRONOMY SERVICE INNOVATION:
HUMAN-CENTRIC VS PRODUCT-CENTRIC APPROACHES

Creative innovation processes that contribute to new gastronomy services are dependent on their HoReCa environmental factors. Gastronomy
services evolve in a complex environment. In order to organize elements
in these environments to give an integrated overview of the interaction
of the creative innovation processes, the transcripts from the 25 interviews were thematically coded using a concordance software, AntConc
(Anthony, 2019). The themes were subsequently sorted in 4 salient
perspectives that include (i) the Individual, (ii) the Community, (iii)
Technology and (iv) Systems network. Factors that contribute to the
development of new gastronomy services can be seen as being created
from a human-centric approach (Perspective A in Table 1) and/or from
a product-centric approach (Perspective B in Table 1).

TAB. 1 – Integrated perspective of gastronomy service from a human-centric ("A" perspective) and product-centric ("B" perspective).

Perspective	Individual	Community	Technology	Systems Network
A	Consciousness	Social practices	Technology enablers in the kitchen for the Chef	Industry structure and network
	Commitment	Organizational support	Digitalisation / Internet for HoReCa	Business Environment Network
	Belief	Culture	New food product	Governance
	Passion	Consumer awareness	Novel ingredients	Logistics Infrastructure
	Inspiration	Intergroup communication and feedback		Trade agreements
	Aspiration	Values		
		Heritage		
B	Terroir	Product-consumer proximity	Geographic proximity and access to raw produce	Industry structure and network
	Product Identity	Product branding through cultural practices, values, food heritage	Geographic proximity of product to consumers	Systems architecture and network
	Country of origin (COO)	New product support through purchase and consumption	Harvesting technologies	Logistics infrastructure
			Food processing technologies	Trade agreements

6. HUMAN-CENTRIC PERSPECTIVE

This is the singular subjective perspective of the Chefs inter-
viewed for this article. It describes the personal journey of the Chefs
in their work experience. For example, from Transcript 19, a Chef
narrates his journey to finding his professional identity in culinary
and gastronomy services. He describes his work as a personal and
individual calling:

> my brother took me there and said / this is the perfect place for you / it's
> the place where you can express yourself through the food / through your
> passion / i said to < name > are you sure / he said / yes this is the perfect
> place / one week later / i was there / because the food world chose me / It's
> not that i chose that / that was the perfect timing / and in that moment / i
> realized i had to put all of myself into this world // and the simplest interest
> for food / step by step became a passion / and through the passion / i realized
> you can transfer emotions / that's what i think food is / and how i interpret
> food-- just transfer emotions

Communities of practice provide the plural intersubjective perspective.
Communities of practice create the language of gastronomy experiences,
and creative innovation forces come from the different stakeholders in
a society that support the HoReCa industry. Stakeholders from food
producers, business owners, Chefs as well as consumers are needed to
support emerging foods and food trends such as phycogastronomy.
Consumers can encourage new gastronomy services by giving positive
feedback to the restaurants that offer seaweed on the menu.

New culinary technologies are also used by humans, where Technology
offers the singular objective perspective in developing new gastronomy
services. Experimenting with liquid nitrogen from Transcript 11 allows
for new products to be served:

> let's see a technique that is a very new technique / you know liquid nitro-
> gen / well that may seem quite strange but it's a very common product / it
> comes in a gas form / in this case we use liquid nitrogen / and in this case
> it allows us to make things that are otherwise impossible / we're making
> pure alcohol sorbet / if you put alcohol in the freezer you know that it won't
> freeze / this is -196 deg C

But technology enablers can also be useful at the production stage of the food service value chain, particularly in the emerging field of phycogastronomy. From Transcript 7, the issue of productivity in seaweed harvest depends on the available harvest technologies, and access to technology. The need for communities of practice and interaction between chefs, food producers and consumers is also highlighted in the following text example, as a means to creative innovations:

> we hire inner-city kids to package / cook / process all of our food / they learn about 3D farming / they learn about sustainability / one of the kids at the school / it's called < name of the school > actually took the kelp and invented a 12 volt kelp powered biodegradable battery // so you know / on the blue green economy / i think we can think much bigger than this / why can't we take my farm and embed it in offshore wind farms / why don't we just harvest wind / let's harvest food / fuel / fertilizer / let's bring it back

7. PRODUCT-CENTRIC PERSPECTIVE

Food products are branded and given characteristics that pertain to their place-of-origin and terroir. For example, when Nordic chefs speak about Nordic foods, they often reflect on how the food produce is influenced by the Nordic climate, the soil, air, and societal values of how the food is processed and served. This is encapsulated in the concept of the "flavours of the North", which is a product-centric perspective.

Local Nordic gastronomy services embody an experiential identity. In the marketing of a relatively new food product, the seaweed pasta, product branding and identity is achieved via association with credible partners such as a bank as business partner, and new food wrapping technology companies that will help decrease the carbon footprint of each package of seaweed pasta sold. From Transcript 15, all branding and product identity building, can be studied from a Systems Network perspective:

> besides the netherlands / the seaweed pasta is also sold in germany / switzerland / denmark / great britain and australia / various other countries are expected to follow / after the crowd-funding the < name of bank > entered

into a partnership with < company name > / the bank not only functions as its personal banker / but even introduces its products at trade fairs abroad // ...the bank is an important bank known for investing in the food and agriculture section // ...as to the transport of the harvest / that is being looked at too / transporters whose trucks would formerly travel back empty after having delivered their flowers in < country name > / in the harvesting months now return to < name of country> with a load of seaweed / [so that] the company's ecological footprint will remain as small as possible

The Systems Network perspective is the broadest perspective to the provision and development of gastronomy service because it includes and transcends all other perspectives i.e., the Individual, the Community and the Technology perspectives.

Another example of a Systems Network perspective that crosses regional borders is digitalisation in gastronomy service. Digitalisation is revolutionizing HoReCa workspaces in the kitchen, and in providing new dining experiences for consumers. The provision of a digital menu for consumers prior to the actual dining event, has made the flow of serving food more efficient. From Transcript 11, the Chef and restaurant owner explains how productivity and dining experiences are enhanced for the consumers by use of the internet:

it's not [the most] logical thing that we'll find in the world / [but] you find long wine lists in restaurants / so if you get there maybe three hours before / [okay] / otherwise you won't have time to read it / in this case the internet can be used very efficiently and wonderfully / you can hang your wine list on internet / and you can look through it at ease / and you get an idea of the wines / and what things are a bit special / and at least you've got an idea when you're out at the restaurant

Because creative innovation is a delicate balance between structure and freedom from structure, project management and management of ideas is important. This can be improved by digital tools that help manage the organization of documents better, whether it's coordinating the food service value chain or enabling smoother table bookings. From Transcript 17, structured innovation is referred to and helped by placing projects in an organisation wide internal digital platform:

by actually bringing these projects to life in a digital platform / you increase your productivity significantly / and further / you also increase the quality of the output of the projects / because you've been efficient in producing something that actually adds value / and when the productivity is there the quality is there / the profitability also sneaks in on you because then you've been efficient in providing something that that creates value to your customers // ...it's also about joint work because it is more fun to go to work every day if you're part of the well-oiled machine / rather than spending most of your day discussing with your colleagues who should do what and when / and why don't I get the information I need when I need it etc.

Systems of technological networks, available software that can be implemented at the organization or between organizations in a shared digital platform, will affect how creative innovation proceeds. The successful acceptance and adoption of new food products and services requires cooperation from both consumers as well as top-down legislation effort, whether in the form of national dietary guidelines, or of the lowering of regional trade barriers to favour access to new food produce.

REFERENCES

AMABILE T. M., and PRATT M. G. (2016), "The dynamic componential model of creativity and innovation in organizations: Making progress, making meaning", *Research in Organizational Behavior*, 36, 157-183.

ANDERSSON T. D., and MOSSBERG L. (2017), "Travel for the sake of food", *Scandinavian Journal of Hospitality and Tourism*, vol. 17, n° 1, p. 44-58.

ANTHONY L. (2019), AntConc (Version 3.5.8) [Computer Software]. Tokyo, Japan: Waseda University. Retrieved November 15, 2019, from Software website: https://www.laurenceanthony.net/software/antconc/

FEULS M. (2018), "Understanding culinary innovation as relational: Insights from Tarde's relational sociology", *Creativity and Innovation Management*, vol. 27, n° 2, p. 161-168.

KURNIAWAN P., HARTATI W., QODRIAH S. L., and BADAWI B. (2020), "From knowledge sharing to quality performance: The role of absorptive capacity, ambidexterity and innovation capability in creative industry", *Management Science Letters*, vol. 10, n° 2, p. 433-442.

MESSENI PETRUZZELLI A., and SAVINO T. (2014), "Search, recombination, and innovation: Lessons from haute cuisine", *Long Range Planning*, vol. 47, n° 4, p. 224-238.

MOURITSEN O. G. (2012), "The emerging science of gastrophysics and its application to the algal cuisine", *Flavour*, vol. 1, n° 1, p. 1-9.

NIVRE J., ALLWOOD J., GRÖNQVIST L., GUNNARSSON M., AHLSÉN E., VAPPULA H.,... OTTESJÖ C. (2004), Göteborg Transcription Standard Version 6.4. Retrieved September 1, 2019, from University of Gothenburg, Sweden website: https://www.researchgate.net/publication/268503487_Goteborg_Transcription_Standard_Version_64

SCHUMPETER J. A. (1947), "The Creative Response in Economic History", *The Journal of Economic History*, vol. 7, n° 2, p. 149-159.

STIERAND M., and LYNCH P. (2008), "The art of creating culinary innovations", *Tourism and Hospitality Research*, vol. 8, n° 4, p. 337-350.

TOHIDI H., and JABBARI M. M. (2012), "Innovation as a Success Key for Organizations", *Procedia Technology*, 1, p. 560-564.

VOETEN J., DE HAAN J., DE GROOT G., & ROOME N. (2015), "Understanding responsible innovation in small producers' clusters in Vietnam through actor-network theory", *European Journal of Development Research*, vol. 27, n° 2, p. 289-307.

WOODMAN R. W., SAWYER J. E., and GRIFFIN R. W. (1993), "Toward a Theory of Organizational Creativity", *The Academy of Management Review*, vol. 18, n° 2, 293-321.

CHINA AS AN OPPORTUNITY
AND A CHALLENGE
FOR WESTERN SERVICE PROVIDERS

Sen Bao[a1]
Marja Toivonen[b2]
[a]Avalance Oy
[b]Helsinki University

INTRODUCTION

Culture is "the collective programming of the mind which distin-guishes the members of one group or category of people from another" (Hofstede, 1991). Cultural differences manifest themselves in many ways: there may be differences in language, social structure, ideology, moral, work ethics, customs, habits and so on. Generally, the impacts of cultural differences have been a popular research topic, but studies in the context of service business are scarce. Those studies that exist have argued that cultural differences lead to higher uncertainty avoidance in services than in manufacturing and technological areas due to the close interaction between the service providers and clients. Because services are often delivered in a direct contact with clients, they are particularly sensitive to cultural issues.

Cultural factors may become significant obstacles in internationa-lization, especially when the home and host markets are very different in their cultural background. The increasing international business

1   sen.bao@outlook.com
2   marja.toivonen-noro@helsinki.fi

and communication between the West and the East has brought these differences to the fore. China is an important representative of the Eastern culture. Because it is nowadays the second largest economy in the world and increasingly a target of Western business efforts, it deserves particular attention. Its socio-political situation and long tradition of Confucianism create a unique cultural climate which is unfamiliar to representatives of Western countries and clearly manifests itself in the service business. In this entry, cultural differences are first discussed generally and thereafter differences between Western and Eastern cultures are characterized. Finally, the Chinese business culture and its implications are opened up.

1. GENERAL IMPACTS OF CULTURAL DIFFERENCES ON SERVICE BUSINESS

In the early categorizations of cultural differences, communication styles were a central phenomenon to which researchers paid attention. It was an important aspect in Hall's pioneering model (1976). This model discriminated between "low context" and "high-context" cultures, which Hall considered to differ in the communication style but to show other differences as well. The analysis of differences in the role of relation-ships and networks – "mutual involvement" of people – is important in particular. Later on, other dimensions have been identified. A widely used model is provided by Hofstede (1980). Originally, it separated four dimensions in cultural differences: power distance, uncertainty avoidance, individualism vs. collectivism, and masculinity vs. femininity. Based on empirical studies in 70 countries, the fifth dimension of long-term vs. short-term orientation was added (Hofstede, 1991).

The first dimension – power distance – reflects the level at which a society accepts an unequal distribution of power and privileges. It influences the hierarchy and dependency relationships in organizations. If the power distance is high, cultures usually rely on centralization and tolerate tight control and vertical top-down communication. If the power distance is low, equality and bottom-up communication are important principles. The second dimension – uncertainty avoidance – refers to the extent to which people feel threatened by unknown or ambiguous situations and try to avoid them. Uncertainty avoidance has been found to lead to change resistance, less risk-taking and conflict avoiding behavior. The third dimension is individualism vs. collectivism. In individualist cultures, the interests of individuals dominate over the group interests whereas in collectivist cultures, the dominance is reversed. The fourth dimension "masculinity vs. femininity" identifies different values linked to gender roles. Masculinity appreciates assertiveness and achievement; femininity highlights caring of others and of the living environment. The fifth dimension separates long-term oriented cultures from short-term oriented ones. It highlights that a culture may be primarily focused on the future, or it may be focused on the past and the present. Long-term oriented cultures foster virtues like perseverance and thrift, whereas short-term oriented cultures value realized benefits or benefits expectable in the near future.

Another well-known model is the categorization of Trompenaars (1996), which includes the dimensions of universalism vs. particularism, individualism vs. collectivism, affective vs. neutral, specific vs. diffuse, achievement vs. ascription, sequential vs. synchronic time orientation, and internal vs. external environment control. The dimension of internal vs. external environment control illustrates the relationship with the environment (nature); the dimension of sequential vs. synchronic orientation deals with the meaning of time; and the other five dimensions interpret relationships with other people. The dimension of individualism vs. collectivism corresponds to the same dimension in Hofstede's (1980) model. The other dimensions can be explained as follows.

In the dimension "universalism vs. particularism", universalism implies the application of general rules and favors standard procedures; particularism encourages flexibility and adaptation to various situations. The dimension "specific vs. diffuse" depicts the extent to which different life spheres are integrated. The relationship between personal life and working life illustrates the extremes of this dimension. These spheres are clearly separated on the one end (specific), whereas a holistic view combining them characterizes the other end (diffuse). The dimension "achievement vs. ascription" focuses on the way in which status is typically acquired in a culture. Achievement-based cultures prefer skills-based judgement and rewards whereas ascription-based cultures promote status based on experience. The dimension "internal vs. external environment control" describes the broadness of the general mindset in a culture. Internal control refers to determination by the inner-directed judgments, decisions, and commitments of a group, organization or community. External control grounds the activities of actors on outside signals, demands, and trends. This dimension influences, among others, the way in which innovations are pursued. Internal orientation aims to stimulate ideas and develop innovations in-house. External orientation favors open innovation practices, seizing ideas that have originated outside (Trompenaars, 1996).

The dimension "affective vs. neutral" refers to the extent in which people openly express what they think. In an affective culture, emotional expressions are usual whereas in a neutral culture, the ability to control emotions is appreciated and leads to the avoidance of direct judgment and conflict. The "affective vs. neutral" dimension has some touch points with the "low-context vs. high-context" dimension (Hall, 1976) as well as with the "masculinity vs. femininity" dimension (Hofstede, 1980). The dimension "sequential vs. synchronic" concerns the structuration of time. Punctuality and planned schedules are highly valued in sequential cultures, whereas multi-tasking and flexibility regarding time are preferred in synchronic cultures. The "sequential vs. synchronic" dimension examines the concept of time like Hofstede's (1991) dimension "long-term vs. short-term orientation", but the focus is different.

All the above-mentioned dimensions have significant impacts on business practices in cross-cultural contexts, and the issues are often particularly sensitive in service business. Communication gaps are typical. Practices that are highly valued in the cultures favoring direct communication, such as frank comments and straightforward assessments, may be regarded as rude and conflict-creating behavior in the cultures of more subtle communication (Ueltschy et al., 2007). Service customers from cultures preferring direct communication evaluate services on the basis of concrete evidence, such as data, efficient delivery and task completion – whereas cultures with indirect communication focus on the quality of the interaction with service providers.

In high-context cultures, the building of relationships and trust are important before any business can be carried out; in low-context cultures, the relationships and trust are expected to develop over time after the business activities have been started (Ueltschy et al., 2007). In cultures with a high degree of individualism, customers usually demand services promptly in terms of responsiveness and reliability but maintain a distance between themselves and providers. In cultures with a collective emphasis, the close relationship during the service process plays a significant role (Liu et al., 2001).

Also the issues of power and status have implications to service practices. For instance, high power distance may appear as high expectations among the customers regarding the behavior of service personnel. Studies have even revealed that in some cultures service personnel are required to show extra courtesy and behave in a manner which shows a "lower status" compared to customers. The dimension "universalism vs. particularism" may be reflected as a different attitude towards standardization and customization. As universalism supports equal treatment, standard services seem compatible with it; particularism with its emphasis on unique treatment can be expected to favor tailor-made services (Ueltschy et al., 2007). Differences in the definition of status may lead to differences in subordinate-superior relationships. If the status is based on the achievement culture, the hierarchy may be lower because younger employees, too, have the possibility to show their competence. In an ascription culture, reliance on the authority – those who possess the "ascribed" knowledge – may be required.

As regards the dimension "masculinity vs. femininity", masculinity can be expected to appear as professionalism, neutral behavior, and presentation of objective facts in the service encounter, whereas femininity may emphasize the ability to internalize the viewpoint of the customer. The dimension "specific vs. diffuse" influences the efforts carried out in the solution of customers' problems. If business is seen as a separate sphere, the answer to the customer need covers the specific request. If the border between business and private life is vaguer, the request is understood in its context, which means that the related needs may be mapped and service personnel is ready to extend the work and invest personal resources in the relationship building.

The time perspective and openness manifest themselves in the behavior of both parties in the service encounter. Customers in long-term oriented cultures may be tolerant to accept modest or even poor services if other rewards can be anticipated in the future. A close and long-lasting relationship with the service provider – involving reliability, responsiveness and empathy – is often such a reward (Liu et al., 2001). The "internal vs. external" dimension plays a role in the realization of this reward: a genuine service attitude is often linked with an external orientation. People in internally oriented organizations may focus too much on the tasks and issues in which they are skillful and competent and neglect the active and rapid response to the needs of customers (Trompenaars, 1996).

2. CHARACTERISTICS OF WESTERN AND EASTERN CULTURES

Researchers have aimed to create understanding on the cultural variability by clustering countries and nations based on their similarity on the cultural dimensions. In Western countries, four clusters have been typically separated: the Anglo-Saxon culture, the Germanic culture, the Latin culture and the Nordic culture (Perlitz and Seger, 2004).

The Anglo-Saxon culture refers to the dominant values and behavioral inclinations in countries like the UK, the US, Canada and Australia. A strong individualism shared in this culture fosters self-interest above the concerns for others. The power distance is low and makes the people in this culture relatively equal. Germanic culture, dominated by German and expanded to Switzerland, Austria and Belgia, is less individualistic than the Anglo-Saxon culture. It fosters the building of long-term cooperative partnerships between owners, managers and workers. Professionalism, with a considerable degree of self-discipline and self-programming, plays a crucial role in this culture. Latin culture, including Spain, Portugal, Greece, and to a lesser degree, France and Italy, shows differences from their neighbors. The power distance is higher and individualism is lower than in most other Western countries (Hofstede, 2001). Outside the Western countries, some countries in Latin America, such as Mexico and Brazil, also share similarities with this culture. Nordic culture (Norway, Sweden, Denmark, and Finland) exhibits even lower power distance and much lower masculinity than the

Anglo-Saxon culture (Perlitz and Seger, 2004). Hierarchical thinking is quite uncommon in the Nordic society and "big chief" seems to be removed in the mentality.

Although variety exists, Western cultures differ from each other much less than they differ from Eastern cultures in Asia. Asia is not only a geographical location, but nurtures value judgments different from Western countries. On the other hand, Asia is not a culturally homogenous Eastern space. Similarly to the Western cultures, there are cultural clusters in Asia, composing of a multitude of cultural features. In addition, East Asia differs from Southeast Asia and South Asia as regards cultural homogeneity within countries. In many countries of East Asia (China, Japan, Korea and Vietnam), cultural homogeneity is high. On the contrary, the postcolonial countries in Southeast Asia and in South Asia are multicultural. Examples of the former are Malaysia, Indonesia, and Thailand; the latter includes India in the first place (Chen and Chua, 2007).

Main differences between the Western and Eastern cultures can be analyzed in the light of the cultural dimensions presented above. The dimension of high vs. low context is a clearly separating factor: most Eastern cultures are high-context societies, whereas most Western cultures have low-context characteristics. Also the dimension of individualism vs. collectivism is important because Eastern cultures show characteristics of collectivism. A high power distance is linked to collectivism; accepting hierarchal structure and preserving harmony are motivators to enable a stable society (Hofstede, 1980). As regards communication, direct opinions are often linked to the fear of "losing face" in Eastern cultures (Ueltschy et al., 2007). (Even though Western cultures generally differ in the communication style, a similar concern is identifiable in the observation that indirect communication maintains the partner's public image.) Finally, Hofstede points out two dimensions that separate the Western and Eastern cultures: uncertainty avoidance and time perspective. He claims that uncertainty avoidance is a uniquely Western dimension that supports the search for "one truth" in the society. On the other hand, long-term orientation is a uniquely Eastern dimension to search for "virtue" in the society (Hofstede, 1991).

According to Hofstede, the dominance of Christian religion in the West has promoted the search for one truth. Christian religion deviates from Eastern religions – Confucianism, Buddhism, Taoism, and Shintoism – which consider that a partial truth does not exclude other truths. A practical implication of this "philosophical" difference is that Westerners are inclined to consider various issues on the "either-or" basis, whereas Asians foster a more dialectical thinking and change their minds in the "both-and" context. In metaphoric terms, Asians accept the existence of both "white" and "black" simultaneously and allow the context and time to determine what will be appropriate.

As a bridge to the discussion about the Chinese business culture, the current stage of global interaction deserves attention. In the aftermath of recent economic crisis, business reality has transformed from "the West leads the East" to "the West meets the East". The rising economies in Asia have generated increasing business communication between the West and the East in the globalization context. China, which represents a typical Eastern culture in Asia, has a dominant impact on East Asian culture due to both its current role and its long history (Chen and Chua, 2007). The Chinese culture can function as a fruitful source in international partnerships if the cultural differences are mutually understood.

3. CHINESE BUSINESS CULTURE
AND ITS IMPLICATIONS FOR SERVICES

In China, the long history and heritage – and the "both-and" mindset – make the situation particularly complex: cultural characteristics depend on the situation, context and time. In addition to research, difficulties arise in practice. Especially foreigners conducting business in China become confused when they meet the local mix of cultural and contextual characteristics. Fang (1999) has summarized the peculiarities of the Chinese culture into two fundamental components: socio-political situation and the long tradition of Confucianism.

China's socio-political situation refers to the distinctive characteristics of the contemporary societal and political system of People's Republic of China. These characteristics influence the behavior of people both in the daily life and in the business practices. The socio-political situation includes several variables: politics, the socialist planned economy, rapid change, great size and uneven development, technology development, bureaucracy, and the legal framework (Fang, 1999).

The influence of politics on services can be traced back far to the history in China. Feudal governments dominating the society in early times ranked the societal status from high to low classes (Liu, 2009). Service employees represented the lowest rank without honor and respect. The situation did not change much before the modern times. A radical change took place when China became a socialist country in 1949; since then, the country has developed under Communist Party's ruling. During thirty years, the attitude towards services was that they are a sector that reflects the values of capitalism. Low price of services combined with non-incentive policy was characteristic until the social and economic reform was implemented in 1978. After that reform, the business environment has been more favorable, but the former impact still exists to some degree. Due to its pervasive influence on every aspect of life, politics cannot be separated from the social system in China (Fang, 1999).

The socialist planned economy is linked to communism. During the years after the reform, the industrial structure has been decentralized. However, key industries (e.g. telecommunication, energy and mining) are still under the governmental control and not open to foreigners. Originally, these industries were dominated by state-owned enterprises. Nowadays, this dominance has diminished as many state-owned enterprises have been sold and become privately owned. However, state-owned enterprises are still significant because of their size – privatization has concerned small- and medium sized enterprises. The end result is that the shares of state-owned and privately owned enterprises are very different in terms of the number of enterprises compared to their share of the gross industrial output. State-owned enterprises form only 5% of all enterprises while the share of privately owned enterprises is 60%. However, the contribution to the gross industrial output is the same: 30% in both cases (China National Statistics Bureau, 2020). Foreign-owned enterprises permeated China's economy along with the "open door" policy, which was linked to the general reform policy and included preferential treatment of foreigners (Ralston et al., 2006).

The economic development in China has been rapid: the country has witnessed miraculous achievements in the past three decades. During the 2000s, the average economic growth has exceeded ten percent every year (China National Statistics Bureau, 2020). The economic reform and growth bring the Western life style to China and change the business environment of services, in particular: demands from customers increase rapidly. On the other hand, the change challenges the dominant ideology and traditional cultural values (Fang, 1999).

The implementation of the reform policy has been regionally uneven in China (Ralston et al., 2006). The Eastern part is developing much more rapidly than inland areas – in general and in terms of service business. In addition, a regional approach and regional segmentation are needed in any case because of the huge size of the country: different regions have their own business characteristics. For example, the business styles in Beijing, Shanghai, and Guangdong differ from each other. In Beijing, the style can be characterized as relational, in Shanghai it is professional, and in Guangdong entrepreneurial (Fang, 2005).

In the area of technology, learning from the West in order to improve people's living standards was one of the reasons why China opened its economy in 1978. However, many Chinese companies have only copied Western technology and neglected the cultural aspects that impact on business practices (Liu, 2009). Consequently, the technological gap has narrowed between China and Western countries, but the gap in carrying out business (and particularly service business) is still large. As generally in transition economies, bureaucracy is characteristic of China. The government intervenes in private business in many ways, e.g. via taxes. The approval of business initiatives may require a long process at various levels of governmental departments with long waiting times. Close relationship with governmental officials helps overcome bureaucracy and may lead to efforts to get preferential treatment. The ability to form an alliance with the partners who have such relationships is often critical for success in China. It is especially crucial for service business due to its immature regulation with a space to deal. The positive aspect is quick decision making if one's products or services meet the government's priority (Fang, 1999).

The legal system in China is still developing and human factors influence its implementation (Fang, 1999). The clause of laws is clear and transparent in most matters in which the mechanisms are intended to protect one's legal rights. However, there is vagueness in local regulations which leaves space for interpretation by local officers. Practices vary and may deviate from published laws and regulations – also regarding the issues that influence service business.

The other fundamental component in the Chinese society – the long tradition of Confucianism – is a philosophical thought of moral ethic and human relationships. Confucianism has shaped Chinese culture for more than 2000 years since it became the state ideology during Han Dynasty. It met serious criticism in early Communist China, especially during the Culture Revolution in 1960s, but recently it has earned back its position. The Chinese government has even started to rebuild and emphasize Confucianism's central role in the policy document "The Construction of a Harmonious Society" (Liu, 2009). Confucianism includes five basic values: moral cultivation, family orientation, respect of hierarchy, harmony, and interpersonal relationships. The last one includes "guanxi", "renqing" and "mianzi" (Fang, 1999).

Moral cultivation maintains the idea that people entrusted with power and responsibility are supposed to show high moral and act as an example to educate their peers and others. It explains why human factors are often more influential than regulations in China. It also reflects the role of particularism and its linkage to the underdeveloped legal system in the country (Trompenaars, 1996). Local governors can interpret various principles according to their own understanding and benefits. This may compensate the immature legal framework in the Confucian "spirit", but it confuses foreigners as the gaps between laws and practices are apparent.

Family orientation is an important social and also economic factor in China. Families have carried much of the social responsibility (e.g. welfare services) during the history and compensated the lack of public systems (Fang, 1999). Consequently, there is a huge number of domestic privately-owned enterprises running businesses in a family style (Ralston et al., 2006). The founder's spouse, children and close relatives have often been working in the same firm as a big family. The diffuse culture in Trompenaars' (1996) categorization corresponds to the situation in China: business is integrated with family life. Family orientation is also linked to the collectivist nature of the Chinese culture (Hofstede, 2001): the group interests are more important than individual benefits.

Hierarchy is emphasized in Confucianism together with the rights and duties attached to the roles at each level. The roles are based on age and past experience, which indicates that "ascription" is included in Confucianism. Although social hierarchies exist in all large-scale societies, the Chinese system shows higher power distance than Western cultures (Hofstede, 1991): unevenly distributed power is accepted in society and business. A practical consequence in service business is the small emphasis put on the empowerment of employees and proactive offering of services.

The aim of Confucian philosophy is to avoid conflicts and to achieve harmonious society (Fang, 1999). This ideal is visible in various principles, regulations and practices in the Chinese business and social life. It also answers the current challenge of balancing the rapidly growing economy and its negative effects. An illustrative example is the governmental goal of promoting sustainable development, which has been included in the newest Five-Year Plans. However, interests of some enterprises may be sacrificed in order to meet the needs of the majority. The cultural features of collectivism and long-term orientation are visible here; short-term orientation is however common in the economic transition.

Interpersonal relationships in China are closely connected to the Chinese word "guanxi" (Davies et al., 1995). It is a way to demonstrate one's position or role within social networks, thus providing security and trust. Based on "guanxi", an individual can secure resources and gain advantages when doing business. The Western concept of networking is inherent in "guanxi", but the latter concept is more specific. Guanxi" works through "renqing" and "mianzi". Renqing describes reciprocity and exchange of favor: the one who accepts renqing from the other is expected to pay it back in certain ways when needed (Davies et al., 1995). Mianzi, so called "Chinese face", refers to enhancing individual's social status or preserving one's dignity. It recognizes the status and moral reputation of a person. In China, it is very important to avoid "losing face", which denounces the status. One should also aim at "giving face", which raises the reputation of collaborators in the guanxi network. Consequently, Chinese people feel obligated to offer renqing as assistance and save business partners' mianzi to maintain guanxi. At the same time, the partners are also expected to reciprocate renqing in one or other ways to maintain trust and cooperation.

The process of building and maintaining guanxi reflects the long-term orientation in the Chinese business culture. In the service context, it implies that providers aim to establish long lasting relationships with customers (Liu et al., 2001). This may lead to free of charge services during the product's life cycle. However, Chinese companies also offer "free" services as renqing to build guanxi with customers. If a customer expects services for free, service managers in the provider company feel that they "lose face" by charging those.

Because markets in China are still taking shape and the institutional set-up is limited, guanxi networks help companies gain information about business opportunities and improve efficiency. On the other hand, along with the rapid development, the legal framework is improving and the whole country is becoming more integrated into global economy. Consequently, it is expected that the impact of guanxi will remain but have less influence in the future. Understanding guanxi is necessary but not sufficient to achieve business success in China. Even good guanxi cannot replace a well-organized business plan.

REFERENCES

CHEN K. H., CHUA B. H. (2007), *Inter-Asia Cultural Studies Reader*, New York, Routledge.

DAVIES H., LEUNG T. K., LUK S. T., WONG, Y. H. (1995) "The benefits of 'Guanxi': the value of relationships in developing the Chinese market", *Industrial Marketing Management*, vol. 24, n° 3, p. 207-214.

FANG T. (1999), *Chinese business negotiating style*, Thousand Oaks, CA, Sage.

FANG T. (2005), "Chinese business style: a regional approach", in MACBEAN A. and BROWN D. (Eds.), *Challenge and Change in China's Development: An Enterprise Perspective*, London, Routledge Curzon, p. 156-172.

HALL E. T. (1976), *Beyond Culture*, New York, Doubleday.

HOFSTEDE G. (1980), *Culture's consequences.* Beverly Hills, CA, Sage.

HOFSTEDE G. (1991). *Cultures and organizations – software of the mind*, New York, McGraw Hill.

HOFSTEDE G. (2001), *Culture's consequences: Comparing values, behaviors, institutions and organizations across nations*, Thousand Oaks, CA, Sage.

LIU B. S. C., FURRER O., and SUDHARSHAN D. (2001), "The relationships between culture and behavioral intentions toward services", *Journal of Service Research*, vol. 4, n° 2, p. 118-129.

LIU C. H. (2009), "Enhance Servitization in Manufacturing Firms of China with Three Main Chinese Inherent Thoughts", *International Journal of Commerce and Strategy*, vol. 1, n° 1, p. 19-39.

NATIONAL STATISTICS BUREAU OF CHINA, *China Statistical Yearbook 2020*, China Statistics Press. http://www.stats.gov.cn/tjsj/ndsj/2020/indexch.htm. Retrieved December 16, 2021.

PERLITZ M. and SEGER F. (2004), "European cultures and management styles", *International Journal of Asian Management*, vol. 3, n° 1, p. 1-26.

RALSTON D. A., TERPSTRA-TONG J., TERPSTRA R. H., WANG X. and EGRI C. (2006), "Today's state-owned enterprises of China: are they dying dinosaurs or dynamic dynamos?", *Strategic Management Journal*, vol. 27, n° 9, 825-843.

TROMPENAARS F. (1996), "Resolving international conflict: Culture and business strategy", *Business Strategy Review*, vol. 7, n° 3, p. 51-68.

UELTSCHY L. C., LAROCHE M., EGGERT, A. and BINDL U. (2007),"Service quality and satisfaction: an international comparison of professional services perceptions", *Journal of Services Marketing*, vol. 21, n° 6, p. 410-423.

ABSTRACTS/RÉSUMÉS

Benoît DESMARCHELIER, Faridah DJELLAL, Faïz GALLOUJ, Luis RUBALCABA, "Inside the black box of public service innovation networks for social innovation (PSINSIs). A Public Service Logic perspective"

This paper is given over to "Public Service Innovation Networks for Social Innovation" (PSINSIs), multi-agent structural arrangements set up for the collaborative production of social innovation in public services. The paper firstly provides an analytical framework that makes it possible to distinguish PSINSIs from other expressions of innovation networks and includes a Public Service Logic perspective. Then, using a set of 24 in-depth PSINSIs case studies undertaken in five European countries, it attempts to enter the black box of PSINSIs in order to better understand the nature of social innovation at work and the modes of formation and functioning of these networks.

Keywords: public services, social innovation, network, public service logic, public innovation.

Benoît DESMARCHELIER, Faridah DJELLAL, Faïz GALLOUJ, Luis RUBALCABA, « Dans la boîte noire des réseaux d'innovation de services publics pour l'innovation sociale »

Cet article est consacré aux réseaux d'innovation de services publics pour l'innovation sociale [« public service innovation networks for social innovation » (PSINSIs)], un arrangement structurel multi-agents constitué pour produire, selon un mode collaboratif, de l'innovation sociale dans les services publics. Il commence par proposer un cadre analytique, qui permet de distinguer, d'un point de vue morphologique et fonctionnel, les PSINSIs des autres expressions du concept de réseau d'innovation. Ensuite, en s'appuyant sur un riche matériau empirique collecté dans le cadre du projet européen COVAL et constitué de 24 études de cas approfondies de PSINSIs dans cinq pays européens, il tente de pénétrer dans la boîte noire des PSINSIs, pour mieux comprendre la nature de l'innovation sociale qui en est l'objet ainsi que les modes de formation et de fonctionnement de ces réseaux.

Mots-clés : innovation networks, public services, social innovation, logique de service publique, innovation publique.

Peter M. SMITH, "Recent developments in European integration for services"

This paper extends and updates the previous estimates for European integration in non-financial commercial services for 2008 with EU-28 results for 2017 and country level results for 2016, the most recent years available. Foreign direct investment is still the dominant form of internationalization for services but some knowledge intensive business services are now being supplied cross-border rather than by FDI. Levels of integration differ markedly between EU countries but there has been some convergence since 2008. On BREXIT the EU market becomes both smaller and less integrated. For the non-financial services covered by this paper, the EU runs a small surplus with the UK on cross-border trade contrary to financial services. The EU also invests much more for services in the UK than the UK invests in the EU.

Keywords: services, European integration, Brexit, FDI, international trade, knowledge intensive business services.

Peter M. SMITH, « Développements récents dans l'intégration européenne des services »

Ce article étend et actualise de précédentes estimations de l'intégration européenne dans les services marchands non financiers pour 2008 avec les résultats de l'UE-28 pour 2017 et ceux au niveau des pays pour 2016, années les plus récentes disponibles. L'IDE reste la forme dominante d'internationalisation pour les services, mais certains services commerciaux intensifs en connaissances sont désormais fournis de manière transfrontalière. Les niveaux d'intégration diffèrent sensiblement entre les pays, mais on observe une certaine convergence depuis 2008. Avec le BREXIT, le marché de l'UE devient plus petit et moins intégré. Pour les services non financiers, contrairement aux services financiers, l'UE enregistre un léger excédent avec le Royaume-Uni (R-U) sur le commerce transfrontalier. L'UE investit également beaucoup plus pour les services au R-U que le R-U n'investit dans l'UE.

Mots-clés : services, intégration européenne, Brexit, IDE, commerce international, services intensifs en connaissances.

Singha CHAVEESUK, Paweensuda DECHAPRASERT, "Covid-19 pandemic and lecturers intention to use learning management system (LMS)"

This study aims to analyse lecturer intention to use the Learning Management System (LMS) in Thailand's Higher Education (HE) establishments. By using the Technology Acceptance Model (TAM) and conducting a survey of lecturers at ten universities, a total of 396 responses have been analysed, using Partial Least Square Structural Equation Modelling. The results show that User-Interface Design was what made the most decisive impact on intention to use LMS. They also show that Perceived Ease Of Use, Perceived Usefulness, and Perceived Interaction are important mediators in the extended TAM model. The research also proved that Perceived Self-Efficacy, User-Interface Design, and Perceived Interaction are essential constructs of the TAM model. The study recommends that in order to improve lecturer-student interaction in the LMS, policymakers should improve the system's interface design.

Keywords: perceived self-efficacy, user-interface design, perceived interaction, perceived ease of use, perceived usefulness.

Singha CHAVEESUK, Paweensuda DECHAPRASERT, « La pandémie de Covid-19 et l'intention des enseignants d'utiliser un environnement numérique d'apprentissage »

Cet article analyse l'intention des enseignants d'utiliser un environnement numérique d'apprentissage (ENA). Il s'appuie sur le modèle d'acceptation de la technologie (TAM), sur une enquête auprès d'enseignants d'universités thaïlandaises (396 réponses), et sur une modélisation par équations structurelles des moindres carrés partiels. L'article souligne que la conception de l'interface utilisateur a l'impact le plus décisif sur l'intention d'utiliser un ENA, que la facilité d'utilisation perçue, l'utilité perçue et l'interaction perçue sont des médiateurs importants dans le modèle TAM étendu et que l'auto-efficacité perçue, la conception de l'interface utilisateur et l'interaction perçue sont des variables essentielles du modèle TAM. Il est nécessaire d'améliorer la conception de l'interface du système afin d'améliorer l'interaction entre les enseignants et les étudiants dans l'ENA.

Mots-clés : auto-efficacité perçue, conception de l'interface utilisateur, interaction perçue, facilité d'utilisation perçue, utilité perçue.

Dagou Hermann-Wenceslas DAGOU, "The quest for the ideal service through collaborative innovation in a public business model with customer stewardship. The case of an Ivorian university hospital"

Abstract : Providing an efficient public service increasingly requires innovation that can take a collaborative form, by involving the clients/patients themselves. Thus, in hospitals, clients/patients who have long been considered captive are now being asked to participate and contribute their experiences. By mobilizing stewardship theory, this article proposes to understand how an ideal quality service can be addressed through cultural effectiveness in a business model. The empirical investigation is carried out with patients in a university hospital in Ivory Coast. The results show that stewardship clients envision the ideal service with the cultural effectiveness attributes of change, team, empowerment, integration and accountability. The surgical service, closer to the ideal service, appears to be an example of collaborative innovation for the emergency and maternity services.

Keywords: ideal service, business model, collaborative innovation, stewardship, hospital services, Ivory Coast.

Dagou Hermann-Wenceslas DAGOU, « La quête du service idéal par l'innovation collaborative dans un business model public avec l'intendance des clients. Le cas d'un hôpital universitaire ivoirien »

Un service public performant nécessite de plus en plus une innovation collaborative, impliquant l'usager lui-même. Ainsi, à l'hôpital, les usagers, longtemps considérés comme captifs, sont désormais amenés à participer et à apporter leurs expériences. En mobilisant la théorie de l'intendance, cet article propose de comprendre comment un service de qualité idéal peut être abordé à travers l'efficacité culturelle dans un modèle d'affaires. L'investigation empirique est réalisée auprès des patients d'un hôpital universitaire ivoirien. Les résultats montrent que les clients intendants envisagent le service idéal avec les attributs de l'efficacité culturelle que sont le changement, l'équipe, la capacitation, l'intégration et la responsabilité. Le service chirurgie, plus proche du service idéal, apparaît comme un exemple d'innovation collaborative pour les services d'urgences et de maternité.

Mots-clés : service idéal, modèle d'affaires, innovation collaborative, intendance, service hospitalier, Côte d'Ivoire.

Abdelmajid AMINE, Audrey BONNEMAIZON, Margaret JOSION-PORTAIL, "The role of norms' conflict among caregivers in shaping care practices with vulnerable elderly patients"

This research explores the care practices carried out by personnel in contact with elderly patients, in a hospital context that is increasingly normative and driven by a managerial paradigm that comes into conflict with the personal values and ethics of caregivers. By using a immersion approach in a geriatric hospital department, this research makes it possible to understand the role of the frailty of the elderly in feeding the tensions of norms experienced by the caregivers. It also makes it possible to identify the strategies used for negotiating and circumventing norms, based on tinkering and cunning, which caregivers put in place to resolve these tensions in order to accomplish their mission. If the mobilization of these strategies makes it possible to preserve the well-being of elderly patients, it makes part of the caregivers' work invisible and is a source of psycho-social risks.

Keywords: caregivers, elderly patients, norms, vulnerability, care practices, bricolage, cunning, health service.

Abdelmajid AMINE, Audrey BONNEMAIZON, Margaret JOSION-PORTAIL, « Rôle des tensions de normes chez les soignants dans la configuration des pratiques de soins avec les patients âgés vulnérables »

Cette recherche explore les pratiques de soins du personnel en contact avec les patients âgés, dans un contexte hospitalier de plus en plus normatif et animé par une logique managériale qui entre en conflit avec les valeurs personnelles et l'éthique des soignants. En utilisant une approche par immersion dans un service hospitalier de gériatrie, elle permet de comprendre le rôle de la fragilité des personnes âgées dans l'alimentation des tensions de normes vécues par les soignants, mais aussi d'identifier les stratégies de négociation et de contournement des normes, fondées sur le bricolage et la ruse, que les soignants mettent en place pour résoudre ces tensions afin d'accomplir leur mission. Si la mobilisation de ces stratégies permet de préserver le bien-être des patients âgés, elle rend invisible une partie du travail des soignants et constitue une source de risques psycho-sociaux.

Mots-clés : soignants, patients âgés, normes, vulnérabilité, pratiques de soins, bricolage, ruse, service de santé.

Cheryl Marie CORDEIRO, Jaap W. VAN HAL, "Creative innovation in gastronomy services"

Creativity and innovation are important elements in the development of new gastronomy services. This article brings insights from interviews with 25 Nordic Chefs, and their view the processes of creative innovation in the field of culinary science and gastronomy service. An integrated human-centric and product-centric perspective of gastronomy service is presented from the consolidated interview transcripts.

Key words: creativity, innovation, gastronomy service, culinary science, service.

Cheryl Marie CORDEIRO, Jaap W. VAN HAL, « Innovation créative dans les services gastronomiques »

La créativité et l'innovation sont des éléments importants dans le développement de nouveaux services gastronomiques. Cet article présente les résultats d'entretiens avec 25 chefs nordiques et leur vision des processus d'innovation créative dans le domaine des sciences culinaires et des services gastronomiques. Une perspective intégrée du service gastronomique, centrée sur l'homme et le produit, est présentée à partir des transcriptions consolidées des entretiens.

Mots-clés : créativité, innovation, service gastronomique, sciences culinaires, service.

Sen BAO, Marja TOIVONEN, "China as an opportunity and a challenge for Western service providers"

This article analyzes the issues of cultural differences in the production and delivery of services in the globalized world. A focus is set on the differences between Western and Chinese cultures. As a framework for the comparison and country-specific analysis, the basic dimensions of cultural differences are presented based on the literature. In the numerous studies carried out during the last decades, the following dimensions have been found to be typical in the Eastern cultures: collectivism, indirect communication style, high power distance, and long-term orientation. In China, these Eastern characteristics are mixed with deep traditions of the Confucian culture, with the socio-political system of the country, and with the rapid, but regionally uneven development in recent years.

Keywords: cultural differences, global business, internationalization of services, Chinese society, "guanxi".

Sen BAO, Marja TOIVONEN, « La Chine, une opportunité et un défi pour les prestataires de services occidentaux »

Cet article est consacré à la question des différences culturelles dans la prestation de services dans un monde globalisé. L'accent est mis sur les différences entre les cultures occidentales et chinoises. Les dimensions fondamentales des différences culturelles, qui constituent le cadre de la comparaison, sont présentées sur la base d'un bilan de la littérature. Dans les nombreuses études réalisées au cours des dernières décennies, les dimensions suivantes sont considérées comme caractéristiques des cultures orientales : collectivisme, style de communication indirect, distance hiérarchique élevée et orientation à long terme. En Chine, ces caractéristiques orientales se mêlent aux profondes traditions de la culture confucéenne, au système sociopolitique du pays et au développement rapide, mais inégal, de ces dernières années.

Mots-clés : différences culturelles, commerce mondial, internationalisation des services, société chinoise, « guanxi ».

Achevé d'imprimer par Corlet,
Condé-en-Normandie (Calvados),
en Avril 2022
N° d'impression : 175755 - dépôt légal : Avril 2022
Imprimé en France

Bulletin d'abonnement revue 2022

European Review of Service Economics and Management /
Revue Européenne d'Économie et Management des Services

2 numéros par an

M., Mme :

Adresse :

Code postal :   Ville :

Pays :

Téléphone :   Fax :

Courriel :

Prix TTC abonnement France, frais de port inclus		Prix HT abonnement étranger, frais de port inclus	
Particulier	Institution	Particulier	Institution
78 €	98 €	90 €	106 €

Cet abonnement concerne les parutions papier du 1ᵉʳ janvier 2022 au 31 décembre 2022.

Les numéros parus avant le 1ᵉʳ janvier 2022 sont disponibles à l'unité (hors abonnement) sur notre site web.

Modalités de règlement (en euros) :

 Par carte bancaire sur notre site web : www.classiques-garnier.com

 Par virement bancaire sur le compte :

Banque : Société Générale – BIC : SOGEFRPP

IBAN : FR 76 3000 3018 7700 0208 3910 870

RIB : 30003 01877 00020839108 70

 Par chèque à l'ordre de Classiques Garnier

Classiques Garnier

6, rue de la Sorbonne – 75005 Paris – France

Fax : + 33 1 43 54 00 44

Courriel : revues@classiques-garnier.com

mis à jour le 26/08/2021

Abonnez-vous sur notre site web :
www.classiques-garnier.com